T3-AKC-120

INTERNATIONAL
BANKING CRISES

INTERNATIONAL BANKING CRISES

Large-Scale Failures, Massive Government Interventions

Edited by Benton E. Gup

QUORUM BOOKS
Westport, Connecticut • London

3 32.15
I 618

Library of Congress Cataloging-in-Publication Data

International banking crises : large-scale failures, massive
   government interventions / edited by Benton E. Gup.
      p.   cm.
   Includes bibliographical references and index.
   ISBN 1–56720–283–7 (alk. paper)
   1. Banks and banking, International.   2. Bank failures.   I. Gup,
Benton E.
HG3881.I5751343   1999
332.1′5—dc21   99–21591

British Library Cataloguing in Publication Data is available.

 Copyright © 1999 by Benton E. Gup

All rights reserved. No portion of this book may be
reproduced, by any process or technique, without the
express written consent of the publisher.

Library of Congress Catalog Card Number: 99–21591
ISBN: 1–56720–283–7

First published in 1999

Quorum Books, 88 Post Road West, Westport, CT 06881
An imprint of Greenwood Publishing Group, Inc.
www.quorumbooks.com

Printed in the United States of America

The paper used in this book complies with the
Permanent Paper Standard issued by the National
Information Standards Organization (Z39.48–1984).

10 9 8 7 6 5 4 3 2 1

To Jean, Lincoln, Andy and Carol, and Jeremy

University Libraries
Carnegie Mellon University
Pittsburgh PA 15213-3890

Contents

Tables and Figures

TABLES

FIGURES

Preface

This is my third book dealing with bank failures. The first book, *Targeting Fraud: Uncovering and Deterring Fraud in Financial Institutions* (McGraw-Hill, 1995), examined domestic and international banks that failed as a result of massive fraud. The second book, *Bank Failures in the Major Trading Countries of the World* (Quorum Books, 1998), was an outgrowth of my research when I was a visiting scholar at the Office of the Comptroller of the Currency in 1997. Part of that research was to determine why banks in the G-10 countries failed during the 1980 to 1997 period. Defaults of real estate loans stood out as being the most common cause of failures, and fraud was a distant second. As I was finishing that book in July 1997, Thailand devalued its currency. That act marked the beginning of crises in other Southeast Asian countries and Russia that impacted the rest of the world. It was feared that the contagion would spread to Brazil and then to other Latin American countries. In the United States, stock prices declined sharply in July and August 1998, but they recovered in the months to come. Long Term Capital Management, a hedge fund, almost failed and had to be bailed out by commercial banks and investment banks with the aid of the New York Federal Reserve Bank. Several other hedge funds did fail, and some major banks had huge trading losses from the dealings in foreign currencies. There was a flight to quality investments away from risky bonds and mortgage debt, and the fear of a credit crunch. Intervention by the International Monetary Fund in the crises was cheered by some and strongly criticized by others. The Federal Reserve and other central banks cut interest rates to bolster their respective economies. In December 1998, at the time this is being written, it appears that the worst is over, and that the world economy is not going to collapse, but the jury is still out. Indonesia, Malaysia, Russia, and other countries are in a weakened state, and it would not take much to push them over the brink into a deep recession.

Growth in Southeast Asia was hailed as an economic miracle until it came to a screeching halt in July 1997. No one that I am aware of predicted the crises that followed or the speed at which events occurred. That raises the obvious questions of why no one saw those dark storm clouds on the horizon, why the crises occurred, and what can be done to prevent them in the future. This book provides some insights into those issues, but you will not find all of the answers here. The book is divided into three parts. Part I provides an overview of why banks fail. Part II examines the crises in selected countries. These countries are Thailand, Indonesia, South Korea, Russia, and Argentina. Information about crises in other countries was not sufficient to include here. Part III deals with bank regulatory issues from an international perspective.

PART **I**

WHY BANKS FAIL

1

Bank Growth and Failure

Benton E. Gup

This chapter explains three major reasons why individual banks fail. The reasons are credit risk, interest rate risk, and foreign exchange risk. Two other potential sources of failure are bank runs and fraud. Bank runs occur when depositors or other creditors fear for the safety of their funds and try to withdraw them. This is most likely to occur with uninsured deposits. During the financial debacle in Russia in August 1998, CNN and other television stations showed long lines of Russians trying to withdraw their funds from local banks. Most banks do not keep sufficient funds on hand to meet unanticipated large-scale withdraws. Under these circumstances, the banks cannot pay off all depositors. A "silent run" occurs when large creditors withdraw their funds. This occurred in the case of Continental Illinois bank in 1974 (Gup 1998). International banks had uninsured deposits of tens and hundreds of millions of dollars in Continental.

If the run is on an illiquid but solvent institution, that institution may be able to borrow from the lender of last resort. Insolvent institutions may fail. The depositor's lack of confidence in the bank is because they believe that the bank has large losses due to credit risk, interest rate risk, or foreign exchange risk and that their deposits are at risk. Finally, fraud is a legal concept, and what constitutes fraud in one country may be standard business practice in another. What was called "crony capitalism" in Indonesia is called fraud in the United States. Therefore, fraud is not addressed here.[1]

CREDIT RISK

Banks' primary source of income is interest income from their loan portfolios, and their primary risk is credit risk. According to the Comptroller of the Currency, credit risk is "the risk of repayment, i.e., the possibility that an obligor will fail to perform as agreed" (*Loan Portfolio Management* 1998, 4). Credit risk also applies to on- and off-balance-sheet exposures, such as acceptances, derivatives, guarantees, and securities investments. In this section, we examine the credit risk associated with loans. Bankers know that lending is a risky business, and they set aside a reserve for expected losses, usually 1 to 2 percent of total loans and leases. When losses exceed that amount, the losses reduce bank capital. If the losses are sufficiently large, the bank will fail.

The amount of bank capital relative to the loans is important. Banks' ratio of capital to assets declined from over 50 percent in the 1840s to under 10 percent in the 1990s. During the 1930s, when banks experienced the most bank failures, the ratio was about 15 percent. Thus, a small capital base puts banks at a greater risk of failure if there are large losses.

Asymmetric information between borrowers and lenders and adverse selection in the process of granting loans are not an important part of the process of growth and failure that is described here.[2] But they are not inconsistent with it either. Asymmetric information means that the borrowers know more about the risks associated with the expected cash flows from their investment projects than the lenders. Because of asymmetric information, the lenders charge interest rates on loans that reflect the average risk in the market. The average interest rate is too high for borrowers with low-risk projects, and too low for borrowers with high-risk projects. The expected returns on the projects are related to the degree of risk. Thus, high-risk projects expect high returns. Adverse selection occurs before the loans are made, when high-risk borrowers try to borrow at the relatively low average rate, while the low-risk borrowers may be unwilling to do so at the average rate of interest. The end result is that the lender's portfolios may have above-average risks. After the loans are made, there may be a moral hazard problem. That is, the borrower may use the borrowed funds to engage in increasingly risky activities to increase expected returns. This is most likely to occur when the lender cannot monitor the borrowers behavior effectively.

In order to examine the process of growth and failure, we make five simplifying assumptions. First, the stakeholders in a bank include shareholders, employees, customers, and the communities they serve. Each of these stakeholders wants to maximize their own utility. They see higher growth of assets, loans, and profits as a means to an end. Simply stated, everyone wants the bank to grow in order for them to be better off. Second, in developed capital markets where competition prevails, bankers do not intentionally make bad loans. However, they do make loans that can go bad over time because of factors that are unique to a borrower. Alternatively, changes in macroeconomic or international conditions might adversely affect a large number of borrowers, and then they default. Such macroeconomic and international factors include but are not limited to shocks in interest rates and exchange rates, widespread asset price deflation, and global contagion. Third, the bank in the example that will follow has an excess concentration of loans to a group of borrowers, and it is not adequately diversified. In countries with developed capital market, this is considered poor management. In a developing country with repressed financial markets, there may not be any alternatives. Financial repression implies that the government intervenes heavily in the economy and in the financial markets. In South Korea, for example, nationalized banks in the 1960s were told by the government to make loans to *chaebols* to finance government-directed investment projects. *Chaebols* are large conglomerate business groups. Also, banks in repressed financial markets do not have the same opportunities to diversify their portfolios as banks in developed capital markets. Finally, the creditworthiness of borrowers is not an issue because of the government involvement in the lending process. Fourth, the loans are not backed by collateral. Fifth, the loan-to-value ratio is 100 percent.

Bank Growth

Consider the hypothetical bank that is shown in Panel A of Table 1.1. It has a single loan as its sole asset, and it is funded by deposits and stockholders' equity. The ratio of equity capital to risk assets (E/A) is sufficiently large so that the bank is "well-capitalized" at 10 percent, and it has an ample loan loss reserve. In addition, the bank is very profitable. It has a return on assets (ROA) of 2.88 percent, more than twice the 1.23 percent ROA for all FDIC-insured commercial bank in the United States in 1997 (*FDIC Quarterly Banking Profile* 1997). As previously noted, the stakeholders of the bank want it to grow so that they get higher returns on their investment, higher salaries, and so on.

In order to grow, the bank raises an additional $20 million in deposits and it invests those funds in two loans of $10 million each (Panel B of Table 1.1).[3] No additional loan loss reserves are required. In this period, the ROA is 2.73 percent, and the E/A is 8.33 percent, meaning that the bank is "adequately capitalized."

In the next period, which is shown in Panel C of Table 1.1, one of the $10-million loans goes into default. The reason for the default in this example resides exclusively with the borrower; no external factors were

Table 1.1
Bank Growth and Losses: Credit Risk

Panel A

Assets ($ millions)		Liabilities	
Loan	$102@ 9%	Deposits	$90 @ 7%
Loan loss reserve	- 2		
Net loans	$100		
		Stockholders' equity	$10
Totals	$100		$100

Net income	$9.18 - $6.30 = $2.88
Return on assets (ROA)	$2.88/$100 = 2.88%
Equity/Assets (E/A)	$10/$100 = 10% Well capitalized

Panel B

Assets ($ millions)		Liabilities	
Loan	$102@ 9%	Deposits	$110 @ 7%
Loan	10@ 9%		
Loan	10@ 9%		
Loan loss reserve	- 2		
Net loans	$120		
		Stockholders' equity	$10
Totals	$120		$120

Net income	$10.98 - $7.70 = $3.28
Return on assets (ROA)	$3.28/$120 = 2.73%
Equity/Assets (E/A)	$10/$120 = 8.33% Adequately capitalized

Panel C

Assets ($ millions)		Liabilities	
Loan	$102@ 9%	Deposits	$110 @ 7%
Loan	10@ 9%		
Loan Default	**- 10**		
Loan loss reserve	2		
Net loans	$112		
		Stockholders' equity	$2
Totals	$112		$112

Defaulted loan $10 exceeds loan loss reserve by $8, which is deducted from stockholders' equity.

Net income	$10.08 - $7.70 = $2.38
Return on assets (ROA)	$2.38/$112 = 2.13%
Equity/Assets (E/A)	$2/$112 = 1.79% Critically undercapitalized = Bank Failure

at work. The $10 million default exceeds the loan loss reserve by $8 million. That difference is deducted from stockholders' equity, leaving only $2 million. Now the bank has a tangible E/A of 1.79 percent and it is "critically undercapitalized." In this scenario, the bank fails.

Reducing Credit Risk

What could the bank have done to reduce its credit risk? First, there was undue loan concentration in this example. As previously noted, banks in repressed financial markets may not have a choice about loan concentration. Banks in well-developed capital markets, however, usually do not lend more than 25 percent of their capital and surplus to a single borrower, or to a group of borrowers closely related to the same business (*Core Principles for Effective Banking Supervision* 1997, 60). Of that total, 15 percent may be unsecured lending and 10 percent secured lending. Despite such limits, Folkerts-Landau and Lindgren (1998) note that banks can have large concentrations with respect to particular industries, economic sectors, or geographical regions or by having loans with characteristics, such as highly leveraged transactions, that makes those banks vulnerable to economic factors. For example, in a study of bank failures in the 1980s and early 1990s, Hanc (1998, 9), found that the incidence of bank failures was particularly high in states characterized by

- severe economic downturns related to the collapse of energy prices (Alaska, Louisiana, Oklahoma, Texas, and Wyoming).
- real estate related downturns (California, the Northeast, and the Southwest).
- the agricultural recession of the early 1980s (Iowa, Kansas, Nebraska, Oklahoma, and Texas).

Second, the loan-to-value ratio and collateral are important determinants of a borrower's vested interest in an loan. The lower the vested interest, the higher the moral hazard problem. From the borrowers point of view, a high loan-to-value ratio (i.e., 100%) is desirable. From the bank's point of view, a lower loan-to-value ratio, say 70 to 80 percent is desirable to reduce risk. In a competitive environment, some banks will compete on the terms of the loan as well as interest rate and forgo safety in order to grow.

Third, the bank could have reduced its risk by requiring collateral that could be sold in the event of default. Borrowers have a positive incentive not to lose valuable collateral.

Fourth, the creditworthiness of the borrower was not an issue at the time the loan was made. Nevertheless, over time the creditworthiness of the borrower deteriorated to the extent that the loan went into default. Regular monitoring of the loan may give the bank sufficient early warning to deal with the borrower's problems and avoid the default.

Fifth, the bank could have hedged some of its credit risk with credit derivatives (Moser 1998). Credit derivatives are a new and growing part of the derivatives market. Credit derivatives include credit default contracts, total return swaps, credit spread contracts, and credit linked notes.

Finally, there is credit risk due to asset price deflation over an extended period. During the 1990 to 1998 period in Japan, real estate prices declined more than 80 percent. There is little that banks can do to reduce that risk.

INTEREST RATE RISK

Interest rate risk is the risk to earnings or capital arising from movement of interest rates. It arises from differences between the timing of rate changes and the timing of cash flows (repricing risk); from changing rate relationships among yield curves that affect bank activities (basis risk); from changing relationships across the spectrum of maturities (yield curve risk); and from interest-rate-related options embedded in bank products (option risk). (*Interest Rate Risk* 1997, 2)

Yield curves are usually positively sloped. This means that long-term market rates of interest are higher than short-term rates. Banks take advantage of the yield curve by borrowing short-term funds and lend over a longer term. The difference between their borrowing and lending rates is their net interest income. In the example shown in Panel A of Table 1.2, the bank is borrowing for thirty days at 7 percent and lending for five years at a fixed rate of 9 percent, a 200-basis-point spread. As previously noted, the bank is very profitable and highly capitalized in the initial period.

Suppose that there is an instantaneous 500-basis-point increase in market rates of interest. Large increases in interest rates are not uncommon in the United States or elsewhere. During the late 1970s and the early 1980s, the Federal Reserve declared war on inflation by tightening the money supply. Short-term interest rates soared from 10 to 19 percent in a relatively short time period. While this shock therapy cured the inflation, it also triggered a recession that resulted in the highest rate of unemployment since the Great Depression and large-scale defaults of bank loans. In Indonesia, the central bank (Bank of Indonesia) increased the one-month interest rate from 22 to 45 percent *in one day* to help slow the rate of inflation (Thoenes 1998). In May 1998, Russia hiked interest rates to 50 percent as investors fled the falling

Table 1.2
Bank Growth and Losses: Interest Rate Risk

Panel A

Assets ($ millions)		Liabilities	
Loan	$102@ 9% fixed	Deposits	$90 @ 7%
(5 years)		(30 days)	
Loan loss reserve	- 2		
Net loans	$100		
		Stockholders' equity	$10
Totals	$100		$100

Net income	$9.18 - $6.30 = $2.88	
Return on assets (ROA)	$2.88/$100 = 2.88%	
Equity/Assets (E/A)	$10/$100 = 10% Well capitalized	

Panel B

Market rates of interest increase 500 basis points.

Assets ($ millions)		Liabilities	
Loan	$102@ 9%	Deposits	$90 @ 12%
(5 years)		(30 days)	
Loan loss reserve	- 2		
Net loans	$100		
		Stockholders' equity	$10
Totals	$100		$100

The loss is subtracted from stockholders' equity.

Net income	$9.18 - $10.80 = - $1.62	
Return on assets (ROA)	-$1.62/$100 = Negative	
Equity/Assets (E/A)	$8.38/$100 = 8.38% Adequately capitalized	

ruble (down 41.3% relative to the U.S. dollar in five months), and their stock prices declined 16.5 percent in one week ("Emerging Market Indicators" 1998).

An unexpected increase in interest rates has four potential effects on banks. First, it will effect net interest income. Second, it will effect the market value of bank assets; in the case of our example, it is a single loan. Third, it may affect the borrowers ability to repay the loan. Finally, it may affect the value of put and call options that are embedded in some bank products. For example, customers with early withdrawal rights on low-yielding deposits may put the deposits back to the bank and reinvest those funds in the market at higher rates. In addition, interest rate caps on loans act like puts when interest rates increase.

Net Interest Income

As shown in Panel B of Table 1.2, the interest rate on thirty-day deposits increased from 7 to 12 percent as a result of the 500-basis-point increase in market rates of interest. However, the income from the five-year fixed-rate loan is still 9 percent. Because of the increased cost of funds, the bank has a negative net interest income of $1.62 million. The loss reduces the bank's equity to 8.38 percent. The bank is adequately capitalized, but further losses in net interest income will put the bank at risk.

Market Value of Loans

Assume that the market value of a loan is the present value of expected annual cash flows (an annuity) during the term of the loan, discounted by the market rate of interest. The market rate of interest at the time the loan was made was the 9-percent fixed-loan rate. The market value of the loan or annuity PV_a is

$$PV_a = PMT \sum_{t=1}^{n} \left[\frac{1}{(1+i)^t} \right]$$

where

$$PMT = \text{expected annual cash flow (income)}$$
$$n = \text{number of years}$$
$$i = \text{interest rate}$$

The initial market value of the loan (annuity) is $102 million, the amount shown on the bank's balance sheet at the time the loan was made. At 9 percent for five years, the expected annual cash flows from the loan are $26,223,102.[4]

When market rates of interest increase 500 basis points, the bank cannot increase the rate charged on the fixed-rate loan. Had it been able to do so, it would have charged 14 percent, which is 200 basis points over its cost of funds (12%). Therefore, we can assume that the market rate on the loan should be computed at 14 percent. Accordingly, the new market value of the loan can be determined by multiplying the expected annual cash flows ($26,223,102) by the present

value of an annuity interest factor of 14 percent for five years (3.4331).
It is $90,026,531.

$$PV_a = \$26,223,102 \times 3.4331 = \$90,026,531$$

The lower market value of the loan has two effects on the bank.
First, if bank regulators considered market value accounting, the bank
would be technically insolvent because the market value of the loan
declined $11,973,469 ($102,000,000 – $90,026,531 = $11,973,469), thereby
eliminating the bank's capital. Second, Ambrose and Capone (1996)
consider bank loans to be compound options containing the rights to
prepay loans (a call option) and to default on loans (a put option).
When the value of the loan is less than the amount owed, the put option is in the money, and the borrower may have an incentive to exercise his or her put option to default on the loan. This decision depends,
in part, on the loan-to-value ratio.[5] If the bank did not require any
borrower equity in our example, a loan-to-value ratio of 100 percent,
the borrower's put option would be in the money. However, if the
bank required the borrower to put up 20 percent of the $102 million, it
would have lent $81.6 million to the borrower, and the value of the
put option would be out of the money. Thus, the loan-to-value ratio is
an important determinant of a bank's credit risk. Third, we relax the
assumption that the loan is made at a fixed rate. If there is an interest
rate shock and the rate on the loan increases, the borrower may not be
able to service the loan at the higher rate. In this case, the interest rate
risk has been converted into credit risk.

Reducing Interest Rate Risk

The proximate cause of interest rate risk in the example presented
here was a large unexpected increase in market rates of interest. The
increase is usually a result of central bank activities to raise rates for
domestic economic policy reasons, such as fighting inflation, or attempts to stabilize foreign exchange rates. Accordingly, a stable economic environment, including stable interest rates, could eliminate
interest rate risk for banks.

The initial impact of an interest rate shock is on net interest income.
Banks can reduce this risk by properly managing their dollar gaps,
the difference between their interest rate sensitive assets and interest
rate sensitive liabilities. A neutral dollar gap, where rate sensitive assets and liabilities are equal, eliminates interest rate risk, but it also
reduces the opportunity to profit from expected changes in interest
rates. As an alternative, they can hedge the interest rate risk by using
derivatives.[6]

The second effect of the interest rate shock was that the market value of the loan declined because it had a fixed rate of interest. This problem can be reduced, but not eliminated, by using floating interest rates. Such floating rate loans usually have caps and floors that limit their usefulness. Moreover, it is highly unlikely that banks would adjust loan rates to match the large rate hikes that were described at the beginning of this section. Even when they make smaller adjustments in interest rates, it could exceed the borrower's ability to repay the loan, thereby contributing to a default.

A large decline in interest rates also may create interest rate risk. Suppose that a bank has a positive net interest income funded by long-term fixed rate deposits, and there is a large decline in interest rates. If borrowers exercise their options and pay off their loans in order to refinance them at lower rates, the net interest income could be negative due to the high fixed costs of funds.

FOREIGN EXCHANGE RATE RISK

Foreign exchange rates can be volatile. For example, the yen/dollar exchange rate was 142 yen/dollar in June 1991. It fell to 81 yen/dollar in April 1995, and rebounded to 136 yen/dollar in early 1997.[7] Between December 31, 1997, and May 20, 1998, the Russian ruble declined 41.3 percent in terms of the U.S. dollar, the Indonesian rupiah declined 50.4 percent, and the Portugese peso gained 55 percent ("Emerging Market Indicators" 1998).

Foreign exchange rate risk arises in the bank that we will examine when it borrows in one currency and lends in another, without hedging that risk. Well-managed banks have internal controls and limits on their foreign exchange exposure. This is not a well-managed bank. Neither were the institutions in Thailand in 1997 that failed for the reasons that will be demonstrated. They did not hedge their foreign exchange risk because they believed that the Thai government would defend the fixed exchange rate. They were wrong.

In South Korea, investment banks borrowed dollars short term and lent won longer term (Feldstein 1998). As a result of the borrowing, Korea's short-term debt exceeded its foreign exchange reserves. Investors, fearing a currency crisis, sold won. The exchange rate declined from 950 won/dollar in October 1997 to 1,900 won/dollar by year end. The IMF, trying to stem the decline, wanted higher interest rates. However, the higher interest rates adversely affected highly leveraged *chaebols*.

Consider the bank shown in Panel A of Table 1.3. The bank borrows funds in U.S. dollars and lends in a foreign currency (FC1). That is, the loans are denominated in the foreign currency, and interest payments

Table 1.3
Bank Growth and Losses: Foreign Exchange Rate Risk

Panel A

Assets ($ millions)		Liabilities	
Loan	FC102@ 9%	Deposits	$90 @ 7%
(In Foreign		(In U.S. dollars)	
Currency, FC)			
Loan loss reserve	- 2		
Net loans	FC100		
		Stockholders' equity	$10
Totals	FC100 = $100		$100

Exchange rate FC1 = $1

Net income	$9.18 - $6.30 = $2.88	
Return on assets (ROA)	$2.88/$100	= 2.88%
Equity/Assets (E/A)	$10/$100	= 10% Well capitalized

Panel B

FC depreciates relative to the dollar
Exchange rate: FC2 = $0.20

Assets ($ millions)		Liabilities	
Loan	FC102@ 9%	Deposits	$90 @ 7%
(In Foreign		(In U.S. dollars)	
Currency, FC)			
Loan loss reserve	- 2		
Net loans	FC100		
		Stockholders' equity	- $70
Totals	FC100 = $20		$20

Net income	$1.84 - $6.30 = - $4.46	
Return on assets (ROA)	-$4.46/$20	= Negative
Equity/Assets (E/A)	-$70/$20	= Critically undercapitalized

are also in that currency. We assume that the initial exchange rate is that one unit of the foreign currency is equal to one dollar. We know from the previous examples that the bank is profitable.

In the next period, Panel B of Table 1.3, the foreign currency depreciates relative to the dollar. In 1997, the Indonesian rupiah, the Thai baht, and the Korean won all fell sharply against the dollar. Now FC2 is equal to $0.20. In this case, the value of the bank's assets, denominated in foreign currency units, is $20 million, while its liabilities are worth $90 million. This means that the bank has an equity of negative $70 million. If the bank's shareholders had unlimited liability, they would have to fund that amount. At the current exchange rate, the net income is a negative $4.46. The bank fails. This is what happened to a number of financial institutions in Thailand in 1997. Notice that in this example the borrowers did not default on their loans. They did, however, repay the loans in a foreign currency.

Changes in foreign exchange rates may adversely affect borrowers and their ability to repay loans. Silverman (1998) gave the following scenario of how currency contagion might spread. Russia defaults on its foreign debts and suspends payments on currency hedges. A hedge fund manager who used Russian treasury bills as collateral to buy more Russian securities gets a margin call from his U.S. bank. The fund manager and other highly leveraged borrowers are forced to sell securities, say, bonds in Latin America, to meet the margin calls. However, the forced selling depresses the prices of those bonds and they are sold at a loss. Because of the losses and overleveraged positions, the hedge fund fails, and defaults on the bank loan.

The currency crises in Southeast Asia and Russia in 1998 contributed to large foreign exchange losses at banks and dealers. Bankers Trust lost $350 million, Chase Manhattan $200 million, Citicorp $200 million, and Salomon Smith Barney $150 million. BankAmerica suffered trading losses of $220 million that were attributed to Russia, and another $110 million in connection with trading in Latin America (Brooks 1998).

Reducing Foreign Exchange Risk

A recent study revealed that about 60 percent of the nonfinancial firms surveyed did not hedge their foreign exchange rate exposure (Bodnar, Hayt, and Marston 1996). Although there are no similar studies of banks, it is a safe bet that many banks in foreign countries do not hedge this risk. As noted, bank managers in Thailand and Korea who borrowed in one currency and lent in another were wrong in their beliefs about the stability of their domestic currencies.

Banks can hedge their foreign exchange risk using traditional money market and derivative instruments such as forward contracts, futures contracts, and swaps. On the other side of the coin, Knight (1998) argues that using derivatives to hedge against short-term currency risk is misguided for global companies that deal in a continuous stream of cash flows. He claims that futures prices contain no additional information over spot prices. Therefore, the policy of hedging cash flows is like rearranging the deck chairs on the Titanic. Some large international banks may use natural hedges, having facilities located in foreign countries and borrowing and lending in the local currencies. However, this solution is not open to small banks. The solution to their problem is sound internal controls concerning foreign exchange operations, and prudential regulation to enforce them. Nevertheless, as previously noted, large losses occur even in well-managed banks.

The failure of Barings Brothers and Co., Ltd. in 1995 is an example of what can happen to a bank that had foreign exchange dealings and lacked internal controls (see Gup 1998). The chief trader of Barings Futures Singapore, a subsidiary of the London parent holding company Barings PLC, traded stock index futures contracts on Singapore's stock exchange (SIMEX). In a twenty-eight-day period, he bet more than $1 billion on the direction of the Nikkei Index of Japanese stocks. He lost $1.4 billion and the bank had only $500 million in capital. Barings Bank failed.

CONCLUSION

There are three major reasons why banks fail: credit risk, interest rate risk, and foreign exchange risk. These risks are minimal in stable economic environments, and they increase exponentially in unstable economic environments. To a very large degree, the economic environment depends on government economic polices and the effects of contagion. Thus, a bank can make a "good" loan that turns "bad" because of changes beyond the control of both the borrower and the lender. While there may be a sound economy in the United States, turmoil in Indonesia or Russia did result in large bank losses at some U.S. banks. Because of such unanticipated shocks, banks must consider the methods suggested here for reducing risks. Even taking those methods into account, some banks will fail.

NOTES

1. See Gup (1995) for a discussion of frauds that led to bank failures.
2. Mishkin (1991) places a lot of emphasis on the role of asymmetric information in contributing to financial crises.
3. Haubrich (1998) provides an interesting discussion of the relationships between bank growth, diversification, and risk. In very general terms, banks

grow by adding risky loans. Using the weak law of large numbers, Haubrich shows that diversified banks have a reduced expected failure rate. However, they are not necessarily less risky overall.

4. The present value of an annuity interest factor for five years at 9 percent is 3.8897. The annual cash flow is determined by $102 million/3.8897 = $26,223,102.

5. The decision to exercise the put option is influenced by the borrower's ability to increase the returns on the investment project that are commensurate with the higher market rates of interest.

6. For further discussion of interest rate risk, see Gup and Brooks (1993) and *Interest Rate Risk* (1997).

7. Foreign exchange rate and market data are published in *The Economist*, "Financial Indicators" and "Emerging Market Indicators."

REFERENCES

Ambrose, B. W., and C. A. Capone. 1996. "Cost-Benefit Analysis of Single-Family Foreclosure Alternatives." *Journal of Real Estate Finance and Economics* 13: 105–20.

Bodnar, G. M., G. S. Hayt, and R. C. Marston. 1996. "1995 Wharton Survey of Derivative Usage by U.S. Non-Financial Companies." *Financial Management* Winter, pp. 113–33.

Brooks, Rick. 1998. "BankAmercia Puts Trading Losses at $330 Million." *Wall Street Journal*, 16 September, p. A3.

Core Principles for Effective Banking Supervision. 1997. Basle, Switzerland: Basle Committee on Banking Supervision, Bank of International Settlements.

"Emerging Market Indicators." 1998. *The Economist*, 23 March, p. 98.

FDIC Quarterly Banking Profile. 1997. Washington, D.C.: Federal Deposit Insurance Corporation.

Feldstein, M. 1998. "All Is Not Lost for the Won." *Wall Street Journal*, 2 June, p. A22.

"Financial Indicators." 1998. *The Economist*, 23 March.

Folkerts-Landau, D., and C.-J. Lindgren. 1998. *Toward a Framework for Financial Stability*. Washington, D.C.: International Monetary Fund, World Economic and Financial Surveys.

Gup, B. E. 1995. *Targeting Fraud: Uncovering and Deterring Fraud in Financial Institutions*. Oakbrook, Ill.: Irwin-McGraw Hill.

Gup, B. E. 1998. *Bank Failures in the Major Trading Countries Around the World: Causes and Remedies*. Westport, Conn.: Quorum Books.

Gup, B. E., and R. Brooks. 1993. *Interest Rate Risk Management: The Bankers Guide to Using Futures, Options, Swaps, and Other Derivative Instruments*. Oakbrook, Ill.: Irwin-McGraw Hill.

Hanc, G. 1998. "The Banking Crises of the 1980s and Early 1990s: Summary and Implications." *FDIC Banking Review* 11: 1–55.

Haubrich, J. G. 1998. "Bank Diversification: Laws and Fallacies of Large Numbers." *Economic Review* (Federal Reserve Bank of Cleveland) 34, no. 2: 2–9.

Interest Rate Risk: Comptroller's Handbook. 1997. Washington, D.C.: Office of the Comptroller of the Currency.

Knight, R. 1998. "Global Finance, The Great Equalizer." *Financial Times, Mastering Global Business,* part 8, pp. 2–5.

Loan Portfolio Management: Comptroller's Handbook. 1998. Washington, D.C.: Office of the Comptroller of the Currency, A-LPM.

Mishkin, F. S. 1991. "Asymmetric Information and Financial Crises: A Historical Perspective." In *Financial Markets and Financial Crises: A National Bureau of Economic Research Project Report,* edited by R. Glenn Hubbard. Chicago: University of Chicago Press.

Moser, J. 1998. "Credit Derivatives: The Latest New Thing." *Chicago Fed Letter* (Federal Reserve Bank of Chicago), June.

Silverman, Gary. 1998. "Up the Volga Without a Calculator." *Business Week,* 14 September, p. 46.

Thoenes, S. 1998. "Indonesia in Big Interest Rate Increase." *Financial Times,* 24 March, p. 4.

2

International Banking Crises: The Real Estate Connection

Benton E. Gup

The default of long-term real estate loans has been associated with banking crises in Japan, Spain, Sweden, Thailand, the United States, and elsewhere. This study extends the literature on banking crises and failures by examining the effects of unexpected increases in interest rates and asset price deflation on borrower's behavior. We show that while interest rate shocks may have little direct impact on banks today, they increase the value of borrowers' put options to default on loans to the point that they are in the money. That is, the value of the assets financed by borrowing is less than the amount of the loans due. Macroeconomic deflationary effects and an oversupply of real estate provide the borrowers with incentives to exercise their put options. In addition, borrowers with variable rate loans may have interest costs in excess of their income. The in-the-money values of put options and incentives are less for shorter-term borrowers. If a sufficiently large number of borrowers exercise their options default, the banks will fail en masse.

   During the 1980 to 1996 period, more than 130 of the International Monetary Fund's 181 members experienced significant banking-sector problems or crises (Lindgren, Garcia, and Saal 1996). Fluctuations in real estate conditions were specifically mentioned in connection with banking problems in Finland, France, Japan, Malaysia, Norway, Spain, Sweden, the United States, and Venezuela. In a World Bank study of bank restructuring during the 1980s, Sheng (1996) identified real estate losses associated with banking problems in Argentina, Chile, Columbia, Ghana, Malaysia, Spain, the United States, and Yugoslavia. A Federal Deposit Insurance Corporation study concluded that booms and busts in commercial real estate markets were the main causes of losses at failed and surviving banks during the U.S. banking crises in the 1980s and early 1990s (*History of the Eighties* 1997, vol. 1).

Studies of individual bank failures in the G-10 countries by Bartholomew and Gup (1997) and Gup (1998) identified real estate loans as contributing to more bank failures than any other single category of loans. The countries where problem real estate loans could be identified with individual bank failures included Canada, France, Japan, Netherlands, and the United States. Losses in real estate loans and other long-term loans also played an important role in the 1977 banking crises in Southeast Asia. Berg (1993, 441), commenting on the banking crises in Finland, Norway, and Sweden, stated that real estate bubbles "are a common characteristic of banking crises almost everywhere." Seidman (1997, 58), former Chairman of the FDIC, said, "Everywhere from Finland to Sweden to England to the United States to Japan to Australia, excessive real estate loans created the core of the banking problem." Why do real estate loans stand out as being such a problem? To help answer that question, this chapter examines why borrowers default on real estate loans, thereby contributing to bank failures and crises.

In option-pricing theory, bank loans are considered compound options containing rights to prepay (call options) and to default (put options) on each of the scheduled payment dates (Ambrose and Capone 1996). When the put options are in the money (the value of the asset is less than the loan amount), borrowers have an incentive to exercise their put options and default on their loans. In the sections that follow, we examine why some borrowers have greater incentives than others to exercise their put options.

There are three key parties involved in banking crises: borrowers, banks, and the government, including bank regulators. The term "bank" is used in the general sense of the word, and it includes other types of lenders. In general terms, government policies intended to stimulate economic growth encourage borrowing and lending. The borrowing and lending may become excessive, resulting in an oversupply in real estate and excess productive capacity in some industries. At some point, the government recognizes that the rate of growth must be slowed, and its policies become restrictive. The adverse effects that follow include higher interest rates, asset price deflation, reduced demand, and lower expectations of future business revenues. The combination of these effects and other factors that will be presented affect borrowers' incentives to exercise their put options to default. If a sufficiently large number of borrowers default, banks fail.

GOVERNMENT

Three ways in which government policies affect banks are examined in this section. These include monetary policy, state-directed investment policies, and foreign exchange rate policies. Although fiscal policies also affect banks, they are not considered here. The role of bank regulators is explained later.

Monetary Policy

Benjamin Friedman (1995) examined the effects of monetary policy on real economic activity and found that they are systematic, significant, and sizeable. Milton Friedman (1997) argues that monetary policy deserves much of the blame for the current "parlous state of the Japanese economy." Since 1973, the growth rate of money has declined on average, contributing to the current low level of interest rates (the discount rate is 0.5%). The growth rate of money remains at its lowest level in the postwar period. In contrast, the Bank of Japan argues that since 1995 it has taken an easy stance. Whichever view is correct, it is clear that monetary policy matters. More to the point, monetary policy has a direct effect on banks. Goodhart (1995, 294) states that monetary authorities and commercial banks share the responsibility for asset price/banking cycles in the 1980s and early 1990s.

With that in mind, Lindgren, Garcia, and Saal (1996, 55) state that "experience has shown that although a loosening of monetary policy could be to the advantage of banks in the short-term, an excessively loose policy may contribute to asset price bubbles and inflation and to future banking system problems." Stated otherwise, loose monetary policy encourages borrowing, and its counterpart, lending. One consequence of continued borrowing is that oversupply or excess capacity may develop. In Bangkok, Thailand, for example, overbuilding resulted in 300 thousand housing units that were unoccupied in early 1997. In a good year, about 120 thousand units are needed. In addition, an array of luxury hotels and the world's tallest building stood empty (Bluestein 1997). The oversupply drives down the prices of real estate and rents. Excess capacity in Southeast Asia developed in the production of automobiles, computer chips, steel, textiles, and other industries.

Problems with banks occur when monetary authorities suddenly reverse their expansive policy and it becomes restrictive. This is characterized by a sharp increase in interest rates and monetary contraction. That is what happened in the late 1970s, which marked the beginning of the United States savings and loan (S&L) crises.[1] Government-mandated institutional rigidities, including borrowing short term and lending long term, limits on rates that could be paid for funds, and limits on investments, all had adverse affects on S&Ls. Similar institutional rigidities caused problems in 1997 for Thailand's fifty-eight finance companies that specialized in real estate finance. The Thai finance companies funded their long-term lending activities by borrowing short-term fixed rate deposits and notes. The problem was exacerbated by borrowing in dollars and lending in the local currency (the baht). More will be said about this shortly. Fifty-six of the fifty-eight finance companies were closed by the central bank (the Bank of Thailand) in late 1997.[2]

Restrictive monetary policy may result in asset price deflation over time. Accordingly, the demand for real estate and other assets is reduced. The deflation can be exacerbated by the oversupply and excess capacity that was referred to earlier. During the 1990 to 1997 period, the value of real estate in Japan is estimated to have declined 70 to 90 percent.

State-Directed Investment Policies

Banks have been tools of state industrial policies in countries including, but not limited to, Japan, Philippines, South Korea, Thailand, and the United States. State industrial policies directed banks to invest in government-approved firms, industries, and projects. In Japan, conglomerate companies, or *keiretsus*, are linked together by crossholdings of shares. The *keiretsus* include banks and industrial firms. In South Korea, *chaebols*, family-run business groups, played a similar role. The *chaebols* are highly leveraged. When the Halla *chaebol* filed for bankruptcy in December 1997, its debt was twenty times the group's equity. Debt-to-equity ratios of 4 to 1 or more are not uncommon.

Although banks are not formally part of the *chaebols*, they are tied to them through long-term relationships and government pressure. In fact, *chaebols* were banks' largest customers, and they could not turn off the credit. Accordingly, banks invested heavily in *chaebols*, such as Hanbo steel group, Kia automobiles, and Halla shipbuilding. Although initial investments in these industries spurred economic growth in South Korea, more recent investments resulted in excess capacity. All three groups went bankrupt, which, in turn, affected the banks that lent to them.

In Indonesia, President Suharto directed investments toward banks and firms owned by family and friends. In the United States, government-sponsored enterprises (GSEs) direct funds to particular sectors of the economy. The Federal Home Loan Banks and the Farm Credit System are two examples. In the early 1980s, the Farm Credit System lent aggressively in real estate until it failed, and was then recapitalized by Congress.

Foreign Exchange Rates Policies

Governments in Indonesia, Malaysia, Philippines, South Korea, and Thailand assumed that foreign exchange rates would remain stable. They further assumed that they could borrow more cheaply in dollars than they could in their own currencies. Thus, banks borrowed dollars to make loans in their local currency. The large influx of foreign currency contributed to record economic growth and speculative bubbles.

The governments tried to manage their exchange rates and monetary policies independently, but they did not succeed. Governments can manage either the exchange rate or domestic prices, but not both at the same time. The local currencies became overvalued, and their current account deficits exhausted their foreign currency reserves. Borrowers repaid their loans in local currencies, and banks were hard pressed to meet their dollar-denominated obligations. This and other factors made conditions ripe for international speculation in the local currencies (Suzuki 1997). As a result of the speculation and downward pressure on the baht, Thailand abandoned its peg against the dollar in July 1997. By October, the value of the baht depreciated 60 percent against the dollar. Following sharp declines in its currency, South Korea permitted the won to float in December 1997. Currencies in other Southeast Asian countries followed a similar pattern of declines against the dollar.[3]

CAUSES OF FAILURES

Banks

The primary reasons for bank failures are credit risk, interest rate risk, and fraud. We will consider the first two, but fraud is beyond the scope of this chapter.[4]

Credit Risk

Privately owned banks attempt to maximize their shareholder's wealth by making profitable loans and increasing the size of their loan portfolios. Expected profits can be increased by making riskier loans. Loans are the primary source of bank income, and bad loans are the primary reason for bank failures. Credit risk is the risk that loans may not be repaid.

It is generally recognized that most bankers are honest, and they do not intentionally make bad loans. Nevertheless, they do make loans that do not perform over time as expected. If the number of nonperforming loans is sufficiently large and they are charged off, the bank's capital can be eroded and the bank may fail.

Loan defaults are a result of borrowers' decisions to exercise their put options. This decision depends, in large part, on how the loan is structured. More will be said about that shortly.

Interest Rate Risk

Interest rate risk is the risk to earnings or capital as a result of changes in interest rates. It is used in two ways in this chapter. First, with respect to the entire bank, it is the negative effect on net interest income from a mismatch between the dollar amounts of interest rate sensitive assets and interest rate sensitive liabilities. For example, in the 1970s, savings and loan associations borrowed short-term funds and lent them at fixed rates for long-term mortgage loans. When interest rates soared in the late 1970s, their interest expense exceeded their interest income. Second, with respect to earnings assets, such as mortgage loans, interest rate risk is the negative effect of interest rate changes on the intrinsic value of those assets. If market rates of interest increase, the value of the assets declines but liabilities remain unchanged. Thus, capital is affected adversely. In the late 1970s and early 1980s, the S&Ls were technically insolvent as a result of interest rate risks. That is, the market value of their assets was less than the market value of their liabilities. Firms that are insolvent can operate as long as their cash flow is positive. Leveraged buyouts are a case in point (Samson and Gup 1989).

Borrowers

Investors seek to maximize their wealth by borrowing to the maximum extent that they can from banks and other investors. In this chapter, the borrowed funds are used to invest in short-term, intermediate-term, and long-term investments. Borrowing here is limited to 100 percent. However, some home equity loans in the United States are made for 125 percent or more of the value of the underlying property.

Characteristics of Borrowers

Borrowers in countries with developed capital markets have a choice of borrowing from banks or issuing public debt. Various studies (Leland and Pyle 1977; Cambell and Kracaw 1980; Diamond 1984, 1991; Ramakrishnan and Thakor 1984; Bensanko and Kanatas 1993) have found that firms with good reputations and adequate equity positions commonly issue public debt. Such firms require minimum monitoring by the investors who buy such debt. In contrast, firms of lesser quality that do require monitoring tend to borrow from banks. Dewatripont and Tirole (1994) report a study by Daltung (1994) which shows that excessive risk taking is a natural consequence of the private information obtained by banks in their delegated monitoring functions.

In countries without developed capital markets, borrowers who do not have access to global capital markets depend primarily on banks for debt financing. A World Bank study revealed that bank loans in the United States are equal to 50 percent of the Gross Domestic Product. In contrast, banks loans are 100 percent in Malaysia, 150 percent in Japan, and 170 percent in Germany (World Bank 1997).

Put Option

Borrowers have a put option to default on their loans. We make the assumption that the loans are used to invest in an earning asset. The valuation of the earning asset is explained in the next section. The put option is in the money when the amount of the loan exceeds the intrinsic value of the earning asset. The intrinsic value of the assets may decline for one or more of the following reasons:

1. oversupply or excess capacity, such as overbuilding of real estate or too many automobile factories.
2. an unexpected increase in interest rates.
3. asset price deflation.
4. reduced demand resulting in actual or expected lower cash flows.

The excess supply develops during the "boom" period. The other factors are a result of restrictive economic policies and they occur with some lags. In discussing conditions in Japan, for example, Milton Friedman (1997) observed that in 1990 the Bank of Japan reduced monetary growth from 13 to 3 percent, which then resulted in lower stock prices, lower nominal incomes, and lower growth. By 1994, the low inflation turned into actual deflation. Real estate values in Japan plunged during this period. The largest Japanese banks had huge portfolios of nonperforming loans, but the government did not let them fail.

Borrowers, like banks, are subject to interest rate risk. If the loan has a variable interest rate and rates increase unexpectedly, the higher interest expense on the loan could exceed the actual or expected income from the earning asset. VanderHoff (1996) found the default rate for adjustable rate home mortgages in the United States is affected more by anticipated increases in rates than by actual increases in payments. Phillips, Rosenblatt, and VanderHoff (1996) examined terminations of fixed and adjustable rate home mortgage loans. They found that the default rates were higher for adjustable rate mortgages, due to reductions in equity associated with depressed local housing markets. Differences may also be due to increased payments from "teaser" rates to higher interest rates and the qualification process that results in adverse selection for adjustable rate mortgages. In 1997, the delinquency rate for adjustable rate single-family mortgages was about twice as high as for fixed rate mortgages in Fannie Mae mortgage-backed securities (Fannie Mae 1997). These studies suggest that banks may be converting their interest rate risk into credit risk by using adjustable rate mortgages.

Elmer and Seelig (1998a) developed a choice-theoretic model to examine single-family mortgage defaults in the United States. They found that income and real estate price shocks, along with insolvency, play a central role in mortgage defaults. They also found (Elmer and Seelig 1998b) that house appreciation rates and loan-to-value ratios explain some of the rising long-term trends in single-family mortgage foreclosure rates.

Finally, some real estate loans are made without recourse. Thus, the borrower is not at risk if he or she defaults on the loan.

All these reasons provide incentives for borrowers to exercise their put options to default. However, not all borrowers are equally likely to default. A large corporation, such as Exxon, is less likely to exercise its put option on one loan than a small firm or an individual investor or speculator.

INTEREST RATE SHOCK

Assume that the economy has been growing at a rapid pace, and that the monetary authority wants to retard the growth rate by raising interest rates sharply. We will examine the effect of an instantaneous 200-basis-point parallel shift in the yield curve on both banks and borrowers. The yield curves before and after the rate increase are shown in Figure 2.1.

Impact on Banks

Table 2.1 shows a hypothetical bank with a negative dollar gap. That is, the dollar amount of the interest rate sensitive liabilities exceeds the dollar amount of the interest rate sensitive assets. The assets earn a fixed rate. The bank has invested in securities at 4.5 percent, a one-year working capital loan at 5 percent, a five-year equipment loan at 6 percent, and a twenty-five-year real estate loan at 7 percent. The loans are secured by the assets they fund. The bank's principal source of funds is floating rate deposits.

There are important differences between long-term real estate loans and shorter-term loans. First, in contrast to working-capital loans, real

Figure 2.1
Yield Curves

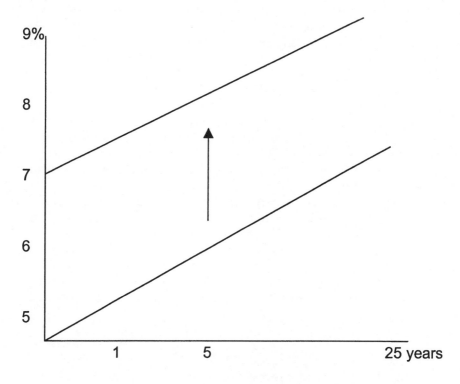

estate is the end product of a real estate loan. Second, a long lead time is required to develop large commercial and multifamily real estate projects, and economic conditions can change during the development process. Third, typically the developer of the projects is not the end user, but hopes to sell them at a profit. Finally, large commercial and multifamily real estate projects lack liquidity, especially when economic conditions change for the worse. Along this line, we know from the experiences of the Resolution Trust Corporation and the FDIC that the liquidation of assets from failed banks can take years and losses from those assets are substantial. James (1991) found that losses from bank failures in the mid-1980s were about 30 percent of failed banks' assets.

The bank shown in Table 2.1 is well capitalized, with an equity/risk asset ratio of 10 percent at the beginning of the period. The bank expects its net interest income (interest income minus interest expense) to be $56,500. Its return on assets will be 1.41 percent, and its return on equity (ROE; net interest income/equity) will be 16.14 percent. This is a profitable bank, if everything goes as planned. However, if there is

Table 2.1
Bank with a Negative Dollar Gap

ASSETS			LIABILITIES AND EQUITY		
Secur.	$500,000	@ 4.5% Fixed	Deposits	$3,650,000	@ 4% Floating
1-Year Working Capital Loan	$1,000,000	@ 5% Fixed			
5- Year Equip. Loan	$1,000,000	@ 6% Fixed			
25-Year Real Estate Loan	$1,000,000	@ 7% Fixed			
Non earning Asset	$500,000		Equity	$350,000	
	$4,000,000			$4,000,000	

an instantaneous 200-basis-point parallel shift in the yield curve, the bank will have a net interest income of negative $16,500, a negative ROA, and a negative ROE. The equity/risk assets ratio will fall to 9.57 percent if the loss is subtracted from the equity and risk assets. The bank will survive, but it is not profitable.

The bank could have eliminated the interest rate risk by hedging with a swap, where the bank received floating rates and paid fixed rates. Similarly, banks can eliminate their interest rate risk by hedging using other derivatives, or by having a neutral dollar gap. Thus, interest rate risk is not a real threat to this bank, but it does have a negative impact on the borrowers that are examined next. The effect of the increase in interest rates on the market value of the bank's securities and loans is not considered here, but it is addressed in connection with the borrowers.

Impact on Borrowers

Before we can examine the impact of the 200-basis-point increase in market rates of interest on the borrower, we have to make some assumptions about the valuation of the borrower's assets. As mentioned, the borrower made the loan to invest in an earning asset. The value of the earning asset is the present value of expected future cash flows (an annuity), discounted by the market rate of interest. The market rate of interest at the time that the loans were made was the loan rate for each of the three loans. The holding period of the asset is equal to the term of the loan. There are no taxes. The present value of an annuity PV_a is

$$PV_a = PMT \sum_{t=1}^{n} \left[\frac{1}{(1 + i)^t} \right]$$

where

$$PMT = \text{expected annual cash flow (income)}$$
$$n = \text{number of years}$$
$$i = \text{interest rate}$$

Panel A of Table 2.2 shows the initial intrinsic value of the real estate asset for various loan-to-value ratios. The loan is for $1 million. If the loan-to-value ratio is 100 percent, then the value of the asset is $1 million. If the loan-to-value ratio is 90 percent, the value of the asset is $1,111,111 ($1,000,000/0.90), and so on. The difference between the value of the asset and the amount of the loan represents the borrower's equity in the asset. Studies by von Furstenberg (1969, 1970) and Vandell (1978) reveal that loan-to-value ratios and the amount of borrowers' equity accumulation were statistically significant determinants of mortgage loan defaults. The higher the loan-to-value ratios, the greater the default rates. Panel A of Table 2.2 also shows expected annual income (PMT) for each initial asset values based on a 7-percent interest rate.

Panel B of Table 2.2 demonstrates the effects of the 200-basis-point increase in market rates of interest to 9 percent on the present value of the annuity, which is the intrinsic value of the real estate asset. It also reveals the difference between the loan amount and the intrinsic value of the asset. When the loan-to-value ratio is 100 percent, the loan exceeds the value by $157,123, and the put option is deep in the money. The put is also in the money when the loan-to-value ratio is 90 percent. The put is out of the money at lower loan-to-value ratios.

Table 2.3 presents the effects of the 200-basis-point increase in interest rates on the asset values and the differences between these values and the loan amounts for all three categories of loans. The data reveal that when the loan-to-value ratio is 100 percent, the put options are in the money for the three loans. However, the twenty-five-year real estate loan is in the money for $157,123, whereas the five-year and one-year loans are in the money for $52,577 and $18,690, respectively. Only the twenty-five-year loan is in the money when the loan-to-value ratio is 90 percent.

Table 2.2
Real Estate Values

Panel A

25 Year, $1,000,000 Real Estate Loan at 7% Fixed Rate

	Loan/ Value 100%	Loan/ Value 90%	Loan/ Value 80%	Loan/ Value 70%	Loan/ Value 60%
25-Year Real Estate Loan	$1,000,000	$1,000,000	$1,000,000	$1,000,000	$1,000,000
Initial Asset Value*	$1,000,000	$1,111,111	$1,250,000	$1,428,571	$1,666,667
Expected Annual Income from Asset**	$85,810	$95,345	$107,263	$122,586	$143,017

Panel B

Interest Rates Increase 200 Basis Points to 9%

	Loan/ Value 100%	Loan/ Value 90%	Loan/ Value 80%	Loan/ Value 70%	Loan/ Value 60%
25-Year Real Estate Loan	$1,000,000	$1,000,000	$1,000,000	$1,000,000	$1,000,000
PV_a @ 9%	$842,877	$936,5361	$1,053,602	$1,204,113	$1,404,798
Asset Value Less Loan	- $157,123	- $63,464	$53,602	$204,113	$404,798

*At 90% loan/value, $1,000,000/0.90 = $1,111,111.11; $1,000,000/0.80 = $1,250,000, etc.
**PMT derived from initial asset values being discounted at 7%.

When the put is deep in the money, which is the case for the twenty-five-year real estate loan, the borrower may default, given the incentives that have been mentioned. Simons (1994) found that industrial real estate mortgage defaults were strongly associated with negative equity and bankruptcy. Kau and Kim (1994, 550), analyzing defaults on property, concluded, "If the house price has fallen low enough, one

Table 2.3
Values When Market Rates of Interest Increase 200 Basis Points

	Loan/ Value 100%	Loan/ Value 90%	Loan/ Value 80%	Loan/ Value 70%	Loan/ Value 60%
PV$_a$ @ 9% 25-Year Real Estate Loan	$842,877	$936,536	$1,053,602	$1,204,113	$1,404,798
Asset Value Less Loan	-$157,123 Default likely	-$63,464 Default possible	$53,602	$204,113	$404,798
PV$_a$ @ 8% 5-Year Equipment Loan	$947,623	$1,053,186	$1,184,833	$1,354,096	$1,579,780
Asset Value Less Loan	-$52,577 Default possible	$53,186	$183,833	$354,096	$579,798
PV$_a$ 7% 1-Year Working Capital Loan	$981,310	$1,090,345	$1,226,636	$1,401,872	$1,635,517
Asset Value Less Loan	-$18,690 Default not likely	$90,345	$226,636	$401,872	$635,517

will then default immediately." Conversely, if the put option is out of the money, and the borrower has a positive equity investment in the asset, defaults are highly unlikely.

Duration also can be used to explain price changes in financial assets (Bierwag 1987). Duration is the weighted average time to maturity necessary to receive all cash flows from an investment. The price changes in the intrinsic value of the investment depend directly on the term to maturity of the cash flows, and inversely on the level of interest rates. Simply stated, for a given change in market rates of interest, long-term investments experience greater price changes than shorter-term investments with the same cash flow. In our example, the twenty-five-year loan/asset had much larger price changes than the shorter-term loans/assets.

Duration theory also reveals that for a given change in market rates of interest, assets with low coupon rates experience greater price changes than assets of the same maturity that have high cash flow. The difference in rates between the twenty-five-year loan and the one-year loan did not have much of an effect on the intrinsic value in this case.

To review, the data suggest that long-term loans/assets, such as mortgage loans, are more price sensitive to changes in market rates than short-term loans/assets. Therefore, when market rates of interest increase, put options on such loans are more likely to be deep in the money than puts on shorter-term loans. Other reasons for declining asset values have already been mentioned. They include oversupply, asset price deflation, and reduced demand. If the borrower of the long-term loan in our example exercises the put option to default for these or other reasons, the bank will probably fail.

DOES BANK REGULATION MATTER?

Macroeconomics

A basic theme in this chapter is that government policies combined with concentrations of long-term real estate loans contributed to bank failures and crises. An IMF study by Sheng (1996, 14) found, "Evidence suggests that while fraud and bank mismanagement were responsible for many individual bank failures and losses, macroeconomic factors, such as external shocks, policy mistakes, and inadequate risk management at all levels—institutional, sectoral, and national—created conditions of financial imbalance that led to widespread bank distress." He goes on to say that the banking problems of the 1980s were a result of a combination of bad policies, bad management, and a bad institutional framework. Benston and Kaufman (1997, 3), in discussing the causes of the S&L crisis, said, "Both the duration mismatch and the interest rate increases can be blamed on government policy."

The Basle Committee on Banking Supervision (1997) recognized the importance of macroeconomic policies with respect to banking supervision. Their preconditions for effective banking supervision recognize that providing stable economic conditions are not within the purview of banking supervisors. Nevertheless, banking supervisors "will need to react if they perceive that existing policies are undermining the safety and soundness of the banking system. In the absence of sound macro-economic policies, banking supervisors will be faced with a virtually impossible task" (p. 11).

Even if governments have stable macroeconomic polices, external factors over which they have no control can raise havoc with banks. The impact of oil shocks on banks in the Southwest United States and speculative attacks on currency in the European exchange market in the early 1990s are two examples (Gerlach and Smets 1994).

Supervision Can Matter

While it is true that banking supervisors cannot control macroeconomic stability or external shocks, they can mitigate the adverse effects of them by encouraging or requiring sound banking policies. The less-developed-country (LDC) debt crisis of the 1980s provides an example. In this case, regulatory forbearance granted to the largest banks with respect to loan-loss reserves against past-due LDC debt saved those banks from being deemed insolvent. The regulator's believed that the failure of these banks may have precipitated an economic and political crisis (*History of the Eighties* 1997, 207). However, there are counterexamples. The regulatory forbearance of financially distressed S&Ls in the early 1980s is one example. Well-intended regulatory actions to forestall failures and other factors contributed to the S&L debacle (*History of the Eighties* 1997, Chapter 4).

Finally, bank regulators can learn from the mistakes. In the United States, bank regulators are trying to improve their effectiveness with off-site monitoring and more effective internal examinations. However, bank regulators in Thailand failed to learn lessons from our S&L crisis. As mentioned, Thai finance companies that specialize in real estate lending borrowed short-term funds and lent long term. As a result of their banking and currency crises, the Thai government closed fifty-six of fifty-eight finance companies. Greenspan (1997) stated, "Crises would have been better contained if long-maturity property loans had not accentuated the usual mismatch between maturities of assets and liabilities of domestic financial systems."

Currently, this study identified long-term loans and high loan-to-value ratios as complementary factors that add to banks' credit risks. The Federal Deposit Insurance Corporation Improvement Act of 1991 (FDICIA) required federal banking regulators to develop uniform banking regulations with respect to real estate lending standards. The regulations include the maximum loan-to-value ratios for various real estate loan categories.[5] Although no supervisory limit was established for owner-occupied home mortgage loans, the average loan-to-price ratios for new homes in 1997 was about 80 percent.[6] Unfortunately, there is no similar legislation for state-supervised financial institutions. Accordingly, some lenders are making home equity loans (second mortgages) that bring the loan-to-value ratio up to 125 percent or higher (Bleakley 1997; U.S. General Accounting Office 1998). Regulated depository institutions were not heavily involved in such lending. Moreover, the total amount of the High Loan to Value (HLTV) lending in 1998 was estimated to be about $12 billion, a small fraction of the $3.8

trillion of outstanding residential mortgage debt. Nevertheless, the put option is deep in the money on these HLTV loans.

CONCLUSION

Government economic policies may inadvertently contribute to economic booms and speculative bubbles that ultimately burst, resulting in large-scale bank failures. The government policies presented here include monetary policy, government-directed investments, and foreign exchange rate policies. This does not mean that these policies have the same effect on all geographic sectors of the economy. In most countries, for example, commercial real estate cycles tend to be local in character. This suggests that other factors, such as demographics, oil shocks, and so on also influence lenders and borrowers.

Borrowers attempting to maximize their wealth borrow as much as possible to finance their investments, some of which are speculative. Such borrowers favor high loan-to-value ratios. The borrowers have a put option to default on their loans. The put option is in the money when the value of the asset financed by the bank loan is less than the amount of the loan. This can happen because of an unexpected increase in interest rates, asset price deflation, or other reasons. The greatest price changes occur in long-term loans, such as real estate loans. Given the proper incentives, borrowers will exercise their put options and default on their bank loans. Banks fail when this occurs in sufficient numbers. The incentives include reduced demand, lower expectations of income, interest expense in excess of income, nonrecourse loans, and so on.

Private banks are for-profit corporations that attempt to maximize shareholder wealth. They attempt to do this by increasing their loans and returns by taking on higher risks. Several ways in which this can be accomplished include offering high loan-to-value ratios, lowering credit standards, and increasing loan concentration in high-risk loans. During periods of rapid economic growth, banks may ignore sound lending practices, believing that strong growth will provide revenues to fund their increased problem loans. Nevertheless, an excess concentration of long-term loans, such as real estate loans, with high loan-to-value ratios increases the chances of bank failures and crises when there are large interest rate shocks, economic conditions deteriorate, or there is deflation or other problems in the economy.

NOTES

Earlier versions of this chapter were presented at seminars at the University of Alabama and at the Office of the Comptroller of the Currency. I am indebted to the participants of those seminars and to Catharine Lemieux (Federal Reserve Bank of Chicago) and Pat Rudolph (University of Alabama) for helpful comments and suggestions.

1. The causes of the savings and loan crisis have been examined extensively by Barth (1991), Bartholomew (1993), Benston and Kaufman (1997), and others.

2. For further discussion of the financial crises in Thailand, see Gup (1998) and Moreno (1997).

3. Hong Kong did not suffer from this problem because of its currency-board arrangement. For a discussion of currency boards, see Báliño and Enoch (1997).

4. For a discussion of bank fraud and bank failures, see Gup (1995).

5. The details are reported in 12 CFR (Code of Federal Regulations), Subpart D.

6. Mortgage market data are published monthly in the *Federal Reserve Bulletin*.

REFERENCES

Ambrose, B. W., and C. A. Capone, Jr. 1996. "Cost-Benefit Analysis of Single-Family Foreclosure Alternatives." *Journal or Real Estate Finance and Economics* 13: 105–20.

Báliño, T., and C. Enoch. 1997. *Currency Board Arrangements: Issues and Experiences*. Washington, D.C.: International Monetary Fund.

Barth, J. R. 1991. *The Great Savings and Loan Debacle*. Washington, D.C.: American Enterprise Institute.

Bartholomew, P. F. 1993. *Resolving the Thrift Crises*. Washington, D.C.: Congressional Budget Office.

Bartholomew, P. F., and B. Gup. 1997. "A Survey of Bank Failures, Near Failures, and Significant Incidents in the Foreign G-10 Countries Since 1980." Paper presented at the annual meeting of the International Trade & Finance Association, 23 May, Porto, Portugal.

Basle Committee on Banking Supervision. 1997. *Core Principles to the Governors on Banking Supervision*. Basle, Switzerland: Bank for International Settlements.

Bensanko, D., and G. Kanatas. 1993. "Credit Market Equilibrium with Bank Monitoring and Moral Hazard." *Review of Financial Studies* 6: 213–32.

Benston, G. J., and G. G. Kaufman. 1997. *FDICIA After Five Years: A Review and Evaluation* (WP-97-1). Chicago: Federal Reserve Bank of Chicago.

Berg, S. A. 1993. "The Banking Crises in the Scandinavian Countries." In *Proceedings, 29th Annual Conference on Bank Structure and Competition*. Chicago: Federal Reserve Bank of Chicago.

Bierwag, G. O. 1987. *Duration Analysis: Managing Interest Rate Risk*. Cambridge, Mass.: Ballinger.

Bleakley, F. R. 1997. "A 125% Solution to Card Debt Stirs Worry." *Wall Street Journal*, 17 November.

Bluestein, P. 1997. "Asian 'Miracle' Loses Its Gleam as Economy Falters." *Washington Post*, 3 November, p. A1.

Cambell, T. S., and W. A. Kracaw. 1980. "Information Production, Market Signalling, and the Theory of Financial Intermediation." *The Journal of Finance* 35: 682–83.

Daltung, S. 1994. Risk, Efficiency and Regulation of Banks. Ph.D. diss., Stockholm University, Institute for International Economic Studies Monograph Series 25.

Dewatripont, M., and J. Tirole. 1994. *The Prudential Regulation of Banks.* Cambridge: MIT Press.

Diamond, D. 1984. "Financial Intermediation and Delegated Monitoring." *Review of Economic Studies* 51: 393–414.

Diamond, D. 1991. "Monitoring and Reputation: The Choice Between Bank Loans and Directly Placed Debt." *Journal of Political Economy* 99: 689–721.

Elmer, Peter J., and Steven A. Seelig. 1998a. "Insolvency, Trigger Events, and Consumer Risk Posture in the Theory of Single-Family Mortgage Default." Working Paper 98-3, FDIC Division of Research and Statistics.

Elmer, Peter J., and Steven A. Seelig. 1998b. "The Rising Long-Term Trend of Single-Family Mortgage Foreclosure Rates." Working Paper 98-2, FDIC Division of Research and Statistics.

Fannie Mae. 1997. *Monthly Summary* (December). Washington, D.C.: Federal National Mortgage Association.

Friedman, B. M. 1995. "Does Monetary Policy Affect Real Economic Activity? Why Do We Still Ask This Question?" Working Paper 5212, National Bureau of Economic Research, Cambridge, Mass.

Friedman, M. 1997. "Rx for Japan: Back to the Future." *Wall Street Journal,* 17 December, p. A22.

Gerlach, S., and F. Smets. 1994. "Contagious Speculative Attacks." Working Paper 23, Bank for International Settlements, Basle, Switzerland.

Goodhart, C.A.E. 1995. *The Central Bank and the Financial System.* Cambridge: MIT Press.

Greenspan, A. 1997. "Statement by Alan Greenspan, Chairman, Board of Governors of the Federal Reserve System, before the Joint Economic Committee, U.S. Congress, October 29, 1997." *Federal Reserve Bulletin,* December, 975–77.

Gup, B. E. 1995. *Targeting Fraud: Uncovering and Deterring Fraud in Financial Institutions.* New York: McGraw-Hill.

Gup, B. E. 1998. *Bank Failures in the Major Trading Countries of the World: Causes and Remedies.* Westport, Conn.: Quorum Books.

History of the Eighties—Lessons for the Future: An Examination of Banking Crises of the 1980s and Early 1990s. 1997. Washington, D.C.: Federal Deposit Insurance Corporation.

James, C. 1991. "The Losses Realized in Bank Failures." *Journal of Finance* 46: 1223–42.

Kau, J. B., and T. Kim. 1994. "Waiting to Default: The Value of Delay." *Journal of the American Real Estate and Urban Economics Association* 22: 539–51.

Leland, H. E., and D. H. Pyle. 1977. "Informational Asymmetries, Financial Structure and Financial Intermediation." *The Journal of Finance* 32: 371–87.

Lindgren, C., G. Garcia, and M. I. Saal. 1996. *Banking Soundness and Macroeconomic Policy.* Washington, D.C.: International Monetary Fund.

Moreno, R. 1997. "Lessons from Thailand." *FRSB Economic Letter* (Federal Reserve Bank of San Francisco), 7 November.

Phillips, R. A., E. Rosenblatt, and J. H. VanderHoff. 1996. "The Probabilty of Fixed- and Adjustable-Rate Mortgage Termination." *Journal of Real Estate Finance and Economics* 13: 95–104.

Ramakrishnan, R.T.S., and A. V. Thakor. 1984. "Information Reliability and a Theory of Financial Intermediation." *Review of Economic Studies* 51: 415–32.

Samson, W. D., and B. Gup. 1989. "The Hidden Side of Corporate Restructuring." *Tax Notes* 45: 877–84.

Seidman, W. L. 1997. "Lessons of the Eighties: What Does the Evidence Show." In *History of the Eighties—Lessons for the Future: An Examination of Banking Crises of the 1980s and Early 1990s*. Vol. 2, 55–64. Washington, D.C.: Federal Deposit Insurance Corporation.

Sheng, A. 1996. *Bank Restructuring: Lessons from the 1980s*. Washington, D.C.: International Monetary Fund.

Simons, R. A. 1994. "Industrial Real Estate Mortgage Default Experience of the New York State Job Development Authority Second Loan Program: A Preliminary Investigation." *Journal of the American Real Estate and Urban Economics Association* 22: 632–46.

Suzuki, Yoshio. 1997. "What Lessons Can Be Learned from Recent Financial Crises." Remarks made at a Federal Reserve Bank of Kansas City Symposium on "Maintaining Financial Stability in a Global Economy," 29 August, Jackson Hole, Wyoming.

U.S. General Accounting Office. 1998. *High-Loan-to-Value Lending: Information on Loans Exceeding Home Value* (GAO/GGD-98-169). Washington, D.C.: U.S. General Accounting Office.

Vandell, K. D. 1978. "Default Risk Under Alternative Mortgage Instruments." *Journal of Finance* 33: 1279–96.

VanderHoff, J. 1996. "Adjustable and Fixed Rate Mortgage Termination, Option Values and Local Market Conditions: An Empirical Analysis." *Real Estate Economics* 24: 379–406.

von Furstenberg, G. M. 1969. "Default Risk on FHA Insured Home Mortgages as a Function of the Terms of Financing." *Journal of Finance* 24: 459–77.

von Furstenberg, G. M. 1970. "The Investment Quality of Home Mortgages." *Journal of Risk and Insurance* 37: 437–45.

World Bank. 1997. *Private Capital Flows to Developing Countries*. Washington, D.C.: World Bank.

3

International Bank Lending and the Southeast Asian Financial Crisis

Philip F. Bartholomew and Nancy A. Wentzler

The financial crises in Thailand, Indonesia, and Korea that unfolded in the last half of 1997 now seem to be recognized as part of a larger story related to financial and economic difficulties in Japan and subsequent difficulties in other parts of the world.[1] As all of these crises had root causes predating public recognition of the Southeast Asian crises, economists for some time to come will debate fundamental and ancillary causes, timing, and the degree to which global financial difficulties among the affected countries were related.

Many financial and economic commentators have characterized the East Asian problems as a contagion. Bartholomew and Caprio (forthcoming) challenge this view, arguing that problems in Thailand, Korea, and Indonesia could be characterized as systemic with international spillover consequences, but there is little evidence of the presence of a contagion in these financial markets—at least up to April 1998. While all three economies shared many common characteristics, it is not clear that financial crisis in one country caused financial crises in others. Rather, all three economies were headed in a similar precipitous direction, and all three were affected by at least one common phenomena that may have triggered the inevitable. Although the argument may seem purely semantic, the distinction among types of financial crises is important in order to prescribe policy solutions.

This chapter only looks at one part of the East Asian crisis. By examining international bank lending data, it can be seen that problems in Thailand, Korea, and Indonesia were probably fueled by expansive international bank lending. Changes in that lending contributed to the bursting of these three economies' bubbles.

TWO VIEWS OF THE EAST ASIAN CRISIS

Discussion of the East Asian crisis was not focused on the presence of contagion. As well described in Moreno (1998), there were two initial views of the East Asian crisis. One view held that there was nothing fundamentally wrong with the East Asian economies. They merely experienced a surge in capital inflows to finance productive investments that made them vulnerable to financial panics. When international reserves were used up, exchange rates could no longer be pegged and a currency crisis ensued. Others argued that the financial systems of East Asian economies were the problem. Weaknesses were caused by lack of incentives for effective risk management (including poor bank supervision). These weaknesses were masked by rapid growth and were exacerbated by large capital inflows which themselves were partly encouraged by pegged exchange rates.

It could be argued that adherents of the first view would advocate international intervention to deal with the currency crisis. The problem with this view is that it ignores the importance of the second view. Problems in these emerging countries' financial systems resulted in a major financial crisis that will probably require long-term structural solutions. The second view has been characterized by some as a systemic-event view. However, because of the debate over the nature of systemic events and financial crises, one must be careful how to characterize the nature of the East Asian systemic problem.

SOME FUNDAMENTALS ABOUT SYSTEMIC RISK, CONTAGION, AND SPILLOVER

Systemic risk is a term used by financial and economic commentators, but still lacks a consensus definition.[2] To some, it is the risk of what is referred to as a classic bank contagion or widespread bank runs. Presently, contagions can refer to financial instruments and markets as well. Under this view, the East Asian crisis did not comprise a systemic event, as no financial contagion was at first present and therefore did not precipitate financial crisis. To others, however, a contagion is not necessary for a systemic event.[3] It is argued that if a substantial portion of a financial industry becomes insolvent, and this insolvency has real economic consequences, this too can comprise a systemic event. Under the second view, the East Asian crisis comprised a systemic event without a contagion.

The reason the distinction matters is that the policy prescription for each type of systemic event is different. Central bank provision of liquidity can stop a contagion; deposit and other liability guarantees can reduce the threat of a contagion. But such policies create a moral hazard that uncontained can cause substantial damage to a financial system. Although these policies are not necessary to create a systemic event of the second type, caution must be used in addressing a systemic event where a substantial insolvency of institutions generates real consequences. Less consensus exists on policy prescriptions for systemic events of the second type. It could be argued that the U.S. thrift crisis, massive industry insolvencies in the Nordic countries during the early 1990s, and the Japanese banking problems of the late 1990s characterize the second type of systemic event. A general-resolution strategy to process failures and return assets back to the marketplace seems appropriate. But failure of a less-sophisticated financial industry may pose peculiar difficulties. One general prescription for massive financial-industry insolvency accompanied with financial asset deflation is reflation of asset prices. To date, however, systematic development of such a policy prescription is not available.

Discussion of the East Asian crisis centers on the notion of contagion and spillover. Although it is unclear that economists have formally defined either term, and it is true that definitions are unfortunately arbitrary, the terms "contagion" and "spillover" seem to have particular meanings to economists. Both may be related to systemic risk and financial crisis, but they are certainly not synonymous. To students of banking, contagion has a very specific meaning.[4] As discussed, contagion refers to the transmission of a financial disturbance from one financial institution, market, or other arrangement to other financial players. Such disturbances may or may not have subsequent long-term effects, but the disturbance affects financial activity and there are probably at least short-term consequences.

A contagion, in financial terms, relates to a collapse of confidence by creditors to financial intermediaries. Absent deposit guarantees or other regulatory safety nets, if a single bank runs into financial difficulty its depositors would be rational to withdraw their funds as soon as possible in order to assure themselves that the troubled institution would make good on the deposit. This isolated bank run turns into a contagion if the failure of one institution undermines depositor confidence in general and runs ensue at other institutions.

Such a contagion can occur at nonbank financial institutions or in financial markets where information is asymmetric. For example, if the collapse of the Korean banking system undermines creditor confidence in other countries with regard to their banks, then it can be said that there is a contagion. But if banking systems in both countries were insolvent or in serious trouble in the first place, then it cannot be said that the collapse of one caused a collapse of public confidence leading to the collapse of the other. If, on the other hand, devaluation of the

Indonesian rupiah reduced confidence in other Southeast Asian currencies, it could be said that the Indonesian devaluation had a contagion effect. Such an effect, however, should be distinguished from the expected adjustments in foreign exchange markets.

FINANCIAL COLLAPSE AND THE ROLE
OF EXTERNAL LENDING

One way to look at the East Asian crisis is through looking at the role external lending had on the three economies. The Bank for International Settlement (BIS) collects data on lending by banks in G-10, European Monetary Union, and Scandinavian countries to all other countries. The BIS data do not show borrowing and lending within either of the two groups of countries. Here is a ranking of the largest bank borrowers as of year-end 1997 from BIS reporting banks:

Country	Billions of U.S. Dollars
South Korea	94
Former USSR	80
Brazil	76
China	63
Mexico	62
Argentina	60
Thailand	59
Indonesia	58
Greece	39
Portugal	31
Turkey	29
Malaysia	28
Taiwan	26
Chile	21
South Africa	21

Here is a list of the countries whose banks are the largest lenders, including consolidated crossborder claims in all currencies and local claims in nonlocal currencies:

Country	Billions of U.S. Dollars
Germany	190
Japan	163
United States	127

France	120
United Kingdom	95
Netherlands	56
Spain	50
Italy	38
Canada	28
Austria	24
Belgium	21
Luxembourg	5
Sweden	5
Denmark	2
Ireland	2
Finland	1
Norway	1

Finally, here are the amounts owed to U.S. banks by the largest foreign borrowers as of December 1997 after adjustments and external borrowings, as indicated by the Country Exposure Lending Survey:

Country	Billions of U.S. Dollars	Percentage Change Since 12/88
Japan	28.8	−53.9
United Kingdom	23.1	12.8
Germany	22.6	254.3
France	19.5	60.6
Brazil	17.4	−15.0
Canada	15.9	53.4
Mexico	13.8	−21.4
South Korea	13.5	168.5
Netherlands	11.4	181.3
Belgium–Luxembourg	10.4	39.8
Swizerland	10.3	120.6
Spain	9.1	246.4
Argentina	8.5	6.8
Italy	8.5	−14.7
British West Indies (Offshore Banking Center)	8.2	1083.5
Sweden	6.1	187.8
Hong Kong (Offshore Bankng Center)	5.1	84.9

Country	Billions of U.S. Dollars	Percentage Change Since 12/88
Australia	5.0	84.9
Chile	4.9	4.2
Former Soviet Union	4.4	794.3
Indonesia	4.3	388.1
China (Taiwan)	3.7	41.4
Colombia	3.4	63.7
Denmark	3.3	82.3
Singapore (Offshore Banking Center)	3.1	132.3
Venezuela	3.1	−59.4
South Africa	3.0	17.0
Norway	3.0	42.8
Thailand	2.8	144.4
Ireland	2.8	315.3

Thailand, Korea, and Indonesia were some of the world's largest borrowers. All three countries reduced international bank borrowings, some substantially, during the last half of 1997. Korea dropped $9 billion from $103 billion borrowed; Thailand, which had been the third-largest borrower behind Brazil reduced its borrowings by $10 billion; and Indonesia, which had been the sixth-largest borrower, fell $1 billion.

The major lenders to Thailand and Korea were Japanese financial institutions. Japanese financial institutions were also large lenders to Korea. As can be seen in Figure 3.1, there is an interesting pattern in this lending to the three countries in question. Loan growth in general in all three of these countries was substantial—in retrospect, some would say excessive. Much of the loan growth came from a single country, Japan.

Figure 3.2 shows as well that an unusually high proportion of the international bank lending was short term (i.e., less than one year in maturity). Chang and Velasco (1998) argue that this indicates the liquidity-crisis nature of the East Asian crisis. However, as argued in Bartholomew and Caprio (forthcoming), the fact that the short-term nature of the lending persisted for such a long period suggests that the crisis was not a liquidity crisis. In fact, it appears that these countries were quite capable of obtaining short-term funding. Certainly, such high proportions of short-term funding made them vulnerable to liquidity problems, but the greater problem is the cost of liquidity. Such a problem is fundamentally a solvency issue, which all three countries seem to have suffered.

Beginning in 1995, when Japan began to acknowledge problems in their financial sector, lending to Southeast Asia from Japanese institutions leveled. As can be seen in Figure 3.3, this was true for Japanese

Figure 3.1
Loans from Banks to Various Asian Countries

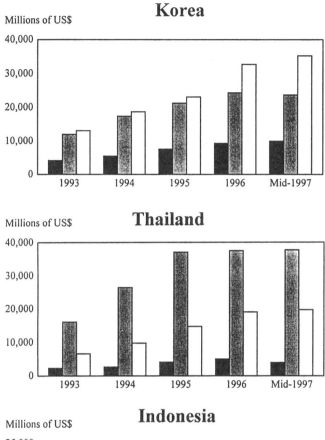

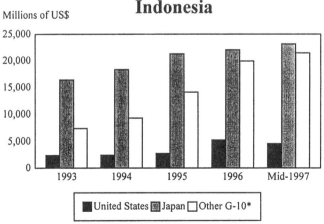

Source: Office of the Comptroller of the Currency using data from Bank for International Settlements.
*Not including Switzerland in 1993 through 1997 and not including Canada in 1993.

Figure 3.2
Percentage of Total Consolidated Crossborder Claims in Maturities of Up to and Including One Year

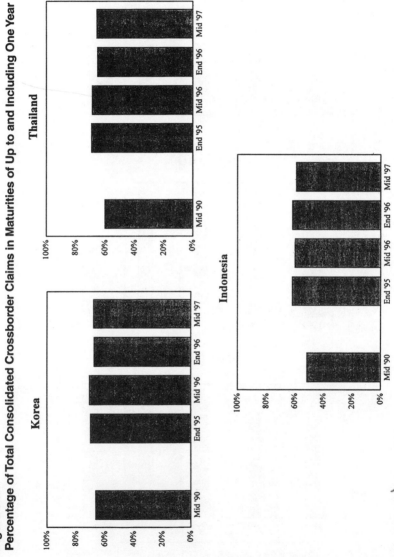

Source: Office of the Comptroller of the Currency using data from Bank for International Settlements.
Note: Total consolidated crossborder claims in all currencies and local claims in nonlocal currencies.

Figure 3.3
International Bank Lending by Japanese Banks to Asian Countries

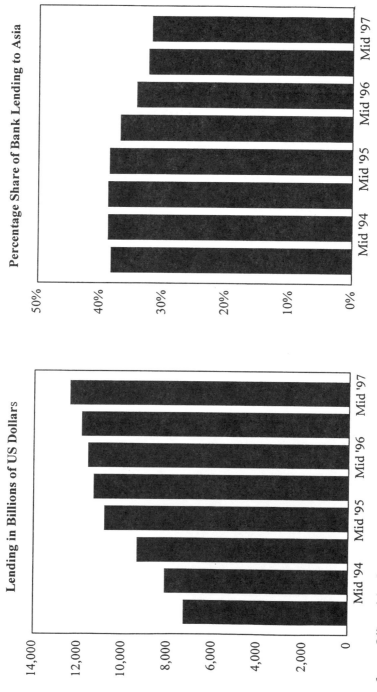

Source: Office of the Comptroller of the Currency using data from Bank for International Settlements.

bank international lending in general. Whereas overall Japanese international bank lending continued to increase through mid-1997, its rate of increase declined considerably and Japan's share of bank lending to East Asia declined abruptly. More recent data show Japan's lending to the region now dropping in absolute terms.

One explanation for the Southeast Asian crisis is that there were three speculative bubbles developing in three countries with similar export-based economies. Speculative bubbles require continued increased financing. Although other countries substituted for the reduced loan growth to Korea, Thailand, and Indonesia, the change in Japanese financing may be a probable trigger for the collapse of the bubbles.

In that the external financing of each of the three countries is similar, it is possible to conclude that the crises in the three countries were fairly simultaneous events. Rather than a collapse in one leading to a collapse in another or both, the three economies appear to have collapsed together. All bubbles collapse eventually—that is why they are bubbles—and in this case the rapid expansion of lending by Japanese banks appeared to be a factor in the run up, so the leveling off of lending can be argued to have played a role in the timing of the collapse. Although problems in Southeast Asia may spill over to Japan and other countries, subsequent revelations about problems in the Japanese financial sector have their roots prior to the Southeast Asian crisis.

ASIAN CONTAGION?

An alternative explanation for the Asian contagion is that the economies in Thailand, Korea, and Indonesia were suffering speculative bubbles that finally burst. All three economies suffered these bubbles and their financial sectors were weak and vulnerable to shocks. There were spillover consequences from the economic problems and devaluations of mid-1997, but there was no spread of the problem. Similarly, all three compared unfavorably with a sample of East Asian and Latin American countries in the adequacy of their financial regulatory environment, another problem in common.

The exchange rates, relative to the United States, of Korea, Japan, Thailand, and Indonesia are shown in Figure 3.4. Korea, Thailand, and Indonesia obviously devalued from a pegged or managed pegged exchange rate regime. It is unclear, however, from looking at exchange rates alone that the devaluations were related in a causal sense or whether they moved together.

Figure 3.5 shows the coefficient of variation for the same currencies. Except for Japan, it seems that in general the variation in these exchange rates were fairly harmonious. One should expect that if a con-

Figure 3.4
Daily Exchange Rates

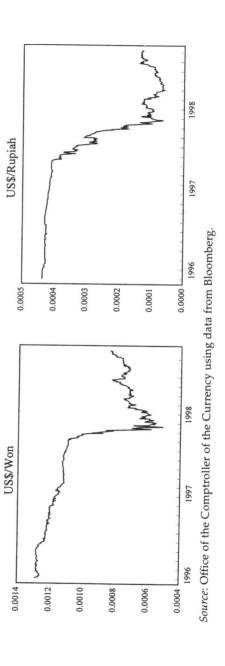

Source: Office of the Comptroller of the Currency using data from Bloomberg.

Figure 3.5
Monthly Coefficient of Variation for Selected Asian Daily U.S.-Dollar Exchange Rates (1996 to 1998)

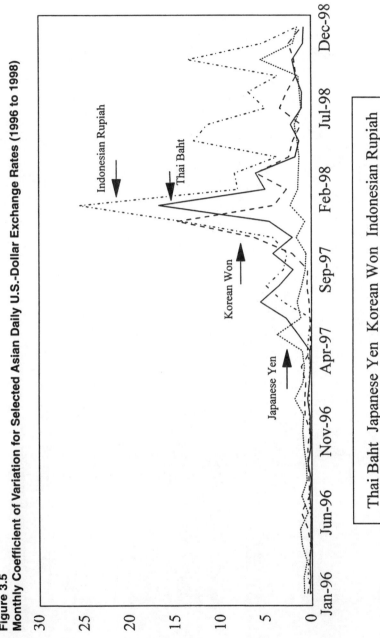

Source: Office of the Comptroller of the Currency using data from Bloomberg.

tagion had occurred, substantial variation would be seen in one market before being transmitted to others.

A similar analysis can be made using information on the same four countries' stock markets. Figure 3.6 shows declines in the stock market indices of Korea, Japan, Thailand, and Indonesia. Figure 3.7 shows the coefficient of variation associated with the movements of these indices. Again, it can be seen that except for Japan the indicator in the three countries moved together; the decline in the yen, as well as the banking crisis in Japan (usually dated as having commenced in 1991), clearly preceded the Thai crisis.

CONCLUSION

More detailed analysis is required to fully sort out how the exchange rates and stock markets of Korea, Thailand, and Indonesia moved over time during the crisis. It is probably the case that because of information disruptions and experience gained with this crisis that Southeast Asian markets will suffer some contagion effects.[5] For example, disturbances occurring well into the crisis will probably cause some confidence loss to varying degrees in all Southeast Asian financial markets. Such contagion effects will dissipate if greater information about these markets is obtained by financial players.

If one country's interest rates and/or exchange rates adjust, there will be consequences to its trade and capital flows. Depending upon the volume of flows, countries with trade and financial relationships with the devaluing country will suffer spillover effects. Spillover effects can be considered the indirect consequences of an economic action. In the case of the Southeast Asian financial crisis, spillover effects from the devaluation are not yet fully realized, as exchange rates in these markets have not yet stabilized.

Certainly, the global difficulties of the past two years provide a considerable amount of data to help sort out the nature of the financial crises, contagion, and spillover effects. This will be ever more important as financial institutions, instruments, and markets become more internationalized and global.

NOTES

This chapter was first prepared for the Financial Management Association Meetings, 15 October 1998, Chicago, Illinois. The authors thank Sarah C. Clark for research assistance.

1. Much has been written on the unfolding global financial crisis. For discussion of the East Asian financial crisis see, for example, Bartholomew and Caprio (forthcoming), Chang and Velasco (1998), Makin (1998a, 1998b), Mayer (1998), Meltzer (1998), and Moreno (1998).

Figure 3.6
Daily Stock Indices

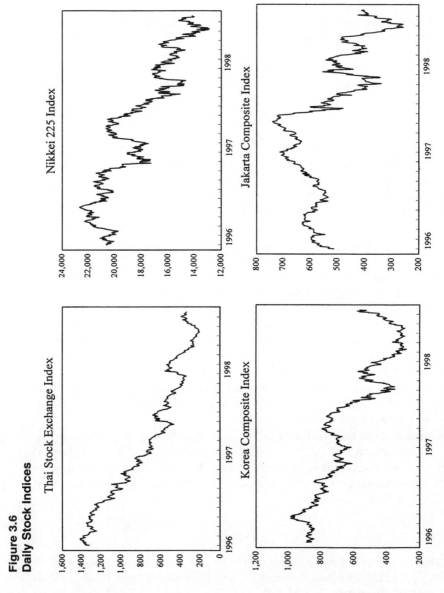

Nikkei 225 Index

Jakarta Composite Index

Thai Stock Exchange Index

Korea Composite Index

Source: Office of the Comptroller of the Currency using data from Bloomberg.

Figure 3.7
Monthly Coefficient of Variation for Selected Asian Daily Stock Market Indices (1996 to Present)

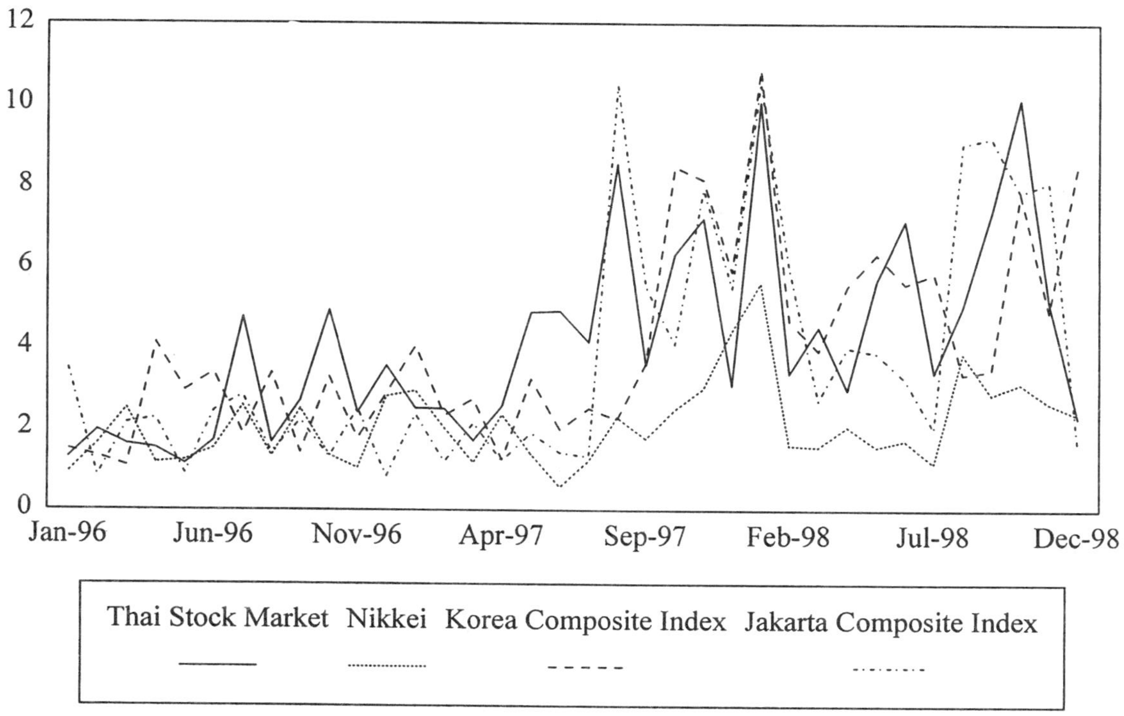
12
10
8
6
4
2
0
Jan-96
Jun-96
Nov-96
Apr-97
Sep-97
Feb-98
Jul-98
Dec-98
Thai Stock Market
Nikkei
Korea Composite Index
Jakarta Composite Index

Source: Office of the Comptroller of the Currency using data from Bloomberg.

2. See, for example, Davis (1992), Baer and Klingbiel (1995), Barth (1995), Bartholomew and Whalen (1995), Bartholomew, Mote, and Whalen (1995), Caprio and Klingbiel (1996), Eisenbeis (1997, 1995), Goldstein (1995), Gup (1998), Kaufman (1995, 1996), Mishkin (1995), Schwartz (1995), Lindgren, Garcia, and Saal (1996).

3. See, for example, Bartholomew and Whalen (1995), Bartholomew, Mote, and Whalen (1995), and Bartholomew and Caprio (forthcoming).

4. For discussion of contagion, see, for example, Gilbert (1988) and Kaufman (1996, 1992, 1986).

5. Some contagion effects may have been involved in latter stages of the East Asian crisis. Certainly, events late in the summer of 1998 suggest that financial contagion may have taken place where Russia's sovereign default may have affected government securities in Latin America (see Arias, Hausmann, and Rigobon 1998).

REFERENCES

Arias, Eduardo Fernandez, Ricardo Hausmann, and Roberto Rigobon. 1998. "Financial Contagion in Emerging Markets." Paper presented at conference, Crisis and Contagion in Emerging Financial Markets: The New Policy Agenda, 7 October, Inter-American Development Bank, Washington, D.C.

Baer, Herbert, and Daniela Klingbiel. 1995. "Systemic Risk When Depositors Bear Losses: Five Case Studies." In *Research in Financial Services and Public Policy*, edited by Philip F. Bartholomew and George G. Kaufman, vol. 7. Greenwich, Conn.: JAI Press.

Barth, James R. 1995. "Comment on Sources of Risk." In *Research in Financial Services and Public Policy*, edited by Philip F. Bartholomew and George G. Kaufman, vol. 7. Greenwich, Conn.: JAI Press.

Bartholomew, Philip F., and Gerard Caprio, Jr. Forthcoming. "Systemic Risk, Contagion, and the Southeast Asian Financial Crisis." In *Restructuring Regulation and Financial Institutions*, edited by James R. Barth and R. Dan Brumbaugh Jr., Milken Institute.

Bartholomew, Philip F., Larry R. Mote, and Gary Whalen. 1995. "The Definition of Systemic Risk." Presentation at the Annual Meetings of the Western Economic Association, 8 July, San Diego, California.

Bartholomew, Philip F., and Gary Whalen. 1995. "Fundamentals of Systemic Risk." In *Research in Financial Services and Public Policy*, edited by Philip F. Bartholomew and George G. Kaufman, vol. 7. Greenwich, Conn.: JAI Press.

Caprio, Gerard, Jr., and Daniela Klingbiel. 1996. "Bank Insolvency: Bad Luck, Bad Policy, or Bad Banking?" Paper presented at the World Bank Annual Bank Conference on Development Economics, 25–26 April, Washington, D.C.

Chang, Roberto, and Andres Velasco. 1998. "The Asian Liquidity Crisis." Working Paper 98-11, Federal Reserve Bank of Atlanta.

Davis, E. P. 1992. *Financial Fragility, and Systemic Risk*. Oxford: Oxford University Press.

Eisenbeis, Robert A. 1995. "Systemic Risk: Bank Deposits and Credit." In *Research in Financial Services and Public Policy*, edited by Philip F. Bartholomew and George G. Kaufman, vol. 7. Greenwich, Conn.: JAI Press.

Eisenbeis, Robert A. 1997. "Bank Deposits and Credit as Sources of Systemic Risk." *Economic Review*, Federal Reserve Bank of Atlanta, Third Quarter, 1997.

Gilbert, R. Alton. 1988. "A Re-Examination of the History of Bank Failures, Contagion, and Banking Panics." *Bank Structure and Competition*, Federal Reserve Bank of Chicago.

Goldstein, Morris. 1995. "International Aspects of Systemic Risk." In *Research in Financial Services and Public Policy*, edited by Philip F. Bartholomew and George G. Kaufman, vol. 7. Greenwich, Conn.: JAI Press.

Gup, Benton E. 1998. *Bank Failures in the Major Trading Countries*. Westport, Conn.: Quorum Books.

Kaufman, George G. 1986. "Banking Risk in Historical Perspective." *Bank Structure and Competition*, Federal Reserve Bank of Chicago.

Kaufman, George G. 1992. "Bank Contagion: Theory and Evidence." Working Paper, Federal Reserve Bank of Chicago working papers series.

Kaufman, George G. 1995. "Comment on Systemic Risk." In *Research in Financial Services and Public Policy*, edited by Philip F. Bartholomew and George G. Kaufman, vol. 7. Greenwich, Conn.: JAI Press.

Kaufman, George G. 1996. "Bank Failures, Systemic Risk, and Bank Regulation." *Cato Journal* 16.

Lindgren, Carl-Johan, Gillian Garcia, and Matthew I. Saal. 1996. *Bank Soundness and Macroeconomic Policy*. Washington, D.C.: International Monetary Fund.

Makin, John H. 1998a. "The Benefits of Devaluation in a Deflationary World." *Economic Outlook*, No. 9520, American Enterprise Institute for Public Policy Research.

Makin, John H. 1998b. "Interference with Free Markets Causes Global Crisis." *Economic Outlook*, No. 9625, American Enterprise Institute for Public Policy Research.

Mayer, Martin. 1998. "The Asian Disease: Plausible Diagnoses, Possible Remedies." *Public Policy Brief*, No. 44A, Jerome Levy Economics Institute of Bard College.

Meltzer, Allan. 1998. "Time for Japan to Print Money." *On the Issues*, No. 9435, American Enterprise Institute for Public Policy Research.

Mishkin, Frederic S. 1995. "Comment on Systemic Risk." In *Research in Financial Services and Public Policy*, edited by Philip F. Bartholomew and George G. Kaufman, vol. 7. Greenwich, Conn.: JAI Press).

Moreno, Ramon. 1998. "What Caused East Asia's Financial Crisis?" *Economic Letter*, Federal Reserve Bank of San Francisco, No. 98-24.

Schwartz, Anna J. 1995. "Systemic Risk and the Macroeconomy." In *Research in Financial Services and Public Policy*, edited by Philip F. Bartholomew and George G. Kaufman, vol. 7. Greenwich, Conn.: JAI Press.

PART **II**

CRISES IN
SELECTED COUNTRIES

Chapter 4 is the first of two chapters that deal with the crisis in Thailand from two different points of view. Chapter 4 is an updated version of Benton E. Gup and Doowoo Nam, "Crises in Thailand: A Case Study," in *Bank Failures in the Major Trading Countries of the World: Causes and Remedies* (Westport, Conn.: Quorum Books, 1998). It presents a broad overview of the Thai crisis and its causes.

Chapter 5, by Kiyoshi Abe of Chiba University in Japan, presents an insider's point of view. Professor Abe spent time in Thailand, and his chapter deals extensively with the Nukul Commission report that focuses on internal economic and political problems in that country. The Nukul Commission was a Thai government commission charged with examining the causes of the economic collapse. The report was completed in May 1998.

4

Thailand: A Tale of Sustained Growth and Then Collapse

Benton E. Gup and Doowoo Nam

Following months of speculative attacks against the Thai baht, which was closely pegged to the U.S. dollar, the Bank of Thailand allowed the baht to float in July 1997. That event is generally considered to be the beginning of the crisis in Thailand that spread to other nations in Southeast Asia. Huh and Kasa (1998) argue that the crisis was a result of external factors—depreciation of the Japanese yen and Chinese yuan—that led to a loss of export competitiveness which necessitated the devaluation. Kaminsky (1998) reveals that currency and banking crises are frequently but not always closely associated with each other. According to Mankin (1998), the crisis in Asia was due to massive excess capacity and the accompanying deflationary pressure. What really happened in Thailand, and what can we learn from that experience? This chapter attempts to answer these questions. The remainder of this chapter is divided into three parts. The first part provides a general description of Thailand. The next part examines the growth, prosperity, and real estate bubble that ultimately burst. The final part examines the lessons to be learned from this crisis.

THAILAND

The Kingdom of Thailand, located in Southeast Asia, has a population of about 60 million people, and the country is about the size of Texas. It is a constitutional monarchy. Its major markets include the United States, Japan, Singapore, and Hong Kong. The Thai legal system combines traditional Thai civil law and Western laws. However, their legal system was not designed to deal with modern financial institutions. For example, their laws impede efforts to restructure companies and liquidate real estate. In addition, their bankruptcy laws do not adequately protect creditors, especially when there are multijurisdictional claims. The law does not distinguish between secured and unsecured creditors, and foreclosure may take several years (*Thai Legal Issues and Financial Recovery* 1998).

Commercial banks are the largest financial institutions in Thailand. There are fifteen domestic banks, of which the three largest account for more than half of the market. There are also five special-purpose banks that finance particular sectors of the economy, such as agriculture and private housing. In December 1996, real estate loans accounted for 8.8 percent of total loans (Salomon Brothers 1997).

Ninety-one finance and securities companies are the second-most-important group of financial institutions. These companies specialize in real estate lending, financial lease and hire–purchase (car leasing) activities, and securities (margin lending) activities. Real estate loans accounted for about 24 percent of finance-company loans. They also accounted for 46 percent of total loans to the real estate sector at the end of 1996, compared to 35 percent three years earlier. Unlike banks, finance companies do not have checking or savings deposits or provide trade finance. They fund their activities through short-term fixed rate deposits and notes. Thus, they borrow short term and lend long term, a prescription for disaster.

Real estate finance companies (*credit-froncier*) finance the purchase of real estate. These firms are financed primarily with long-term debt.

There is no formal deposit insurance scheme in Thailand; but the Financial Institutions Development Fund (FIDF) collects annual contributions from all financial institutions at a rate of 0.1 percent of deposits.

DEJÀ VU

The financial system in Thailand faced a crisis during the first half of the 1980s. An IMF study by Johnston (1991, 274–75) concluded that distressed financial institutions in Thailand "had their origins mainly in weak managerial practices and inadequate legal, regulatory, and supervisory framework for the financial institutions." He goes on to say that, in 1985, the Thai authorities "took a variety of remedial actions as the problems with the institutions emerged, including substantial strengthening of the legal, regulatory, and supervisory arrangements."

According to Johnston (1991, 251), the Bank of Thailand summarized some of the management problems of their commercial banks:

- Several managers were not bankers, but were involved in commercial enterprises and gave little attention to running their banks.
- Extending credit to businesses in which the bank's directors and shareholders were directly involved.
- Inadequate internal controls and operating procedures.
- Concentration of lending to a few, large interrelated enterprises.

For example, Wong (1998) states that the Sophonpanich family controlled a banking, insurance, and securities empire. The empire included the nation's largest bank, Bangkok Bank, which holds more than 20 percent of the country's savings, the third largest insurance company, a major securities firm, and a portfolio of office buildings.

These same conclusions and concerns could have been written for the banking crisis in 1997–1998. They did not learn from their mistakes!

ECONOMIC GROWTH AND BUBBLES

Labor Costs

During the 1970 to 1990 period, Thailand had a competitive advantage in low labor costs. Low-cost labor produced clothing, shoes, and other labor-intensive goods for export. Except for economic problems in the mid-1980s associated with oil price shocks, the exports brought growth and prosperity. In the late 1980s, Thailand was one of the fastest growing economies in the world.

Unfortunately, Thailand did not have a sustainable competitive advantage in low labor costs. Factories in China produced low-cost goods at prices that undermined Thailand's ability to compete in low-cost manufacturing. In 1994, China devalued the yuan against the dollar, which facilitated Chinese exports. In Japan, monetary authorities cut interest rates and weakened the yen in the early 1990s in order to boost Japanese exports. Huh and Kasa (1998) consider these major factors, but they fail to adequately explain the long time delay between the 1994 devaluation of the yuan and the crisis in 1997. Liu and colleagues (1998) found that the Chinese devaluation may have been a contributing factor, but it was not the proximate cause.

Because of the changing dynamics of the market, Thailand was forced to move toward more sophisticated manufacturing. It attracted Seagate Technology, which produces disk drives. Likewise, Mitsubishi Motors Corp., Bridgestone Corp., and Komatsu produce automobiles, tires, and construction machinery in Thailand. The latter three companies are Japanese, suggesting that Japan had invested heavily in Thailand. Despite their success in attracting sophisticated manufacturing, such as electronics and household appliances, competition from other nations, to attract such firms, was intense.

A shortage of skilled labor resulted in increased labor costs. General Motors, for example, invested $750 million in a factory in Thailand to produce automobiles, but it had to send 500 Thai employees overseas for training ("South-East Asia's Learning Difficulties" 1997, 30).

Exports declined as a result of the rising costs and increasing competition. According to data from Krung Thai Bank, export growth was a negative 0.1 percent in 1996, compared to 23.6 percent in the previous year. The slowdown in economic growth in Thailand was not unique. World trade slowed in 1996. The International Monetary Fund (IMF) estimated the growth of world trade in 1996 was 6.4 percent compared to 8.7 percent in 1995.

Foreign Capital

The strong demand for foreign goods was reflected in Thailand's current account deficit, which increased from 5.1 percent of GDP in 1993 to over 8 percent in 1995 and 1996. The current account deficit was financed by foreign investment reflecting private-sector decisions to invest more heavily in Thailand. Since these were private-sector decisions, Eichengreen and Portes (1997, 213) ask why markets did not draw back sooner and more smoothly before events got out of hand. Their answer is that private investors believed, albeit incorrectly, in the exchange rate peg, and that banks would not be allowed to fail.

In the early 1990s, the Bank of Thailand implemented a comprehensive program of financial reforms, including deregulation. According to the Bank of Thailand, the deregulation program "was carefully designed to ensure that local financial institutions are well prepared for the new competitive environment."[1] Perhaps more important is that this fast-growing economy with large current account deficits needed substantial inflows of foreign capital to sustain their domestic growth. The deregulation was one effort to attract foreign capital.

Part of the deregulation program included the establishment of offshore banking facilities known as Bangkok International Banking Facilities (BIBFs). The purpose of BIBFs was to facilitate the flow of investment funds into the country. Deregulation also permitted the expansion of bank branches. By the end of 1994, there were 2,870 branches, subbranches, and agencies.

Many firms in Thailand borrowed heavily in foreign currencies, mostly U.S. dollars, to finance their growth. From 1991 to 1996, the ratio of external debt to GDP increased from 41 to 51 percent. Most of the firms did not hedge their foreign exchange risk because they believed that the government would defend the baht. They were wrong.

Real Estate

The early 1990s was a period of easy money and aggressive lending in the real estate sector by banks and finance companies. In 1993 and 1994, for example, the money supply grew at 18.6 percent and 17.0 percent, respectively. Total loans grew at 21.9 percent and 30.1 percent during the same period.[2] Banks and finance companies borrowed dollars, converted to bahts, added 7 percent onto their borrowing costs, and lent the funds for real estate and consumer loans. One report stated that "the forest of [building] cranes dominated the skyline" (Butler 1997). More than 300 thousand housing units were built that were unoccupied. In a good year, 120 thousand new housing units are needed. The world's tallest building was empty. There was excess capacity in luxury hotels. In 1996, office vacancy rate in Bangkok exceeded 20 percent (Moreno 1997). The growth rate of construction peaked at 13.8 percent in 1994, and then slowed to 8 percent by 1997 when the real estate bubble burst.

Estimates of nonperforming loans (real estate and other loans) in 1997 ranged from 9 to 14 percent or more of total loans outstanding at commercial banks and 30 percent of the loans outstanding at finance companies. Because banks and finance companies understate nonperforming and nonaccrual loans, and have inadequate loan loss reserves (LLR), it is not possible to get an accurate number.[3] Nevertheless, in the aggregate, nonperforming loans exceeded 20 percent of Thailand's GDP.

Failures in the Financial Sector

In June and August 1997, the Bank of Thailand had suspended fifty-eight of the nation's ninety-one finance and securities companies.[4] They had to restructure their operations and/or merge with stronger finance companies or banks. They also had to increase their capital. Two of the companies were permitted to resume operations and fifty-six were closed (*Resolution of Closed Finance Companies* 1998).

In October 1997, the Thai government approved various measures to support the sagging real estate sector. These measures included the establishment of the Financial Restructuring Agency (FRA) (i.e., a resolution trust fund) to administer the liquidation of the fifty-six closed finance companies. The government established a state-owned bank, the Radhanasin Bank, and a finance company to bid on some of the auctioned assets. Finally, the Asset Management Company (a bad bank) was established to buy assets that were not sold from closed finance companies and other financial institutions.

In the banking sector, losses and write-downs exceed the capital of some banks. The Bank of Thailand nationalized five of the nation's fifteen banks (Sherer 1998a). Two of the banks, Bangkok Bank of Commerce and Krung Thai Bank, were already under government control or ownership. The central bank's Financial Institutions Development Fund injected 32 billion bhat into First Bangkok City Bank by converting previously extended loans into equity. The Bank of Thailand claims to have spent more than $25 billion since mid-1996 to support troubled financial institutions, but a large portion of the money is expected to be unrecoverable ("Asian Banks in Throes of Reform" 1998).

It is estimated that banks have about $80 billion in nonperforming loans, about one third of their portoflios (Knecht 1998), and the banks need to restructure. In June 1998, the central bank identified 353 companies with problem loans and offered them special tax incentives to restructure their debts. As of October 1998, not one company had done so. No effort has been made to sell off the bad loans. Also, one part of restructuring is to reduce bank costs by reducing personnel. However, there have been no layoffs because layoffs are not part of the Thai culture. One positive note is that the government has been injecting funds into the banking system. That is a starting point, but there is still a long way to go.

Pegged Currency

For a thirteen-year period, the Thai baht was pegged to a basket of currencies that was dominated by the U.S. dollar. The U.S. dollar accounted for 80 percent of the basket, the Japanese yen 15 percent, and the German mark and others 5 percent. It ended on July 2, 1997, when the Thai government unpegged the currency.

Because the Thai baht was tied to the dollar, it was affected by the course of interest rates in the United States. During the 1992–1993 period, the Federal Reserve kept interest rates low to help U.S. banks and thrifts strengthen their balance sheets. The discount rates at the Federal Reserve Bank of New York were 3.25 percent and 3.00 percent in 1992 and 1993. Thus, for several years, the nominal exchange rate vis-à-vis the U.S. dollar was stable. However, in terms of the real exchange rate that takes inflation into account, the baht appreciated against the dollar. During that same period, the Japanese yen depreciated against the dollar. The result was that the baht appreciated more against the yen than against the dollar. Dr. Yoshio Suzuki (1997, 172–73), a member of the House of Representatives in Japan, in discussing Thailand, Malaysia, and Indonesia, said

This appreciation in real terms against the currencies of the two major capital exporting countries, under systems that were nominally pegged against the dollar, attracted massive inflows of capital and caused domestic economic booms. The other consequences of this process were (1) the loss of aggregate demand control, (2) a further increase in the current account deficits, and (3) real estate bubbles. These three factors, together with (4) over-valued currencies and (5) deregulation of international financial transactions, provided sufficient motive for international speculation against the currencies. These five conditions were most extreme in the case of Thailand. That is why the Thai baht was attacked first, followed by substantial declines in the value of the Malaysian ringgit and the Indonesian rupiah.

The increased strength of the U.S. dollar against the yen and German mark in 1996–1997 adversely affected the value of the bahts. Thai exports were no longer competitive because of the rising cost of labor. Stated otherwise, the baht was overvalued relative to Thailand's economy. The Thai government depleted its foreign currency reserves, spending more than $5 billion to combat currency speculators who were short selling the falling baht.

Part of the government's defense was to raise the interest rates that banks charge each other to 40 percent in order to entice them to buy the baht. In addition, they tried to cut offshore borrowers' supply of the baht. However, on July 2, 1997, the Bank of Thailand unpegged the baht from the U.S. dollar and allowed the baht to float. At that time, the exchange rate was about 25 baht/dollar. The Bank of Thailand tried to support the baht until early July. Then it let the value collapse to 29 baht/dollar. While that seemed like a large collapse at that time, the value reached a historic low of 57 baht/dollar in January 1998. By June 1998, it rebounded to about 40 baht/dollar.

Despite the fall in the baht, the devaluation failed to trigger significant inflation. This appears to be due to a sharp decline in economic activity, falling prices and wages, and soaring unemployment (Sherer 1998b).

The Economy

The economy was subjected to a number of economic policy changes during the mid-1990s. In mid-1995, monetary authorities imposed a restrictive monetary policy to control inflation. The growth rate of the money supply slowed from 17.1 percent in 1995 to 12.1 percent in the following year. The inflation rate was 5.7 percent in 1995, and interest rates were 13.75 percent. The real growth in GDP slowed from 8.6 percent in 1995 to 6.4 percent in 1996. Then economic policy changed, and the money supply increased 20.5 percent in 1996. There was another reversal of policy in 1997, when the money supply slowed to an estimated 12.0 percent in 1997.

Fiscal policies also changed. The 1996 budget increased by 11 billion baht, contributing to inflation and the current account deficit. In addition, tariffs on selected luxury goods were reduced, hurting some domestic industries.

The stock market is a mirror of investor sentiment about the economy. During the 1990 to 1992 period, increases in stock prices reflected the rapid growth of the economy. However, in 1996, concerns about the economy were reflected in lower stock prices. In 1997, the stock market crashed. The plummeting stock market and the currency crises that began in Thailand during the early summer spread to other financial markets throughout the world in October 1997.

International Monetary Fund

In August 1997, the IMF agreed to provide a $17-billion emergency international financial package, including loans and standby credits as well as technical assistance. The loans and standby credits would come from the IMF, World Bank, Asian Development Bank, and the Bank for International Settlements. The IMF's recovery plan involves balancing the budget, retaining the managed float of the baht, and closing insolvent financial institutions. Other features include strengthening bank regulation and supervision, eliminating government support of ailing institutions, and ending subsidies of state enterprises. In September 1998, a study by Hartman and Wongchirachai reported that Thailand was about to pass legislation concerning amendments to their bankruptcy, reorganization, and foreclosure laws that would provide a foundation for debt restructuring.

Despite the IMF's best efforts to rejuvenate the exports and stocks, the economic outlook for Thailand was that the economy was expected to contract in 1998. Estimates of the contraction of the Gross Domestic Product ranged from 4 to 7 percent (Engardio et al. 1998; "Thai Cabinet Offers IMF Latest Pledges for Rescue" 1998). Nevertheless, the economy was forecast to recover faster than other affected economies in the region. Some of the key reasons given for the faster recovery were closure of failed financial institutions, the sale of bad debts, the allowance of 100-percent foreign ownership of financial institutions, the use of public funds, and bankruptcy law reforms (Hartman and Wongchirachai 1998).

LESSONS

Thailand is a small economy that pegged its currency primarily to the U.S. dollar. The financial markets were not well developed, and the government encouraged foreign capital investment. According to Yoshio Suzuki (1997), the fact that Thailand pegged its currency instead of letting it float contributed to the baht being overvalued. This, in turn, resulted in a loss of control of aggregate demand in the economy, increased current account deficits, and capital inflows that financed an asset price bubble. The partial deregulation of the financial system, without controls over aggregate demand or strengthening the safety net of the payments system, may have triggered the instability that occurred.

Nobel laureate Gary Becker (1997) claims that fragile economies and floating exchange rates do not mix well. With floating exchange rates, the value rises and falls as a nation's competitive position changes. However, nations can debase their currency by printing more money. Inflation depreciates the value of currencies to maintain parity between the cost of domestic goods and their costs in other countries. On the other hand, fixed exchange rates require local markets to adjust to changing competitive conditions. By eliminating inflationary expansions and having a stable monetary environment, they work well for countries whose governments do not act responsibly in fiscal and monetary matters. Becker cites Hong Kong as one example.

What role did banks and finance companies play in this debacle? The speculators wanted to borrow money and the banks and finance companies wanted to make loans. In some cases, government intervened in the lending process by directing lending to create jobs, to increase industrialization, or because of political and personal relationships. When the Finance Ministry took control of Bangkok Bank of Commerce in 1995 because of bad loans, it was revealed that most of the loans were made to politicians. Thus, there were little or no controls over credit quality or loan concentration in the real estate sector.[5] In April 1997, Malaysia, which also experienced a real estate bubble, capped commercial bank loans to the real estate sector at 20 percent of total loans. However, banks are not the only financial institutions making real estate loans.

The Bank of Thailand, the central bank, is charged with supervising financial institutions to ensure that they are secure and supportive of economic development. It also formulates monetary policy and makes economic policy recommendations to the government. The facts speak for themselves, and the central bank was not effective in either task. By November, Thailand's Prime Minister offered to resign because of criticism of the government's ability to resolve the economic crises.

The crisis in Thailand provides a case study of what happens when there are speculative bubbles in the real estate sector of the economy, inadequate bank supervision, and ineptitude on the part of the central bank. The problem was exacerbated because Thailand's currency was tied to a strong U.S. dollar. This led to rapid economic growth which hid the extent and depth of the increased risks being taken by lenders. When the bubble burst, Moreno (1998) claims that increases in information and financial technology that link countries together facilitated the transmission of one country's financial problems to other markets. Thus, the crisis in Thailand set off a chain of events that was felt throughout the world.

NOTES

1. For additional information, see Bank of Thailand at http://www.bot.or.th.
2. Data are from Krung Thai Bank PLC at http://www.ktb.co.th.
3. In March 1997, the Bank of Thailand introduced a 100-percent LLR on doubtful or irrecoverable loans, a 15-percent LLR for banks, and a 20-percent LLR for finance companies on substandard loans.
4. According to the Bank of Thailand, on December 31, 1994 there were twenty-one finance companies and seventy finance and securities companies.
5. The Bank of Thailand imposed a maximum credit limit for an individual and related parties of 25 percent of the financial institution's first-tier capital.

REFERENCES

"Asian Banks in Throes of Reform." 1998. *China Daily*, 1 April, p. 4.
"Asian Prospects." 1997. *Washington Post*, 19 August.
Bacani, Cesar, and Assif Shameen. 1997. "Devaluation 101: A Layman's Guide to the Turmoil." *Asiaweek*, 25 July.
Becker, Gary S. 1997. "Fragile Economies and Floating Currencies Don't Mix." *Business Week*, 8 September, p. 22.
"Business Focus: Analysis of Thailand's Economic Recovery Plan." 1997. Board of Investment of Thailand, 1 September.
"Business Focus: Economic Restructuring." 1997. Board of Investment of Thailand, 16 September.
"Business Focus: Q and A on Thailand's Road to Recovery." 1997. Board of Investment of Thailand, 23 September.
Butler, Steven. 1997. "It Was Too Easy to Make Money." *U.S. News and World Report*, 28 July, p. 41.
Caves, Richard E., and Ronald W. Jones. 1985. *World Trade and Payments*, 4th ed. Boston: Little, Brown.
Eichengreen, B., and R. Portes. 1997. "Managing Financial Crises in Emerging Markets." In *Maintaining Financial Stability in a Global Economy*, 193–225. Kansas City, Mo.: Federal Reserve Bank of Kansas City.
Engardio, P., B. Bremmer, M. McNamee, and M. I. Hwan. 1998. "Asia: The Global Impact." *Business Week*, 1 June, pp. 52–54.
Financial Development. 1995. Financial Institutions Supervision and Development Department, Bank of Thailand.
Hall, Denise. 1996. *Business Prospects in Thailand*. Singapore: Prentice Hall.
Hartman, Donaldson, and Marcia Wongchirachai. 1998. *Thailand—Laying the Foundations for Financial Recovery*. New York: Salomon Smith Barney.
Huh, C., and K. Kasa. 1998. "Export Competition and Contagious Currency Crises." *FRBSF Economic Letter* (Federal Reserve Bank of San Francisco), 16 January.

International Monetary Fund (IMF). 1997. "IMF Approves Stand-by Credit for Thailand" (Press release no. 97/37). Washington, D.C., 20 August.

International Monetary Fund (IMF). 1984–1997. *International Financial Statistics*. Washington, D.C.: IMF.

Johnston, R. B. 1991. "Distressed Financial Institutions in Thailand: Structural Weaknesses, Support Operations, and Economic Consequences." In *Banking Crises: Cases and Issues*, edited by V. Sundararajan and J. T. Balino, 234–75. Washington, D.C.: IMF.

Kaminsky, G. L. 1998. "Currency and Banking Crises: The Early Warnings of Distress." Working Paper, Board of Governors of the Federal Reserve System, 16 March.

Kengchon, Charl. 1996. "Economic Overview." *The 1996 Guide to Thailand* (supplement to *Euromoney*), September.

Knecht, G. Bruce. 1998. "Signs of Recovery in Thailand Look Hard to Sustain." *Wall Street Journal*, 27 October, pp. A10, A15.

Kochhar, K., L. Dicks-Mireaux, B. Horvath, M. Mecagni, E. Offerdal, and J. Zhou. 1996. *Thailand: The Road to Sustained Growth* (Occasional paper 146). Washington, D.C.: IMF.

Limthammahisorn, Watsaya. 1997. "Financial Crisis in Japan, South Korea and Thailand: A Comparison." *Bangkok Bank Monthly Review*, August.

Liu, L., M. Noland, S. Robinson, and Z. Wang. 1998. "Asian Competitive Devaluations." Working Paper 98-2, Institute for International Economics, http://www.iie.com/98-2.htm.

Mankin, J. H. 1998. *Asia's Crisis Is Not a Currency Crisis*. Washington, D.C.: American Enterprise Institute for Public Policy Research.

Mishkin, Frederic S. 1992. *The Economics of Money, Banking, and Financial Markets*. New York: HarperCollins.

Moreno, R. 1997. "Lessons from Thailand." *FRBSF Economic Letter* (Federal Reserve Bank of San Francisco), 7 November.

Moreno, R. 1998. "What Caused East Asia's Financial Crisis?" *Economic Letter* (Federal Reserve Bank of San Francisco), 7 August.

Muscat, Robert J. 1994. *The Fifth Tiger: A Study of Thai Development Policy*. New York: M. E. Sharpe.

"The 1991 Guide to Currencies: Thailand." 1991. *Euromoney*, September.

"Recent Financial Developments." 1995. Financial Institutions Supervision and Development Department, Bank of Thailand.

"Recent Supervisory Issues." 1995. Financial Institutions Supervision and Development Department, Bank of Thailand.

Resolution of Closed Finance Companies. 1998. New York: Salomon Smith Barney, 5 February.

Sachs, Jeffrey D. 1997. "Asia's Miracle Is Alive and Well." *Time*, 29 September.

Salomon Brothers. 1997. *Thai Finance Companies—To Be or Not to Be*. New York: Salomon Brothers, 8 August.

Seidel, Erica J. 1995. "The Plaza Agreement of 1985." Http://netspace.org/~erica/econ/.

Sherer, P. M. 1998a. "Seizure of 2 More Thai Banks Points to Large Losses." *Wall Street Journal*, 9 February, p. A15.

Sherer, P. M. 1998b. "Thai Baht Devaluation Fails to Trigger Classic Inflation." *Wall Street Journal*, 3 February, p. A17.

"South-East Asia's Learning Difficulties." 1997. *The Economist*, 16 August, p. 30.

"Supervisory System." 1995. Financial Institutions Supervision and Development Department, Bank of Thailand.

Suzuki, Yoshio. 1997. "What Lessons Can Be Learned from Recent Financial Crises." In *Maintaining Financial Stability in a Global Economy*, 169–74. Kansas City: Federal Reserve Bank of Kansas City.

Terdudomtham, Thamavit. 1996. "Year-End '96 Economic Review—The Economy." *Bangkok Post*, December.

"Thai Cabinet Offers IMF Latest Pledges for Rescue." 1998. *Wall Street Journal*, 27 May, p. A17.

Thai Legal Issues and Financial Recovery. 1998. New York: Salomon Smith Barney, 31 March.

"Thailand—Crash of the Baht." 1997. *Pacific Rim Review*, 6 July.

"Thailand Economy at a Glance." Board of Investment of Thailand.

Thapanachai, Somporn. 1996. "Year-End '96 Economic Review—Exports." *Bangkok Post*, December.

"The 'Tigers' of Asia Stumble." 1997. *Los Angeles Times*, 8 September.

Warr, Peter G. 1993. "The Thai Economy." In *The Thai Economy in Transition*, edited by Peter G. Warr. Cambridge: Cambridge University Press.

"WEFA Country Profile." 1997. New York: Bloomberg, 24 September.

Wong, J. 1998. "Bangkok Bank Family Faces Dilemma of New Capitalism." *Wall Street Journal*, 18 February, p. A17.

World Bank. 1997. *Country Brief: Thailand*. Washington, D.C.: World Bank.

"World Economy: Thai Crisis Highlights Lessons of Mexico." 1997. *Financial Times*, 19 September.

5

Financial Crisis in Thailand

Kiyoshi Abe

The "East Asian Miracle" was envied throughout the world. Now, however, it is unexpectedly gone, replaced by a financial crisis. This chapter aims to clarify causes of the financial crisis in Thailand, where the troubles started. It traces mistakes of the Bank of Thailand, commercial banks, and others. It also reveals how deep, intricate, and structural the financial problems there are. Once the causes of the crisis and bank failures are revealed, we can determine a solution for them. Some innovative solutions are being tried.

BACKGROUND

The economic crisis in East Asia first surfaced in Thailand. Thai authorities, recognizing they could no longer defend their currency's peg to the dollar, floated the baht on July 2, 1997. The baht came under selling pressure, weakening from 25 to the dollar before it was floated to about 46 in mid-December 1997, a loss of 47 percent of its value. The baht remained weak during the first nine months of 1998.

The crisis developed from a policy that had allowed procurement of foreign funds at low interest rates through offshore markets. The system worked well when the economy was growing at a fast pace. The easy money from offshore markets was put into the stock market and real estate investments. The result was a huge current-account deficit. Then the Thai economy slowed in 1997, resulting in an economic crisis. Loans soured, especially in the property sector, leading to a financial turmoil never experienced before. The turmoil meant a collapse of the financial sector, especially the banking sector. The financial sector in Thailand continues to be underdeveloped and vulnerable. The financial crisis is serious, widespread, and deep rooted.

The economic crisis in Thailand is composite—a combination of a currency crisis and a financial crisis—as illustrated in Figure 5.1, which shows how the weak Japanese yen since 1995 caused the strong baht under the dollar peg system, leading to the worsening exports and rising trade deficits. The final result was the currency (baht devaluation) crisis. Figure 5.1 also shows how the strong baht supported by the attractive high interests and the lingering myth of the East Asian Miracle brought about the excessive capital inflow and the bubble economy (spending boom), followed by the inevitable collapse of the speculative bubble and the consequent financial crisis. Excessive consumption spurred heavy import demands (worsening trade accounts), which were paid for by the capital inflows. The currency crisis and the financial crisis are interrelated.

The crisis resulted in soaring unemployment, closed factories, a drop in consumer demand, and the loss of investor confidence, leaving the financial sector crippled. Everybody admits that solving the banking mess is essential to getting the economy moving, but there are huge and unprecedented obstacles to face, including sheer desperation.

Thailand appears headed for a depression. The economy may shrink at least 10 percent in 1998, 1999, and 2000. Finance Minister Tarrin Nimmanaahaeminda concedes, "the financial system is not functioning." Banks are not lending because they are afraid of bad loans. Nonperforming Loans (NPLs), now around $12 billion, will reach 47 percent of all bank loans in 1999. Recapitalizing banks could cost at least $23 billion. Tarrin once thought banks could raise most of that by selling shares to foreigners. However, few have succeeded. Turmoil continues in financial and exchange markets, exacerbated by the lack of Japan's help and lack of investors' confidence.

Thai Farmers Bank is one of the strongest banks in Thailand. In March 1998, Thai Farmers Bank raised $850 million in an equity offering reserved for foreign investors, who paid 27 percent over the market to snap up its shares. With those funds, Thailand's third-largest bank hoped to retire bad loans. But since then, Thai Farmers has reported a $100-million second-quarter loss, its stock price has plunged 65 percent, and analysts expect that it will have to turn to the market to raise yet more money, if investors are willing to take another gamble.

The talk in 1998 is not whether smaller, weaker banks can survive, but whether any can be salvaged. Bank failures are ubiquitous. Russel Kopp, a bank analyst at Dresdner Kleinwort Bensen, warns, "We are one step away from nationalizing the banking system." The govern-

Figure 5.1
Composite Crisis in Thailand

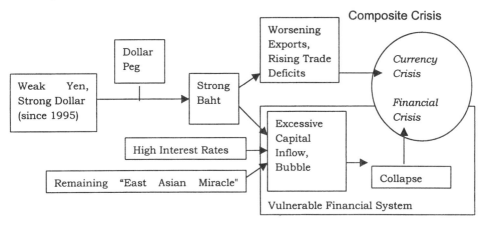

ment may have to take over all but a handful of the country's fifteen major banks. "Nationalization might be needed," says Commerce Minister Supachai Panitchipakdi, who also insists any takeover would be a temporary move "to prepare the banks for reprivatization." The government is expected to issue bonds and use the proceeds to clean up the bank's books. Then they will try to sell stakes in the banks to foreign investors.

MISTAKES OF THE BANK OF THAILAND

Nukul Report

Finance Minister Tarrin Nimmanhaeminda took office in November 1997, and formed a commission headed by former central bank governor Nukul Prachuabmoh. The Nukul Commission, consisting of noted economists, financiers, and civil servants, spent three months interviewing top central bankers and Finance Ministry officials, and examining documents and memos in an effort to reconstruct the events which led to the collapse of the baht in July 1997 and the supervisory failure of the financial system. The main task of the commission was to discover the roots of Thailand's economic collapse and the policy mistakes made by the Bank of Thailand. The commission was instructed to examine at least two crucial issues: the failed defense of the baht in May 1997, and the decision to lend massive financial assistance to ailing finance companies and banks by the Financial Institutions Development Fund. The Nukul report sheds a disturbing light on how those entrusted to regulate the country's financial system responded to the speculative attacks on the baht. It also provides a road map for restructuring the central bank and rebuilding its tattered reputation in local and foreign markets. Mr. Tarrin presented the 205-page report from the Nukul Commission to the cabinet in the first week of May 1998. Widely leaked to the media, the report pinned the greatest blame for the mismanagement of macroeconomic policy squarely on the shoulders of Rerngchai Marakanond, the central bank governor from July 1996 to July 1997.

Misguided Monetary Policies

In 1993, the central bank announced a plan to develop Bangkok as a regional financial center, taking advantage of Thailand's central location in Southeast Asia and competitive exports as a result of industrialization policies implemented in the late 1980s. Foreign exchange controls were relaxed in the early 1990s to encourage freer flow of capital. In 1993, the central bank allowed the establishment of Bangkok International Banking Facilities to help mobilize foreign offshore funds for domestic lending. These measures generated a large influx of foreign capital, with the majority in the form of short-term funds seeking to exploit the higher interest rates available in the Thai local market. Portfolio investments also increased as share prices on the Stock Exchange of Thailand jumped. Thai companies, seeing no exchange risks under the basket, flocked to international markets to borrow at lower interest rates.

As the Nukul Commission noted, in early 1997, the central bank refused to change the relaxed foreign exchange regime. They maintained the basket peg system introduced in the mid-1980s, which effectively fixed the baht to the U.S. dollar. While a stable baht had a beneficial effect in terms of trade and foreign investor confidence, the maintenance of the rigid exchange rate regime while liberalizing capital flows set the stage for greater macroeconomic instability in the future. However, few were aware of the danger. Theoretically, it is well known that it is impossible to realize a fixed exchange rate system, capital liberalization, and an autonomous monetary policy simultaneously.

Financial institutions were beneficiaries of relatively cheap foreign funds. As the economic expansion continued, lending criteria eased as banks and finance companies competed for increasingly risky investment opportunities. The current account deficit reached a peak of 8.2 percent of GDP in 1995. Growing consumerism spurred heavy import demands that were paid for by capital inflows.

The ratio of foreign debt to GNP reached 50.14 percent in 1996, pointing to the country's deteriorating external position. Unproductive investments in property and speculative securities also led to higher costs, wages, and capital goods prices, undermining the competitiveness of Thai exports in global markets. The central bank, then headed by governor Vijit Supinit, failed to push for tighter fiscal policies, which might have slowed investments in the overheating economy. Moreover, no sterilization policy was adopted.

In review, the Nukul report focused on the central bank's failure to recognize the early danger signals confronting the economy. Supervision of financial institutions was lax. Monetary policies and exchange rate policies were misguided. The failed defense of the baht in May 1997 was a costly lesson for Thailand.

Exchange Rate Warnings Ignored

In 1994, the International Monetary Fund warned the Thai central bank about the need for greater flexibility in the exchange rate regime. The IMF argued that allowing greater volatility in the baht versus the dollar would help to curb the inflow of short-term capital. But the central bank was reluctant to introduce any change to foreign exchange policies, arguing that the timing was inappropriate for the framework of the economy. The Nukul Commission noted that this delay proved costly.

After the Mexican peso crisis in early 1995, the baht came under speculative pressure. Following the attack, deputy governor Dr. Chaiyawat argued that maintaining the basket was critical to upholding investor confidence and economic stability. But the economy had already started to slow, as investors became more concerned about the stability of the baht in the face of a growing current-account deficit. Declining economic growth led to declining asset quality held by financial institutions.

Exports posted a sharply lower increase in the second quarter of 1996, a startling development in contrast to the more than 10-percent annual increase posted over the previous decade. The central bank said that the fall was a temporary phenomenon. The baht remained fixed under the basket system.

The IMF, concerned about the high risks of external shock, sent a letter to the central bank in March 1997 about the urgent need to change the basket system, saying, "The present system can hinder adjustment to external shocks. In particular, the heavy weight of the US dollar in the basket has clearly been unhelpful." This IMF concern turned out to be true. The IMF also wrote, "During our discussions you have indicated that you intend to introduce greater exchange rate flexibility at the appropriate time. We encourage you to do so promptly, while at the same time changing the present basket to more closely reflect the pattern of Thailand's foreign trade." Such early warnings were ignored.

The central bank continued its previous stance that changes in the exchange rate regime were inappropriate, particularly given rising fears about the instability of the financial sector and the heavy foreign debt burden of the private sector. Procrastination continued due to the false expectation by overconfident Thai leaders. They were totally unprepared for what was to follow.

In late 1996, Moody's Investors Service downgraded the short-term foreign currency ratings for Thai financial institutions. About that same time there were rumors about an impending devaluation circulated in the market. Poor macroeconomic data and signs of the deteriorating health of local financial institutions placed the baht under pressure early in 1997. From late 1996 to February 1997, the central bank committed $7.8 billion in foreign reserves to defend the baht in the spot market. Forward obligations of $12.2 billion were taken out to avoid increasing domestic interest rates and to conceal the drop in foreign reserves. In May 1997, speculative hedge funds launched a massive attack on the baht, with up to $10 billion committed in an effort to break the basket system and spur a baht depreciation. The central bank fought back through heavy intervention in the spot and forward markets. Capital controls were adopted to deny baht liquidity for offshore speculators. Forward obligations of up to $24.3 billion were taken out by the central bank, where bahts were swapped for dollars in a bid to prop up reserve figures. Net reserves fell to just $2.5 billion, as the Nukul report said, below the legal requirement necessary to back up currency in circulation. The foreign exchange reserves were $39 billion at the end of 1996.

Eventually, in May 1997, the Bank of Thailand's net foreign exchange reserves fell to only $1.14 billion, forcing Thailand to seek a bail-out package from the International Monetary Fund. Thailand had become an insolvent country due to the squandering of almost all Thai foreign exchange reserves.

Unlimited Support for Banks and Finance Companies

The Financial Institution Development Fund under the Bank of Thailand lacked a comprehensive strategy to deal with the systemic risk in the financial system, adopting a no-ceiling policy in its liquidity support to finance companies and banks, which ended up with a total of 1.1 trillion baht (equal to one-fifth of Thailand's GDP) in its loan books in 1996. This rendered the verdict that the Thai financial system had gone broke. The upshot was a complete loss of confidence in the Thai economy and in the financial system. The final outcome was the shift to the managed float on July 2, 1997.

Although the Bank of Thailand recognized that financial-sector liberalization would have to be accompanied by prudent supervision, the measures taken were considered too lax. In 1996, for instance, the central bank announced that financial institutions would have to set aside reserves of at least 7 percent of their foreign borrowings with a maturity under one year. This was a bid to curb short-term capital inflow. But in practice, the measure proved unsuccessful in guarding against the growing instability of the capital account as well as in reducing the dependence on short-term capital. The Bank of Thailand was not influential in the compromising atmosphere of Thailand. At the same time, the credibility of the central bank took a beating for the failure of Dr. Vijit, the governor, to take prompt action against the nonperforming Bangkok Bank of Commerce. The indecisiveness of the central regulators further contributed to declining confidence of foreign investors, who began withdrawing funds in the second half of 1996.

The Nukul Commission highlights the failure of the central bank to take early action to strengthen the financial sector, saying, "In 1993, the central bank ordered financial institutions to meet with the capital-to-risk assets ratio under the standard set by the Bank for International Settlements. But the BIS standard was actually lower than the capital adequacy ratio already achieved by many institutions." As the Nukul report says, accounting and loan classification regulations were more relaxed than international practice, because many banks seemingly more than satisfied the international BIS requirement on capital adequacy. There may have been fraudulent practices. Rather than tighten the regulations, the central bank chose to ease supervisory regulations covering Bangkok International Banking Facilities. The central bank showed lack of prudence. No wonder other banks followed laxly.

In short, imprudence prevailed widely and deeply. The FIDF lendings to banks and finance companies were unlimited and clearly misguided, resulting in a virtual bankruptcy of the Thai financial system. Default as a nation was rumored.

Lack of Expertise and Individual versus Collective Decisions

The Nukul Commission report continues to say, "Despite frequent meetings between the central bank and the Finance Ministry, warnings from the IMF and clear danger signs about the unsustainability of the baht, central bankers refused to make a timely decision. While central bank officials delayed in making a decision about foreign exchange policies, speculators did not hesitate. On the contrary, they increased their attacks." Mr. Rerngchai, central bank governor from July 1996 to July 1997, was particularly singled out for poor performance in dealing with the crisis. In testimony to the Nukul Commission, Mr. Rerngchai acknowledged that he lacked knowledge and expertise regarding foreign exchange policies. He used to supervise administrative duties under Governor Vijit, his predecessor.

The Nukul report blamed the poor leadership and teamwork among senior central bankers as further contributing to the poor decisions of top regulators. The staff of the central bank refrained from expressing disagreement with senior officials. This conforms with a typical Thai tradition, which causes the lack or delay of timely decisions. Mr. Rerngchai failed as a leader.

"It was unfortunate for Thailand that Prime Minister Banharn Silpa-archa appointed Mr. Rerngchai to be the central bank governor," says the Nukul report. During the attack on the baht in May 1997, the Banking Department, which is responsible for handling intervention in the foreign exchange market, urged Mr. Rerngchai to reconsider the present baht defense strategy and the basket system. Mr. Rerngchai passed the task to Dr. Chaiyawat, the manager of the Exchange Equalization Fund. The personal conflicts between Mr. Rerngchai and Dr. Chaiyawat complicated the task of the central bank in reacting to the crisis, thus resulting in decision postponement. Dr. Chaiyawat did not take action for one month, a delay blamed in part by the Nukul Commission. His bad relationship with Mr. Rerngchai hindered important decisions. The Nukul report notes that Dr. Chaiyawat played a critical role in supporting the central bank's stance of maintaining the baht peg.

Given the top central bank officials' irresponsible involvement in the baht defense and the FIDF's unlimited spending, the Nukul report should give us a clear idea as to whether it was poor individual judgment, collective decisions, or the failure of the system that led to the disaster. However, sources said Nukul shied away from pointing the finger at the central bank officials that had made the woeful decisions, leaving the interpretation to the finance minister or readers of the report.

In review, it seems that the poor decisions were not due to individual mistakes alone, but to collective or systemic mistakes. The replacement of one governor with another did not lead to any improvement. Some systemic failures must have been involved, leading to poor leadership and teamwork and suggesting that drastic reforms were needed.

Reforms at the Bank of Thailand

In May 1998, three senior central bankers tendered their resignations: Governor Chaiyawat Wibulswasdi, Deputy Governor Jaroong Nookhwun, and Senior Assistant Governor Siri Ganjarerndee. Hundreds of central bank staff held a rally to implore them to resist growing political pressure to resign. But in his resignation letter, dated May 4, 1998, Dr. Chaiyawat Wibulswasdi said his resignation would break the link between past policies and the future direction of the central bank. He also said, "While the Bank of Thailand has exerted its best efforts to solve the problems, its effectiveness continued to be eroded as there remained questions about past performance which had not been up to expectation. My resignation can pave the way for a new leader to take over without the disadvantage of the haunted past."

Following the resignation of Dr. Chaiyawat, the Chuan government appointed former finance permanent secretary M. R. Chatumongol Sonakul as the next governor of the central bank. He is well known for his outspoken character, progressive management style, honesty, and independence, which was expected to produce some effect. He had the formidable task of restoring the credibility of the central financial institution and of balancing monetary policies in the course of the worst recession in decades. Upon taking office, M. R. Chatumongol announced a broad policy framework aimed at building a service mentality for central bank officials. He recommended that they work at local financial institutions to better understand the workings of the private sector. A monetary policy committee comprised of central bank officials, outside economists, and prominent experts would be established to advise the governor on policy. Auditors and bank examiners would receive additional training to strengthen the regulatory and supervisory role of the central bank. A new litigation department, in coordination with the police department and prosecutors, would be established to oversee criminal prosecution of financiers and bankers who violate the law. M. R. Chatumongol also announced that applications would be accepted for the role of assistant governor to oversee examination of financial institutions. Assistance in drafting a new management structure and policy-setting framework would be given by former central bank officials from the Bank of England, the Bank of Japan, and the U.S. Federal Reserve System.

There is no question that M. R. Chatumongol's style and aggressiveness is in sharp contrast to the low-key, systematic approach of previous indecisive governors. Upon taking up the new position, M. R. Chatumongol called for patience and cooperation from central bank officials while he sought to implement changes and to upgrade the bank toward international levels. It is hoped that his new leadership will lead to better collective decisions and timely due consideration of IMF warnings. The drastic reform of the Bank of Thailand is indeed a long and arduous process, but is something Thailand cannot evade.

Some of the problems of the Bank of Thailand, as revealed by the Nukul report, are summarized in Figure 5.2, which shows how per-

Figure 5.2
Vicious Cycle Inside the Bank of Thailand (Nukul report)

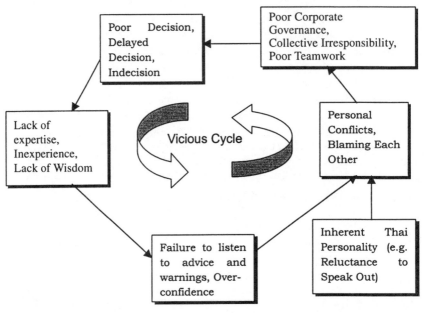

sonal conflicts undermine teamwork and lead to the lack of timely decisions. This reflects the lack of experience as well as expertise in dealing with a crisis. Early warnings were ignored, which, coupled with traditional Thai personalities (e.g., reluctance to be outspoken, reluctance to disagree), again led to personal conflicts, poor teamwork, and low collective efficiency (poor corporate governance) of the central bank.

COMMERCIAL BANKS, FINANCE COMPANIES, AND SECURITIES COMPANIES

Cash-Strapped Consumers and Corporations

The financial sector was hard hit by crisis and it continued to have problems in 1998. The collapse of domestic consumption, a credit crunch, and soaring debt service costs took a harsh toll on the asset quality of commercial banks, finance companies, and securities companies. The liquidity shortage was serious. A Standard and Poor's forecast in May 1998 said that nonperforming loans for Thai banks would likely peak at 35 percent of total outstanding loans by mid-1999. Cleaning up bank balance sheets could cost up to $20 billion in new capital.

Regulatory changes are prompting a sweeping change for the country's financial institutions. The Bank of Thailand, pushed along by the International Monetary Fund and the World Bank, announced new supervisory and capital adequacy guidelines in May 1998. Restrained liquidity and monetary policies tightened the screws further on cash-strapped individual consumers and corporations that were already reeling from higher costs after the fall of the baht. The baht, which held stable at 38 to 40 to the dollar from April to May, began a sharp slide in June toward 45. The decline reflected investor's concerns about the Japanese economy, a medium-term devaluation of the Chinese yuan, and a recession in Hong Kong. Market sentiment cooled off rapidly by mid-1998 on the realization that a long road of structural adjustments and reforms were needed to fix Thailand's economic engine.

A vicious cycle financial sectors, as illustrated in Figure 5.3, shows that banks are unwilling to lend due to the fear of bad loans. The result is a credit crunch. Consumers and corporations are desperately short of liquidity. A long-term stagnation is in store for Thailand. Investor lack of confidence is making bank recapitalization difficult. Small capital inflows coupled with low collateral value make banks unwilling to lend.

Figure 5.3
Financial Crisis and Vicious Cycle

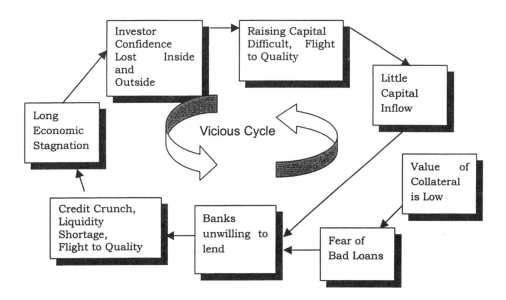

Strengthening the Financial Sector

In March 1998, the central bank unveiled new loan classification, provisioning, and accounting standards aimed at strengthening local financial institutions. From July 1998, all accounts are classified into five categories: (1) pass, (2) special mention, (3) substandard, (4) doubtful, and (5) loss. Provisions were set at 1 percent for pass accounts, where interest was not overdue for more than one month and no loss was likely. Special mention accounts, not overdue for more than three months, would have a 2 percent provision. Substandard accounts, overdue up to six months, require a 20 percent provision. Doubtful accounts, overdue for up to one year, require 50 percent. Loss accounts must have 100 percent provisions or be written off. Collateral would no longer play a role in loan classification, but would help determine the amount of provisioning required for substandard, doubtful, and loss accounts.

The government is expected to issue up to 500 billion baht in local bonds over the next year to restructure liabilities and cover losses of the Financial Institution Development Fund. Total borrowings of the fund at the end of March 1998 were 851.76 billion baht, carrying an average annual interest rate of 20.43 percent.

Commercial Banks: Reconstruction, Write-Downs, and Flight to Quality

Reconstruction Through Write-Downs

In September 1997, an analyst of Moody's Investors Service boldly predicted that as many as five commercial banks could fail and come under regulatory control by the end of 1998. The response by Thai bankers and officials was swift, blasting the analysis as "unfounded," "unprofessional," and "unethical." Midway through 1998, the prediction appeared still optimistic. The blasting now proves to be false. More than the five commercial banks are now doomed.

Small and medium-size banks came under fierce liquidity pressure in the first quarter of 1998, as deposits moved to larger institutions and foreign banks. The flight-to-quality move forced several small and medium-size banks to turn to the FIDF for support. New regulatory policies toward ailing banks began in December 1998.

Bangkok Metropolitan Bank (BMB), Siam City Bank, and First Bangkok City Bank are just three examples of write-downs. Bangkok Metropolitan Bank was taken over by central regulators after failing to secure new equity partners. On January 23, 1998, the central bank ordered the BMB to write off bad debts, writing down 11 billion baht in capital to leave the par value of shares worth just one satang. The

FIDF would take a 99.9-percent stake in the bank by swapping 25 billion baht worth of loans for an equity stake. The recapitalization, the central bank said, would increase the BMB's capital-to-risk assets ratio to 10 percent, comfortably above the 8.5 percent minimum.

On February 6, 1998, regulators took similar actions against Siam City Bank and First Bangkok City Bank, ordering sweeping management changes and a capital write-down followed by a debt-to-equity swap by the Financial Institutions Development Fund. Bangkok Bank of Commerce, seized by regulators in 1995 and managed under contract by the Industrial Finance Corporation of Thailand, was also ordered to write down capital. Siam City Bank had 5.548 billion baht of capital written down, bringing par value of shares to one baht each. The FIDF took a 97-percent stake by swapping 20 billion baht in debt for equity, raising registered capital to 20.616 billion baht. First Bangkok City Bank had 9.99 billion baht worth of capital written down, leaving par value of shares worth one satang each. The FIDF took a 99.9-percent stake by swapping 32 billion baht in outstanding debt for new equity, raising capital to 32.01 billion baht. Remaining banks were given stern warnings to either raise new capital or face similar action.

Although the provisioning standards will be gradually phased in through 2000, all local banks were obligated to submit recapitalization plans by August 15, 1998, with plans by finance companies due on September 15, 1998. In short, such write-downs are expected to accelerate the necessary reconstruction of commercial banks.

Recapitalization

Credit-rating downgrades, tight monetary policy, loss of profitability, collapse of asset prices, and regional volatility all compounded the difficulties for local banks to raise capital funds, although there are exceptions. In late 1997, Thai Danu Bank became the first commercial bank to sell a majority stake to a foreign institution, with the Development Bank of Singapore taking a 50.1-percent stake.

Two of the largest banks, Bangkok Bank and Thai Farmers Bank, managed to raise new capital in international private placements. Bangkok Bank sold 440 million shares at 93 baht each in March 1998 in a global private placement, boosting foreign shareholding to 47.9 percent from 25 percent. The bank's capital-to-risk assets ratio jumped to 16.6 percent. In April 1998, Thai Farmers Bank, one of the strongest banks in Thailand, sold 376 million shares for 88 baht each in a private placement to investors in Hong Kong, Singapore, Europe, and the United States, resulting in foreign shareholders holding 49 percent. The bank's capital-to-risk assets ratio jumped to 16.8 percent.

Siam Commercial Bank placed 588.7 million shares in private placements with Sanwa Bank and Long-Term Credit Bank of Japan. In June

1998, the bank announced plans to raise 40 billion baht in new capital to meet the provisioning requirements and raise capital-to-risk assets ratio to 18 percent.

Recapitalization is one thing, but profitabilty is quite another. Few, if any, commercial banks were expected to post a profit in 1998. With funding costs sharply higher and credit expected to grow little, interest spreads for local banks have been cut almost in half compared with several years ago. With the recession expected to stretch well into 1999, prospects for the banking sector in the medium term remain bleak. Foreign rather than domestic shareholding is expected to increase. In short, a few banks have succeeded in raising capital. However, recapitalization is a remote possibility for the other banks.

Finance Companies

After fifty-six finance companies were shut down in December 1997, the remaining thirty-five firms faced nonperforming loans of up to 50 to 60 percent of total assets. This is the price of extending risky loans to property developers and lower-tier businesses. The Bank of Thailand tried to calm markets by maintaining a full guarantee on creditors and depositors of all financial institutions, but funds continued a flight to quality in late 1997 and 1998. Depositors fled from ailing finance companies to large commercial banks, state institutions, and foreign firms. Liquidity pressures on finance companies continued, as creditors cut lines.

Several firms hurriedly pushed ahead to raise new capital, either by drawing in new foreign partners or turning to deep-pocketed local investors. Asia Credit had a 51-percent stake taken by SG Securities, the investment arm of French bank Societe Generale. In 1998, National Finance successfully raised 7 billion baht in new capital and is looking to buy assets to upgrade to "super-finance" status. Shares for many finance companies are trading below their 10 baht par value. Most analysts have long since recommended investors to sell out because of the poor outlook. With the Stock Exchange of Thailand index testing 300 points by mid-1998, the lowest point in eleven years, raising funds became very difficult for listed finance companies. Overall, the problems faced by finance companies are similar to those faced by commercial banks.

Bleak prospects are in store for the next several years. Even firms successfully raising new capital are not expected to be able to pay dividends or show significant capital gains over the next several years because of their need to set aside provisions against bad loans. There have only been a few foreign partnership deals, and the negotiations were stalled over pricing, management, and so on. In mid-March 1998, the central bank dealt another blow to public confidence in the finance sector, seizing control of seven finance companies which had admitted that recapitalization was impossible. The seven firms (Union Asia Finance, Nava Finance and Securities, Mahatun Finance, Bangkok Asian Finance, Ksit Finance and Securities, Erawan Trust, and Progressive Finance) would have shareholders' equity written down against bad debts. Some analysts predict perhaps only ten or fifteen companies might survive the next several years, as regulators wait for more competitive financial landscape of the future.

In December 1997, the FRA approved rehabilitation plans of two companies (Kiatnakin Finance and Securities and Bangkok Investment). However, preparations for liquidating the assets and repaying the creditors for the fifty-six closed finance companies would preoccupy the FRA. As of December 8, 1997, the total book value of assets of the fifty-six finance companies amounted to 866 billion baht. Estimates on the recoverable value of the assets ranged from a high of 592 billion baht to a low of 363 billion. The FRA began the complicated liquidation process, starting with the automobiles owned by ailing finance companies or seized from delinquent borrowers. In June 1998, the FRA announced that it had raised 10 billion baht from auction sales, with proceeds deposited with the Bank of Thailand to eventually be repaid to creditors in 1999.

The real test for the FRA starts with the sale of core assets (property, consumer loans, securities, etc.). The FRA is expected to auction the core assets of the fifty-six closed finance companies by December 1998 (*Bangkok Post*, September 9, 1998). For the FRA, the slide in exchange rates is actually a boon, as foreign investors gain purchasing power in baht terms. In any case, by mid-1998, Radanasin Bank, the "good bank" set up by the Finance Ministry to support the FRA auctions, faced a cloudy future. Capitalized with 4 billion baht in funds from the Finance Ministry, the bank was authorized to raise another 4 billion if necessary. The bank began accepting deposits, but with only a single branch and limited services, growth was limited.

The FRA consists half of Thais and half of Westerners. Swedish consultants, for instance, receive high consultant fees and help the FRA judge which institutions to kill or not. No Japanese consultants are involved.

Securities Companies

The closure of fifty-six finance firms in December 1997 included thirty-nine securities firms, significantly reducing the competition in securities business. At the time this is written, only twenty-three brokerages and twenty-two subbrokers remain in Thailand. Average trading volume on the Stock Exchange of Thailand was only about 1.5 to 2 billion baht per day in early 1998, resulting in insufficient trading commissions to cover the expenses of local brokerages and subbrokers.

Many securities firms also posted massive losses on portfolio investments and past-due margin loans in the first half of 1998. Fee-based income and underwriting activity also ground to a stop because of the bearish mood of the equity market, thin liquidity, and high interest rates. Investment banking and financial advisory services jumped, reflecting the need by listed companies to restructure debt and secure new capital funding. Further pressure came from the Securities and Exchange Commission (SEC), which pushed forward with the implementation of capital adequacy regulations to strengthen the financial standing of local securities firms. Under the net capital rule (NCR), securities firms are required to maintain sufficient capital funds to cover risk assets. For 1998, the NCR minimum was set at 3 percent, rising to 7 percent in 1999. Five companies were privately warned by the SEC for failure to maintain NCR guidelines. They had their trading operations suspended. Central regulators were concerned about problems in clearing and settlement transactions.

Overall, the problems faced by securities firms are similar to those by finance companies, only smaller in scope. Securities business remains underdeveloped in Thailand, keeping the overall debt–equity ratio relatively low.

The SEC and the government agreed to allow up to 100-percent foreign participation in the securities sector, leading to several deals between local brokerage firms and overseas investment banks. Most prominent was a deal by Phatra Thanakit to sell a 51-percent stake in subsidiary Phatra Securities to Merrill Lynch for 2.6 billion baht. Other transactions included Socgen-Crosby and Asia Credit, AIG and Bangkok Investment, Asia Securities Trading and ABN-AMRO, and Securities One and KG Investment Asia.

Analysts agree that international investment banks will play a major role in the local securities sector, either directly or through majority-controlled joint ventures. Derivatives products and financial advisory services all show opportunities for growth in the local market as authorities proceed with market development plans. Foreign firms, with stronger technology, product depth, product breadth, and global networks, will force local securities firms either to seek partnerships or scale back. In short, foreign involvement is bound to increase in securities business as in banks and finance companies. Flight to quality applies also. The finance companies are expected to grow stronger.

THE UMBRELLA SCHEME (FINANCIAL PACKAGE) OF AUGUST 14, 1998

On August 14, 1998, the Thai government announced a comprehensive financial reform plan. The package was described as an "umbrella" scheme, meaning that its new measures were interrelated and comprehensive enough for banks to resume normal lending.

Thailand is entering a new phase of economic reconstruction marked by the adoption of the comprehensive financial package after going through the macroeconomic stabilization stage in 1998. Anoop Singh, the International Monetary Fund's deputy chief for the Asia Pacific region, says that an "innovative" feature of the comprehensive financial-sector package announced by the Thai government is the built-in linkage of corporate debt restructuring and bank recapitalization. The former will be automatically accelerated by the latter. Both should take place at the same time. About 300 billion baht will be used by the government to help the remaining banks recapitalize to meet new capital-adequacy requirements, 4.25 percent tier-one and 4.25 percent tier-two capital. Anoop Singh, who also oversees the IMF program in South Korea and Indonesia, says Thailand will have to implement a new legal framework (i.e., foreclosure law) and adopt other measures (i.e., market opening) to support a successful reconstruction of the economy.

After the six-month macroeconomic stabilization stage, there is no sequence in implementing policies in the reconstruction stage, since key policy components (bank recapitalization, corporate debt restructuring, a new legal framework, and market opening) will have to be implemented simultaneously. The core measures of the package will force the banks and their shareholders to write down existing capital if they wish to receive assistance in the form of injections of fresh equity from the state. Tier-one capital will be reduced and tier-two capital increased to make room for the government to invest in subordinated loans of ten-years maturity. David Proctor, chairman of the Foreign Banks' Association, says

The measures directly address the key issues affecting the domestic financial system. They clarify the position of local banks where the Financial Institutions Development Fund has intervened, resolve the uncertainty surrounding other small banks and weak finance companies, support an increase in capital at the larger banks, enable a quicker restructuring of corporate debt and an increase in bank lending to the corporate sector while minimizing the cost to taxpayers by ensuring existing shareholders bear appropriate losses.

In essence, the new financial reform measures are innovative, aiming at both bank recapitalization and corporate debt restructuring simultaneously. The umbrella scheme can take several years before results are known. As Prime Minister Chuan Leekpai says, it will be an evolving process and not an automatic quick fix. The success will depend on actual policy implementation and external circumstances. The scheme relies on foreign investors to salvage the ailing economy.

FIRST TALKS BETWEEN CREDITORS AND DEBTORS

On September 10, 1998, bankers and financiers agreed on a framework for easier payment of corporate debt to ensure the survival of struggling firms. The framework outlines an agreed set of guidelines for debtors and creditors engaged in restructuring debts. It is a first step. Both debtors and creditors are expected to cooperate in making the process successful. The Thai Bankers' Association, the Association of Finance Companies, and the Foreign Banks' Association agreed to a memorandum signed with the Corporate Debt Restructuring Advisory Committee. The Federation of Thai Industries and the Thai Chamber of Commerce both support the framework.

Debtors would provide sufficient information to creditors in return for easing repayment terms. Creditors would provide more loans to help the restructuring process. Shareholders of the debtors would be the first to absorb any losses stemming from debt restructuring. David Proctor, chairman of the Foreign Banks' Association, cautioned that the scheme was no magic cure for the country's economic difficulties. It did not mean all debts would be restructured immediately, as it would take time to resolve each case individually. Economic hardship would persist, he warned, with more workers losing their jobs and many more companies folding: "The debt restructuring will not create new investment and job opportunities. It is only an effort to resolve the bad-debt problem."

International Monetary Fund resident representative Reza Moghadam said at the signing that the framework was important but only the first step in a long and arduous process. Thai Bankers' Association chairman Banthoon Lamsam said debt restructuring was difficult, but the framework would help lead the way: "Talks between creditors and debtors are badly needed." He cited the recent court case involving Hotel Nikko Mahanakorn. Creditors had tried to negotiate for debt restructuring, but one of the hotel's major shareholders believed the creditors wanted only to take over the company, so blocked the move. The court ruled in favor of shareholders, as the company's asset value exceeded its debts.

CONCLUSION

The financial sector was the hardest hit in Thailand's economic crisis. Liquidity shortages prevail, and the banks are not functioning. Some even mention a possibility of nationalizing banks. Nonperforming loans for Thai banks will peak at 35 percent of total outstanding loans by mid-1999. The talk is not whether smaller, weaker banks can survive, but whether any can survive. Solving the banking mess is essential to solving the economic crisis.

The Nukul report clarifies why the Bank of Thailand failed. It reveals defects inherent inside the Bank of Thailand (disharmony, poor decisions, delayed decisions, poor leadership, poor teamwork, lack of prudence, misguided policies, etc.). The central bank in the past ignored IMF warnings, refusing to change the foreign exchange regime. Such refusals taught Thailand many things, but at a high price. The central bank's heavy intervention in the foreign exchange market decreased Thailand's net foreign exchange reserves to only $1.14 billion in June 1997, necessitating a bail-out package from the International Monetary Fund. A default as a nation was approaching due to the futile attempt to defend the baht. The Financial Institution Development Fund under the Bank of Thailand used to guarantee "unlimited" financial support to banks and finance companies. The financial system in Thailand was actually broke in June 1997. An insolvency of Thailand as a nation was then rumored. It is hoped that such a no-ceiling policy in the liquidity support to finance companies and banks will not be repeated in the future. Defects are inherent in commercial banks, finance companies, and securities firms.

The Bank of Thailand, pushed along by the International Monetary Fund and the World Bank, has recently announced new supervisory and capital adequacy guidelines. Regulatory changes by the Bank of Thailand prompted a sweeping change for the country's financial institutions. It seems that the Bank of Thailand is changing drastically from the inside, after paying such a high tuition fee for its lessons. The financial crisis has taught Thailand many important things in the borderless age of megacompetition.

On August 14, 1998, the Thai government announced a new financial reform plan which aims at a simultaneous solution of corporate debt restructuring and bank recapitalization. The innovative plan will take several years before results appear. No other East Asian countries are as far along in their reconstruction plans as Thailand. Its success will mean a great deal to the region. The success will depend on actual implementation, external circumstances, and widespread cooperative efforts from within for many years to come.

Thai authorities are seeking to address all the main areas of weaknesses in the financial system. It all depends on the availability of public funds to catalyze the entry of new private capital, as well as strong incentives for banks to restructure corporate debt. A number of burden-sharing safeguards are in place, including the write-down of the value of the assets of existing shareholders. The negotiations between creditors and debtors are expected to be a long and arduous process.

Such direct talks between creditors and debtors will hopefully progress further in the future.

Structural adjustments are constantly needed to fix Thailand's inherent economic disease. Foreign participation is crucial to the success of the programs. However, a potential crisis in China poses both danger and chance. Hopefully, the current reforms will strengthen financial sectors in Thailand. Otherwise, there will be no economic growth. There is still a long road to recovery.

REFERENCES

Abe, Kiyoshi. 1997. "Vicious Cycle and Composite Economic Crisis in Thailand: A Comparison with Japan." In *Japanese Studies*. Vol. 1. Bangkok: Thammassat University, Institute of East Asian Studies.

"Agreement on Easier Payment." 1998. *Bangkok Post*, 11 September.

"Bank Reforms: Last Big Step in Our Recovery." 1998. *The Nation* (Bangkok), 13 August.

"Latin Lessons for Asian Banks." 1998. *The Economist*, 25 July.

"New Reform Measures Bring Relief." 1998. *The Nation* (Bangkok), 15 August.

"Newspapers Voice Optimism Over Comprehensive Package." 1998. *The Nation* (Bangkok), 17 August.

"Nukul to Make Recommendations on BOT Restructuring." 1998. *The Nation* (Bangkok), 13 March.

"Sugisaki Welcomes Thailand's Resolve to Pursue Economic Restructuring Policies—Financial Package." 1998. *IMF Survey*, 31 August.

"Thailand: Banking Chaos." 1998. *Business Week*, 17 August.

"Thailand on Verge of Recovery—IMF." 1998. *The Nation* (Bangkok), 16 August.

6

The Economic Crisis of Indonesia

Doowoo Nam and Benton E. Gup

Since 1985, the growth rate of the Indonesian economy has been above 7 percent per annum, and in 1995 and 1996 it exceeded 8 percent per annum. The economy was transformed from an agricultural society into an industrial economy. Indonesia ranks fifteenth among world oil-producing countries and eighth among the Organization of Petroleum Exporting Countries (OPEC) members, and is the only Asian country that has OPEC membership. It is the world's largest exporter of liquefied natural gas (LNG), accounting for over 40 percent of the world market, and the world's seventh largest producer of natural gas. In addition, it is the world's largest tin producer, and it exports significant quantities of copper ore, nickel matte, coal, and aluminum. Its GDP per capita grew from $50 in 1967 to $1,139 in 1996, although it is still much lower than Malaysia's ($4,758) and Thailand's ($3,058). Nevertheless, it was a booming economy. In early 1997, the World Bank praised Indonesia for its macroeconomic performance (Solomon 1998d). Then, in August 1997, Indonesia caught the "Asian flu" that began when Thailand devalued its currency in the previous month. The value of the Indonesian rupiah plunged from 2,599 rupiah/dollar at the beginning of August to 10,375 rupiah/dollar by the end of January 1998.

The Indonesian government tried to cope with the currency crisis using its foreign reserves, but it failed. Indonesia's foreign exchange reserves were $19.3 billion in 1996, equal to over twenty-five months of the country's monthly requirements of the current account deficit. This appeared to be ample reserves when contrasted with Mexico at the time of its crisis in 1994, which had only two to three weeks of reserves in terms of its monthly current-account deficit requirements (Kuntjoro-Jakti 1997). However, Indonesia had short-term foreign debt of $34.2 billion at the end of 1996, and the ratio of short-term debt to foreign exchange reserves reached to 1.8. The government abandoned the 12-percent intervention band for the rupiah on August 14, 1997, and the rupiah immediately plunged. The value of the rupiah continued to fall, as seen in Tables 6.1 and 6.2. The sharp depreciation in the rupiah caused many problems, such as a sharp decline in stock prices, a significant increase in foreign debt denominated in the U.S. dollar, and the credit crunch resulting from the policy of maintaining high interest rates to stabilize the value of the rupiah.

Was the currency crisis a case of contagion, a reflection of internal mismanagement, or were there other contributing factors? This chapter examines the causes and consequences of the economic crisis in Indonesia.

INDONESIAN ECONOMY

Population

The Republic of Indonesia has 202 million people, giving it the fourth largest population in the world. Although Indonesia consists of more than 17 thousand islands, 60 percent of the population live on the islands of Java and Bali. Jakarta, the capital, is the largest city in the country. It is located on the island of Java, along with 80 percent of the country's in-

Table 6.1
Indonesia's Economic Indicators-1

	1983-88	1989-94	1995	1996
Real GDP (%)	5.2%	6.9%	8.2%	8.0%
Consumer Prices (%)	7.6%	8.6%	8.6%	6.5%
Current A/C Balance	US$-2.9B	US$-2.7B	US$-6.8B	US$-7.8B
External Debt	US$41.4B	US$80.6B	US$107.8B	US$113.1B
Exchange Rate (Rp/$)	1,276.3	1,973.5	2,308	2,383

Sources: "WEFA Country Profile" (New York: Bloomberg, 1997); "International Economic and Monetary Indicators," Bank Indonesia, 25 February 1998.

Table 6.2
Indonesia's Economic Indicators-2

	Exchange Rate		Stock Index		Interest Rate	
	Rupiah/$*	% Change	JSE**	% Change	ICM***	% Change
1993	2,110	—	588.77	—	8.74	—
1994	2,200	4.3	469.64	−20.2	9.74	11.4
1995	2,308	4.7	513.84	9.4	13.56	39.2
1996	2,383	3.2	637.43	24.1	14.06	3.7
1997						
Jul.	2,599	6.1	721.27	−0.5	15.87	16.1
Aug.	3,035	16.8	493.96	−31.5	65.02	309.7
Sep.	3,275	8.0	546.68	10.7	52.61	−19.1
Oct.	3,670	12.1	500.41	−8.5	40.34	−23.3
Nov.	3,648	−0.6	401.70	−19.7	42.15	4.5
Dec.	4,650	27.5	401.71	0.0	40.67	−3.5
1998						
Jan.	10,375	123.1	485.93	21.0	57.18	40.6
Feb.	8,750	−15.7	482.37	−0.7	64.81	13.3
Mar.	8,325	−4.9	541.42	12.2	51.76	−20.1
Apr.	7,970	−4.3	460.13	−15.0	70.80	36.8
May	10,525	32.1	420.46	−8.6	63.54	−10.3

Source: Bank Indonesia at http://www.bi.go.id/statistik.

*Middle rates at Bank Indonesia.
**Composite stock price index of the Jakarta Stock Exchange (JSE).
***Overnight rate of Interbank call money (ICM).

dustries. Bali has 13 percent of the industries. These islands have the most fertile agricultural lands and the most developed infrastructure.

About 95 percent of the population are Malay and 90 percent are followers of Islam. Indonesia has the world's largest Muslim population, with almost as many Muslims as are in the entire Arab world (Wolfowitz 1998). Nevertheless, there are more than 300 ethnic and linguistic groups and the country has a policy of religious tolerance. Like other Southeast Asian countries, Indonesia has an ethnic Chinese minority which constitutes some 3 percent of the population, but they play a disproportionately large role in trade, services, and industry groups (Bhattacharya and Pangestu 1997). They control more than the half of the Indonesian economy. Chinese tycoons own most of the 230 companies sitting on the $62 billion in private corporate debt that has crippled the Indonesian economy (Gilley et al. 1998). The *pribumi*, indigenous Indonesians, blame ethnic Chinese for the current economic crisis.

The imbalance of economic powers between islands, arising from differences in demographics and resource endowment, has created problems in domestic distribution of national wealth. In recent years, the Indonesian government has made efforts to address regional imbalances, particularly in the underdeveloped eastern provinces, including Irian Jaya and East Timor, which are located away from the country's primary areas of economic influence.[1]

The Development Process

The development process of Indonesia can be divided into five subperiods (Hill 1996).

Before 1966

Indonesia proclaimed its independence from the Netherlands in 1945. The economic system remained largely unchanged during the first twenty years of independence. By 1966, Indonesia's agricultural output was not sufficient to meet domestic consumption and the country could barely provide the basic necessities of life for its people. From 1960 to 1966 the annual GDP grew only at 1.7 percent on average, and the per capita GDP fell by 0.5 percent (Bhattacharya and Pangestu 1997). To make matters worse, the economy suffered from intolerable inflation exceeding 600 percent per year.

1966–1970

Suharto took power in 1966, and was formally named acting president in 1967 and president in 1968. The Suharto administration tried to control inflation by eliminating the chronic budget deficit through drastic expenditure cuts. The annual GDP growth rate reached 6.6 percent on average in this period.

In 1969, the government launched five-year development plans (*repelitas*) to establish a framework for systematic national economic planning. This period and the 1970s provided the foundation for industrialization by controlling inflation and starting to build the infrastructure.

1971–1981

There were two oil booms and subsequent crises during this period, a time when Indonesians benefited from the increased prices in oil and other commodities. Net oil and liquid natural gas earnings rose from $0.6 billion in 1973–1974 to a peak of $10.6 billion in 1980–1981 (Bhattacharya and Pangestu 1997). The annual GDP grew at 7.7 percent on average.

1982–1986

Falling oil prices resulted in lower incomes and posed a serious economic problem during this period. The external debts that funded the expansion of the 1980s had to be repaid, but the value of the rupiah declined. It was devalued by 28 percent in March 1983 to help finance the current account deficit, and by 31 percent in September 1986 to improve the competitiveness of the non-oil economy (Bhattacharya and Pangestu 1997).

Since 1983, the Indonesian government has carried out a series of broad measures—such as the elimination of import licensing for some items, a reduction in nontariff barriers as well as in tariffs, the relaxation of controls on foreign investment, and financial deregulation by lowering entry barriers (Bhattacharya and Pangestu 1997)—aimed at reducing the country's reliance on oil revenues through the development of a more diversified and competitive economy. The government continued to take measures to reform the economy, promote investment, increase non-oil exports, and expand the tourism industry and capital markets.

1987–1996

Indonesia successfully reduced its dependence on oil, and it began to export manufactured products. Manufacturing became the largest economic sector in 1991 and continues to keep the leading position. The proportion of oil and gas fell from 80 percent of total exports in 1984, to 43 percent in 1990, and to 23 percent in 1995. In 1996, textile and processed wood accounted for 50 percent of total non-oil and gas industrial products exported, followed by electronics. The main exporting markets for Indonesia are the United States, Japan, and Singapore. On the other hand, the main industrial import products are machinery and automotive and basic chemicals, and the major partners for industrial imports are Japan, the United States, Germany, and South Korea.

In short, during the period under review, the boom and bust of the Indonesian economy was attributable to the rise and fall of oil prices. After oil prices were stabilized from the late 1980s, Indonesia could only depend on foreign investments to finance its economic growth. This external debt problem, coupled with the close adhesion of economy and politics, were major factors in its recent economic crisis.

External Debts

External debt problems are not new to Indonesia. The government rescheduled external debts in the late 1960s. In 1975, there was a surge in the country's foreign debt as a result of the huge government bailout for the debt-stricken state-owned oil company (Bhattacharya and Pangestu 1997; Schwarz 1994).

In the early 1980s, the Indonesian government turned to commercial borrowing in order to finance several large public-sector investments. When oil prices declined in 1982, it borrowed even more to meet the financing gap (Bhattacharya and Pangestu 1997). Both total debt and its proportion of GDP approximately doubled between 1980 and 1986 (Hill 1996). The sharp appreciation of the yen following the Plaza Accord of 1985 caused Indonesian external debts to rapidly rise, since about 40 percent of external debts were denominated in the Japanese yen. Indonesia's external debt amounts to $134 billion (about 56% of GDP) in 1997, of which about $35.4 billion is short term.[2] Table 6.3 shows the external indebtedness of Indonesia, although the data may not be accurate due to the lack of transparency of the economy.

Foreign Exchange System

In 1971, the rupiah was pegged to the U.S. dollar. In 1986, the Indonesian central bank adopted a managed float system (Hill 1996). In the early 1990s, the system was modified to incorporate movements against a basket of currencies. The government changed the exchange rate regime from the managed floating system with a 12 percent intervention band using the weighted basket to the free-floating system in August 1997.

Table 6.3
Indonesia's External Debts

	Total Debt ($ billion)	% of GDP	% of Short-Term Debt
1980	20.9	28.0	13.2
1982	26.3	29.2	13.0
1983	30.0	37.0	10.5
1984	31.9	38.7	12.0
1985	34.3	40.9	10.6
1986	40.1	52.2	9.0
1987	49.7	68.8	7.3
1988	51.4	64.1	7.9
1989	53.5	59.5	9.9
1990	67.0	66.4	16.7
1991	76.1	69.0	18.9
1992	84.4	67.4	21.6
1993	89.2	56.5	21.1
1994	96.5	54.6	22.1
1995	107.8	53.3	25.6
1996	113.1	49.7	30.2
1997	134.0	56.2	26.4

Source: Hal Hill, *The Indonesian Economy Since 1966: Southeast Asia's Emerging Giant* (Cambridge: Cambridge University Press, 1996); and Bank for International Settlements.

Cronyism and Corruption

Michael Dee, the managing director of Morgan Stanley, defines crony capitalism as the allocation of capital to nonefficient mechanisms ("Inside Asia's Whirlwind" 1998). Schwarz (1994) defines crony businessmen in the Suharto regime as a group that has a continuing close, personal relationship with President Suharto. The crony group consists mainly of a few ethnic Chinese businessmen and relatives of President Suharto. Individually, four of Suharto's six children are listed among the biggest of Indonesia's corporate empires, and they have formed an intricate web of business alliances with virtually every major player in Indonesia (Tripathi 1998). Collectively, the Suharto family is the most powerful economic dynasty in the country. Suharto had been in power for thirty-two years when he was replaced in 1998. Maybe one person being in power that long contributed to cronyism?

The crony businessmen obtain an assortment of benefits, including operating without partners, lucrative distribution and supply deals with state-owned companies, no-questions-asked financing from state banks, preferential consideration on government-funded infrastructure projects, and monopolies on importing, exporting, or distributing agricultural commodities like wheat, palm oil, soybeans, or sugar. In the 1990s, hardly a single major infrastructure contract has been awarded without a Suharto relative having a piece of it. The state-owned oil company, Pertamina, has identified 120 companies that supply it that are owned by Suharto's family and friends.

Cronyism and corruption go hand in hand. Until the 1980s, Indonesia's financial system was dominated by seven state banks that often channeled money to projects involving Suharto kin or friends (Brauchli 1998). According to a World Bank report, Indonesia has an "entrenched culture of corruption" (Simpson 1998). As much as 50 to 80 percent of funds budgeted for project land acquisition and resettlement assistance were "diverted" by firms owned or controlled by government officials and their relatives. Corruption deepened in the late 1980s as the business interests of the six children of Suharto began to grow dramatically as a result of government-sanctioned licenses, monopolies, and other privileges. Some of these business empires are barely a decade old, but they rank among the largest corporations in Southeast Asia. During Suharto's time in office, it is estimated that his family amassed as much as $40 billion!

Cronyism did not end when B. J. Habibie succeeded Suharto as president in 1998. Habibie is a protégé of Suharto. According to a *Wall Street Journal* headline, "Indonesia's New Leader Has Commercial Ties Redolent of the Old" (1998). The article goes on to explain that Habibie's sons and relatives are well along the way to replacing the Suharto dynasty.

Cronyism and corruption are a double-edged sword. On the one hand, we condemn them. On the other hand, Indonesia prospered under this system and grew from an agrarian state to an industrial state in a relatively short period of time. The question of whether the country would have grown as fast or by as much without cronyism is beyond the scope of this chapter.

BANKING SYSTEM

Banks dominate the Indonesian financial system. They control over 85 percent of the total assets of financial intermediaries, including insurance companies and nonbank finance companies. Banks provide about 85 percent of total business finance, the stock market accounts for about 15 percent, and the bond market is insignificant (Montgomery 1997).

According to Montgomery (1997), the dominance of bank debts facilitates the operation of monetary policy. However, the dependence of firms on bank finance increases the risk of credit crunch, since the firms have fewer alternative sources of finance than in other countries.

The number of commercial banks increased from 111 in 1989 to approximately 240 in 1994. The total includes 7 state-owned banks, 27 regional government-owned banks, 165 private national banks, 31 joint banks, and 10 foreign banks. The large state-owned banks and the private national banks together accounted for 87 percent of total banking assets as of 1995 (Montgomery 1997). The ownership structure of Indonesian banks influences their lending polices. The state-owned banks make lending decisions on the basis of political considerations. The private national banks are owned by affiliates of large corporate groups. These banks make lending decisions in the interest of their owners.

Government policies also influenced lending policies. The interest rate on dollar-denominated loans (5%) was substantially lower than the interest rate on rupiah-denominated loans (30%). The private sector took advantage of the difference and opted for dollar-denominated loans, as the exchange rate between the dollar and rupiah was controlled by the government and it had been stable. The dollar loans were short term, but they were invested in long-term investment projects. Because the revenues of the borrowers were in rupiah, they were not shielded from exchange risk when the exchange rates changed.

Real estate lending has been one area of concern. Real estate lending grew at an annual rate of 37 percent from 1992 to 1995, far exceeding the growth rate of 22 percent for total bank credit. Bank loans to property developers reached 17 percent of total credit by September 1995, when the property market in Jakarta was reportedly facing a glut of unoccupied apartments and, to a lesser extent, hotels and offices. Risk was further created by problems in the legal system that made it difficult for banks to enforce loan contracts, so that borrowers who purchased real estate or other assets could walk away from the loan if their equity value turned negative (Montgomery 1997).

As of August 1998, the Indonesian Bank Restructuring Agency (IBRA) had either suspended or taken over about one-fifth of the nation's banks, including three large private banks. According to a Salomon Smith Barney ("Indonesian State Banks" 1998) study, most of the banks would be insolvent if they were forced to write off their nonperforming loans. However, while the risk of defaults is high, bank debt maturing up to January 2000 is guaranteed by the IBRA program.

The Indonesian Debt Restructuring Agency (INDRA) provided dollars to Indonesian companies at a fixed exchange rate (12,314rp/dollar) and extended their repayments up to eight years. In return, the companies were to resume making interest payments on their outstanding loans. However, the decline in the value of the rupiah made the fixed exchange rate too expensive for the companies to make their payments (Wagstaff and Solomon 1998). On September 8, 1998, the indirect exchange rate on the rupiah was 11,850 rp/dollar.

The rapid expansion of banks' exposure to real estate lending highlights some of the problems of bank supervision. Government-directed investments and state-owned banks are not conducive to effective bank supervision. Montgomery (1997) suggests that state-owned banks should be privatized in order to reduce inefficiencies and to promote competition. However, uncertainty about delays in reforms have undermined government efforts to privatize state-owned companies (Solomon 1998b).

Finally, in October 1998, the government announced plans to sell off $15 billion in loans from firms that defaulted on their bank debts (Solomon 1998a). However, the IMF expressed concern that the sale of such loans could set off a "fire sale" mentality among investors and make matters worse than they are. The plan also raised fears among ethnic Chinese that the sales would be used to reallocate wealth from Chinese businessmen to indigenous businessmen.

In April 1998, a new commercial court opened in Jakarta to deal with bankruptcies. Bankruptcy provides a means for closing insolvent firms and for rescuing troubled ones by allowing them to restructure their obligations. According the Rivlin (1998), bankruptcy procedures cannot be rapidly invented or first tested during a crisis. There has to be a "culture of bankruptcy," operating in both good and bad times.

ECONOMIC CRISIS

The economic conditions in Indonesia before the economic crisis differed from those in Malaysia, South Korea, and Thailand before their crises. While the severe deterioration of current account balances was one of the main causes for the economic crises in the other countries, Indonesia had a trade surplus of $971 million in May 1997, up from $203 million a year earlier. Although Indonesia's current account deficit rose to $7.8 billion in 1996 (from $6.8 billion and $2.8 billion in 1995 and 1994, respectively) mainly due to a significant rise in imports, it accounted for only 3.5 percent of GDP. It was much lower than Thailand's (8.0%) and South Korea's (4.7%). Inflation averaged 5.1 percent for the first seven months of 1997, compared to 9.8 percent and 8.7 percent for the same period during the two prior years. Therefore, in terms of these two indices, the economy of Indonesia before the turmoil was relatively healthy compared to that of Thailand and South Korea. (The comparative statistics for the countries suffering from financial difficulties are provided in Table 6.4.) This was pointed out in an address by the Minister of Finance of Indonesia, who suggested that the Indonesian crisis was "not the result of domestic policy mismanagement" (Bawazier 1998):

This is not meant as an excuse for what we now recognize were severe domestic weaknesses. Rather, I suggest that a fair reading of the economic data provided little indication to policy makers and to analysts that a crisis was imminent or that an external shock would so severely damage both our real economy and our financial system. Only a year ago Indonesia's macro-economic data showed the operations of a strong, sound, economy. . . . Despite this rapid [economic] growth, inflation remained moderate and even showed signs of declining. Although our current account deficit was large, reaching about 3.5 percent of GDP in recent years, it was not excessively large. But more important, it showed no sign of increasing. . . . While non-oil export growth slackened somewhat in the mid-1990s, the 1997 export data actually showed a slight improvement in their rate of growth. And, our long-standing tradition of balanced budgets meant that domestic government debt was nonexistent. Even viewed from a more comprehensive base, our fiscal deficit was quite modest. These data, I suggest, did not provide evidence of an economy heading into a serious economic crisis.

The early stage of the economic crisis of Indonesia is blamed on the contagion effect (Djiwandono 1997). The early stage of the crisis was divided into two phases: The first phase was sparked by the sharp depreciation of the Thai baht and other Southeast Asian countries' currencies, and the second phase by the abandonment of a managed floating system in Indonesia. In the first phase, Bank Indonesia widened the exchange rate intervention band from 8 to 12 percent on July 11, 1997. Unfortunately, this measure failed to contain the pressure on the rupiah. As soon as the Indonesian government realized that maintaining the managed floating system with an intervention band would have ultimately drained its foreign reserves, Bank Indonesia decided to adopt a free-floating exchange system by removing the intervention band on August 14, 1997.

Table 6.4
Comparative Statistics

	Year	Indonesia	Thailand	South Korea	Malaysia
GDP Growth	1992	7.2	8.1	5.1	7.8
(%)	1993	7.3	8.5	5.8	8.3
	1994	7.5	8.6	8.6	9.2
	1995	8.2	8.8	8.9	9.5
	1996	8.0	5.5	7.1	8.6
	1997	4.7	–0.4	5.5	7.8
Inflation	1992	4.9	4.1	6.2	4.7
(%)	1993	9.8	3.4	4.8	3.5
	1994	9.2	5.1	6.3	3.7
	1995	8.6	5.8	4.5	3.4
	1996	6.5	5.9	4.9	3.5
	1997	11.1	5.6	4.5	2.7
Current	1992	$–2.8	$–6.3	$–3.9	$–2.2
Account	1993	$–2.1	$–6.4	$1.0	$–3.0
Balance	1994	$–2.8	$–8.1	$–3.9	$–4.5
(Billions)	1995	$–6.8	$–13.6	$–8.5	$–7.4
	1996	$–7.8	$–14.7	$–23.0	$–6.1
	1997	$–4.8	$–2.9	$–8.2	NA

Source: "International Economic and Monetary Indicators," Bank Indonesia, 25 February 1998; IMF. *International Financial Statistics* (Washington, D.C.: IMF, 1998).

Melloan (1998) argues that when the rupiah weakened, the central bank should have reduced the money supply in order to increase short-term rates. Instead, they increased the money supply to protect the banks and Suharto's investments. Melloan argues that this approach was not discouraged by the IMF, "which is institutionally inclined toward devaluation as a financial cure-all."

In short, the structural weaknesses of the Indonesian economy, which is mainly due to large external debts (especially the large amount of short-term foreign debt owed by the private corporate sector), made the economy vulnerable to external shocks like the currency turmoil in Thailand, and in turn brought about the financial crisis in 1997. The economic difficulties affected all of society, and the following social disturbances and political instability exacerbated the economic crisis.

What sets Indonesia apart from other Asian countries experiencing economic difficulties is the poor handling of the crisis by its political leadership (U.S. Senate 1998). Since the beginning of 1998, the economic crisis in Indonesia was aggravated by President Suharto's critical mistake on January 6, 1998, when he announced "an overly optimistic national budget that seemed out of line with reality—expectations of 4% annual economic growth, 11% inflation, and an exchange rate of 4,000 rupiah to the dollar—although the currency was then trading at 8,000," ignoring widespread predictions of 15 percent contraction and 55 percent inflation for 1998 (Shari 1998). The proposed budget called for a 23-percent increase in revenue and expenditure over the previous budget. The cost of this untimely announcement, casting doubt on the Indonesian government's will to fulfill the IMF's reform program, was enormous. The rupiah plunged precipitously below 10,000 to the dollar, which was then seen as the psychological barrier. The freefall was precipitated by perceptions that the national budget was not tough enough to meet the IMF-mandated austerity measures and by market rumors that Indonesia might declare a debt moratorium.

In early February 1998, President Suharto made another mistake by announcing a plan for a currency board based on a U.S. economist's (Dr. Steve H. Hanke) suggestion, which would have pegged the rupiah at 5,000 to the dollar and backed it with U.S. dollar reserves (Shari 1998). Indonesia did not have the reserves to guarantee the peg at the suggested rate, creating the likelihood of rapid sovereign bankruptcy (Ford 1998). The plan was widely decried as a way to allow the Suharto family and its cronies to shift funds offshore on favorable terms (Ford 1998). The credibility of Indonesia was adversely affected, and the value of the rupiah fell further.

Like many of his generation, Suharto sees capitalism as the driving force behind colonialism and, as such, has always harbored some suspicion toward it. Being pressured from the outside to do something in the name of capitalism is certain to be associated with colonial behavior by more nationalist-minded officials, and is therefore resisted in principle. Some members of Suharto's inner circle used language to describe the economic policies being pushed by the IMF in terms identical to those used a half-century ago in criticizing the exploitative agenda of the Dutch (U.S. Senate 1998).

IMF PROGRAM

In 1997, the IMF initially agreed to offer $36.6 billion in aid. That amount was increased to $42.3 billion the following year. This package consisted of $11.2 billion from the IMF, $10 billion from the World Bank and the Asian Development Bank, and $21.1 billion from other countries (IMF 1998). The second agreement, the Memorandum of Economic and Financial Policies between Indonesia and the IMF, signed on January 15, 1998, was revised twice, on April 10 and June 24, 1998, reflecting the very strained situation of Indonesia.

The key measures in the economic reform program are as follows: First is financial-sector restructuring, including closing nonviable institutions, merging state banks, and establishing a timetable for dealing with remaining weak institutions and improving the institutional, legal, and regulatory framework for the financial system. Second are structural reforms to enhance economic efficiency and transparency, including liberalization of foreign trade and investment, dismantling of domestic monopolies, and expanding the privatization program. Third are fiscal measures, including cutting low-priority expenditures, postponing or rescheduling major state enterprise infrastructure projects, removing government subsidies, eliminating VAT exemptions, and adjusting administered prices. The memorandum and its supplements have reinforced these key measures to accelerate implementation. The second supplementary memorandum describes the following objectives as the top two priorities of the Indonesian economy: to repair the distribution system and ensure adequate supplies of food and other necessities to all parts of the country, and to move quickly to comprehensively restructure the banking system.

Under the terms of the first IMF package, the Indonesian government closed sixteen insolvent banks in November 1997. Three of them were owned by Suharto's relatives. The bank closures had an adverse effect on the economy. Under the closure order, deposits were guaranteed only up to 20 million rupiah, equivalent to $5,000 at that time. Deposits were shifted into state banks and a few of the better-regarded large private banks and foreign banks. Of more than 200 banks, only twenty have managed to maintain any kind of liquidity. In December

1997, as the rupiah continued to slip, rumors circulated that the government would convert deposits into bonds or impose foreign exchange controls. All Indonesians with sizable deposits immediately transferred them into dollars offshore. The capital flight created almost immediate paralysis of the banking system (Ford 1998). This shows that closing weak banks without a strong and universal guarantee of bank deposits can lead to a serious bank run that critically affects the whole economy. In January 1998, the Indonesian government established IBRA, which is exclusively responsible for restructuring the banking industry.

On May 4, 1998, the Indonesian government removed the subsidy on fuel, and the price of gasoline soared from 700 rupiah per liter to 1,200 rupiah per liter, a 71-percent increase. The price of rice more than tripled. The significance of this is that 40 percent of Indonesians spend more than 20 percent of their incomes on rice ("Indonesia's Agony and the Price of Rice" 1998). About this same time, the first of many social disturbances occurred in Medan, Indonesia's third largest city. Ethnic Chinese were the targets in these riots. Chinese women were raped, and their businesses and properties were looted and burned. The disturbances spread to Jakarta and other cities, and eventually led to the downfall of the Suharto regime. Because of the severity of the situation, the government and the IMF are trying to bring prices down (Solomon 1998c).

On May 21, 1998, B. J. Habibie succeeded Suharto as president. His main mission is to renew confidence in Indonesia's battered economy, persuade the IMF to resume payments under the country's bailout, and woo foreign investors (Templeman 1998). Habibie is a big hit among *pribumi*, indigenous Muslim business leaders. They were cut off from the gravy train operated by Suharto and his family, who preferred ethnic Chinese partners. Habibie's appointments worry foreigners and ethnic Chinese because they are heavily weighted toward the *pribumi* (Templeman 1998).

The social unrest did not stop when Habibie took office. Food riots were fueled by the surging price of rice, that had trebled since the crisis began. Looting and rioting spurred Habibie to instruct the military to use force on those committing criminal acts, such as looting a government-owned warehouse on the island of East Timor.

CONCLUSION

The economic crisis in Indonesia provides important insights about economic crises in general. While contagion may have been the trigger that set off the crises, it could not have occurred without financial-sector weaknesses. According to Marino (1998), such weaknesses appear to reflect the inability of lenders to use business criteria in allocating credit and implicit or explicit government guarantees against risk. While Indonesian capital cronyism directed investments that resulted in economic growth and prosperity for many years, it also contributed to excess capacity in real estate and other areas. Moreover, it did not guarantee banks against the adverse consequences of crony-directed investments. Stated otherwise, perverse economic incentives contributed to this crisis. Congressmen Jim Saxton, Chairman of the Joint Economic Committee, believes that the IMF safety net may be one of these factors. Saxton (1998b) argues that the IMF's Asian bailouts have created a moral hazard problem. Saxton (1998a) goes on to state that "recent IMF lending and prospects for future lending not only reinforce existing risk-promoting incentives in emerging economies but also create incentives for additional risky lending by international financial institutions." One editorial said, "The IMF believes that the sine qua non of recovery is loans being repaid to big Western banks" (Jenkins 1998). This statement is incomplete in the sense that Japanese banks had $23 billion in bank loans in Indonesia in June 1997, and Korean banks had about $9 billion (Jenkins 1998). Finally, Krugman (1998) argues that the IMF plan not only failed to revive the ailing economies, but it actually worsened the situation. Indonesia's GDP increased a respectable 4.7 percent in 1997 (see Table 6.4). At the time of this writing, it was forecast to decline 15 percent in 1998, and the end is not yet in sight.

NOTES

The authors are grateful to Kartono Liano for his helpful suggestions and comments.

1. See "Economy in 1998" at http://www.indonesiatoday.com/a3/j6/y1b.html.

2. Of the total external debt, $66 billion is owed by the public sector, including $53.5 billion by the government, $6.6 billion by state banks, and $5.9 billion by state companies. Of the private-sector debt of $68 billion, private banks owe $9 billion and corporations $59 billion (Ford 1998).

REFERENCES

Bawazier, Fuad. 1998. "Restoring Confidence in the Indonesian Economy." Address to the Annual Conference of the Import–Export Bank, 8 May, Washington, D.C.

Bhattacharya, Amar, and Mari Pangestu. 1997. "Indonesia: Development Transformation and the Role of Public Policy." In *Lessons from East Asia*, edited by Danny M. Leipziger. Ann Arbor: University of Michigan Press.

Brauchli, Marcus W. 1998. "Why the World Bank Failed to Anticipate Indonesia's Deep Crisis." *Wall Street Journal*, 14 July, pp. A1, A10.

Djiwandono, J. Soedradjad. 1997. "Indonesia Facing the Recent Financial Crisis." Bank Indonesia, 21 September.

Ford, Maggie. 1998. "Waking Up to Reality." *Euromoney*, May, pp. 46–48.

Gilley, Bruce, John McBeth, Ben Dolven, and Salil Tripathi. 1998. "Ready, Set . . ." *Far Eastern Economic Review*, 19 February, pp. 46–50.

Hill, Hal. 1996. *The Indonesian Economy Since 1966: Southeast Asia's Emerging Giant*. Cambridge: Cambridge University Press.

Indonesia Industry: Facts and Figures. Ministry of Industry and Trade of the Republic of Indonesia (http://indag.dprin.go.id/INGG/Fact_fig/glcountr.htm).

"Indonesia's Agony and the Price of Rice." 1998. *The Economist*, 19 September, p. 51.

"Indonesia's New Leader Has Commercial Ties Redolent of the Old." 1998. *Wall Street Journal*, 26 May, p. A1.

"Indonesian State Banks." 1998. Salomon Smith Barney, 4 August.

Industrial and Trade Policies of Indonesia. Ministry of Industry and Trade of the Republic of Indonesia (http://indag.dprin.go.id/INGG/industry/Policies.htm).

"Inside Asia's Whirlwind." 1998. *Euromoney*, May, pp. 49–52.

International Monetary Fund (IMF). 1998. *The IMF's Response to the Asian Crisis*. Washington, D.C.: IMF.

Jenkins, Holman W., Jr. 1998. "Let Banks Bail Out Their Indonesian Clients." *Wall Street Journal*, 11 March, p. A21.

Krugman, Paul. 1998. "Saving Asia: It's Time to Get Radical." *Fortune*, 7 September, pp. 75–80.

Kuntjoro-Jakti, Dorodjatun. 1997. "Economic Review: Indonesia's Economy in the Midst of the 1997 Election Politics." *Newsletter* (PT Timah, Indonesia).

Marino, Ramon. 1998. "What Caused East Asia's Financial Crisis?" *FRBSF Economic News Letter* (Federal Reserve Bank of San Francisco), No. 98-24.

Melloan, George. 1998. "Indonesia Faces a Long Road to Recovery." *Wall Street Journal*, 21 April, p. A23.

Montgomery, John. 1997. "The Indonesian Financial System: Its Contribution to Economic Performance and Key Policy Issues." IMF Working Paper WP/97/45, Washington, D.C.

Rivlin, Alice. 1998. "Toward a Better Class of Financial Crises: Some Lessons from Asia." *The Region* (Federal Reserve Bank of Minneapolis), September, pp. 11–16.

Saxton, James. 1998a. "Financial Crises in Emerging Markets: Incentives and the IMF." Joint Economic Committee, United States Congress, August.

Saxton, James. 1998b. "IMF Financing: A Review of the Issues." Joint Economic Committee, United States Congress, March.

Schwarz, Adam. 1994. *A Nation in Waiting: Indonesia in the 1990s*. Boulder, Colo.: Westview Press.

Shari, Michael. 1998. "Up in Smoke: How the IMF's Rescue Plan for Indonesia Exploded." *Business Week*, 1 June, pp. 60–66.

Simpson, Glenn R. 1998. "World Bank Memo Depicts Diverted Funds, Corruption in Jakarta." *Wall Street Journal*, 19 August, p. A14.

Solomon, Jay. 1998a. "Indonesia Asset Sale Raises Eyebrows at IMF." *Wall Street Journal*, 27 October, p. A10.

Solomon, Jay. 1998b. "Indonesia's Privatizations Stumble as Investors Fear Delay in Reform." *Wall Street Journal*, 1 September, p. A12.

Solomon, Jay. 1998c. "Indonesia Unrest Tests if Habibie Can Keep Order." *Wall Street Journal*, 16 September, p. A10.

Solomon, Jay. 1998d. "World Bank Says It Was Wrong on Indonesia." *Wall Street Journal*, 5 February, p. A17.

Templeman, John. 1998. "Indonesia: From One Gang of Cronies to Another?" *Business Week*, 6 July, p. 57.

Tjokronegoro, Paul Soetopo. 1997. "The Indonesian Financial Markets in the Era of Globalization." Bank Indonesia, 15 September.

Tripathi, Salil. 1998. "A Moment of Truth." *Far Eastern Economic Review*, 8 January, pp. 78–79.

U.S. Senate. 1998. Committee on Foreign Relations. *Testimony by Adam Schwarz at a Hearing of the Foreign Relations Committee*. 24 March.

Wagstaff, Jeremy, and Jay Solomon. 1998. "Students Intensify Protests in Indonesia." *Wall Street Journal*, 10 September, p. A16.

Wolfowitz, Paul H. 1998. "Indonesia Challenge." *Wall Street Journal*, 5 February, p. A22.

7

The Economic Crisis of South Korea

Doowoo Nam and Benton E. Gup

The South Korean economy experienced remarkable economic growth for the last three decades. The growth was truly impressive considering Korea's small domestic market and poor natural resources. It came to an abrupt end in 1997, when Korea had a severe economic crisis. Because of the severity of the crisis, the Korean government requested aid from the International Monetary Fund.

The purpose of this chapter is to analyze the Korean boom and bust experience. In one sense, it is analogous to a three-legged stool. The three legs are the *chaebols*, financial institutions, and the government. In simple terms, there were highly leveraged firms, a repressed financial system, and government-directed investments. When external and internal pressures resulted in failures of two of the three legs, the stool collapsed. Thus, we first examine the development of *chaebols* (large conglomerate business groups). Second, we examine the financial system in Korea. We then review the economic development of the Korean economy from the 1960s to the present and investigate the causes of the Korean economic crisis. Later, we examine the economic reforms under the IMF rescue program.

CHAEBOLS

The Korean Anti-Monopoly Regulation and Fair Trade Act defines a *chaebol* as any group of companies whose total assets places it in the top thirty firms. A *chaebol* typically develops when the government grants a firm approval for an industrial project such as building heavy and chemical industries. The project would be financed by 20 percent equity and 80 percent bank loans directed by the government. If the firm succeeds at the project, often with additional assistance on the part of the government, it would normally be granted approval for another project. That project too would be financed largely by new government-provided credits. In this way, a firm, if favored by the government, could rapidly grow and expand its activities from one area into many others with very little original start-up money (Hart-Landsberg 1993). As the companies matured, they increased their financial leverage through borrowing and cross-guarantees of debt. According to the ministry of finance, 170 major Korean firms have debt-to-equity ratios in excess of 500 percent ("Quaking in Seoul" 1997).

The desire on the part of Korean entrepreneurs to form groups of businesses, often in completely unrelated areas, was already established in the 1950s. The Federation of Korean Industries (FKI), which was formed in August 1961, has acted as an interest group representing *chaebols*. The growth of *chaebols* in the 1960s and 1970s was fueled by access to underpriced credit, and closely tied to the government's heavy and chemical industrialization drive (Jones 1994; Hart-Landsberg 1993). The credit came from the banking sector. Five major banks (Cho Hung Bank, Commercial Bank of Korea, Hanil Bank, Korea First Bank, and Seoul Bank) were nationalized in 1961. This gave the government almost total control over the financial system and industrial development (Clifford 1994). Although those banks nationalized in 1961 were privatized later, credit control settled at that time has served as the Korean government's most powerful economic tool, even until now.[1] Gilbert and Wilson (1998) observed that although formal credit allocations by the banking sector were discontinued in 1984, the government continued to influence banks through informal means, called "window guidance," and the appointment of top management. Equally important, Korean credit markets have been characterized by discretionary government allocation of underpriced capital to firms, which means that some firms could borrow at very low interest rates, with extremely high debt-to-equity ratios.

THE FINANCIAL SYSTEM

Financial Repression

According to Noland (1996), structural weaknesses of Korean financial institutions contributed to the economic crisis. First, the Korean economy has repressed financial markets. Financial repression implies that the government intervenes heavily in the economy, segmenting financial markets, placing artificial ceilings on interest rates, and directly allocating credit among enterprises as it sees fit. As mentioned, the government, through the banks, directed the financing of *chaebols*. Banks in repressed financial markets are subject to greater risk because of a lack of portfolio diversification. Restrictions on foreign bank activities further reduce potential diversification from the standpoint of the national economy.

Second, there are lending booms, especially in real estate and equities, as part of an asset bubble. The commercial banking sector was significantly exposed to risks associated with lending to property developers and construction companies during the late 1980s.

Third, government involvement in the financial system has given rise to politicization of lending decisions, moral hazard problems, and so on. As a result, banks could not (and did not) pay much attention to the creditworthiness of borrowers (Goldstein 1998).

Fourth, the problems of liquidity–maturity balance sheet mismatches tend to be magnified by weak reporting standards and provisioning for bad loans. Banks and their corporate customers (mainly *chaebols*), in an effort to lower borrowing cost, undertook most of their foreign borrowing at short maturities and in foreign currency (Goldstein 1998). However, *chaebols* invested in long-term projects. This resulted in liquidity mismatches. On the other hand, currency mismatches also occurred since borrowers have difficulty in repaying loans denominated in foreign currencies such as the U.S. dollar when the value of the Korean won falls.

Fifth, misguided incentives systems, for example, the implicit guarantee of bailouts and the risk-unadjusted form of commercial bank deposit insurance involving risk-unadjusted uniform premiums, allow bank managers to choose inappropriate risk-taking behavior.

Finally, there is inadequately prepared and poorly managed financial liberalization. For instance, public officials who are charged with supervising the liberalized system but have spent their professional careers operating in the environment of a repressed system undergo inadequate retraining. In addition, overly lax loan classification and provisioning practices cause the quality of public disclosure and transparency to be very poor (Goldstein 1998). A by-product of this deficiency of transparency is inadequate bank capital relative to the riskiness of banks' operating environment.

Structure of Financial System

As of the end of August 1997, the Korean financial system consisted of the central bank (Bank of Korea), banking institutions (commercial banks and specialized banks),[2] nonbank financial institutions, and the capital market.[3] The nonbank financial institutions include development institutions, savings institutions, investment institutions, and life insurance institutions.[4] The capital market of Korea is made up of the Korea Stock Exchange, fifty-two domestic securities companies, one joint-venture securities company, and thirteen foreign securities-company branches.

Financial Reform

Financial reform of the Korean system began in the early 1980s to increase competition. The reforms included lowering entry barriers, relaxing government intervention in the management of banks, and deregulating interest rates. These reforms were intended to give more autonomy in management and expand the business scope of financial institutions. An extensive deregulation of interest rates of banks and nonbank financial institutions was announced in December 1988, but it was never implemented.

Two very important initiatives were announced in 1991 and 1993. First, the medium- and long-term plan for interest rate deregulation was announced in August 1991. Interest rates were to be deregulated stage by stage, with the process being completed around the late 1990s. The goal of the first stage (November 1991) was the deregulation of most of the short-term lending rates and some long-term deposit rates. The goal of the second stage (November 1993) was the deregulation of all lending rates, excluding loans financed by the government or by the BOK's rediscounts. The goal of the third stage (1994–1995) was the deregulation of all rates on deposits except for demand deposits and lending rates on policy loans. The second initiative was the announcement of the blueprint for financial deregulation and market opening in June 1993. The three-phase approach, which consisted of the first phase in 1993, the second phase in 1994–1995, and the third phase in 1996–1997, was used to ensure smooth coordination between the process of interest rate deregulation and that of capital market liberalization.

Koreans had long been able to conduct transactions with financial institutions under pseudonyms. This practice led to a lack of equity in the taxation of income, fed the underground economy, and provided room for money laundering. On August 12, 1993, the government implemented a ban on the use of false names in financial transactions. The use of real names in financial transactions, called the real-name system for financial transactions, was regarded as an important step toward Korea's achievement of successful financial liberalization.

Internationalization

Internationalization of the Korean financial markets can be characterized by three factors: the domestic banks' presence abroad and the higher profile of foreign banks in Korea, foreign exchange liberaliza-tion, and capital market internationalization. In 1967, foreign banks were allowed to open branches in Korea and domestic banks were permitted to open branches overseas in order to facilitate inducement of the foreign capital needed for economic progress. Since the mid-1970s, domestic banks' overseas banking networks have expanded rapidly in pace with the rapid growth of crossborder transactions. During the 1970s and 1980s, foreign bank branches in Korea increased rapidly in number and scale, due partly to their relatively advanta-geous business circumstances vis-à-vis domestic commercial banks.

Since 1986, when the current account shifted into surplus, the gov-ernment has pursued an accelerated liberalization of the foreign ex-change market. In March 1990, a market-average exchange rate system was adopted to eliminate any arbitrary influence of the government in the determination of exchange rates.[5] In December 1994, the For-eign Exchange Reform Plan laid out a detailed schedule for the decon-trol of current account transactions, the liberalization of capital account transactions, and the reform of the foreign exchange market structure.

Foreign investors' access to the capital market was substantially widened in 1981. In 1992, foreign investors were allowed to invest directly in Korean stocks, subject to a general ceiling on total foreign holdings of any one company's outstanding shares. Residents were allowed to invest in overseas securities indirectly in 1993, and by 1995 the ceiling has been abolished on the domestic institutional investors' overseas portfolio investment. International organizations were al-lowed to issue Korean won-denominated bonds in the domestic mar-ket in 1995.

Against this background, we now examine the economic develop-ment of Korea from 1960 to the present time. This is the third leg of the stool that was referred to previously. This section shows the key role that government-directed investment and macroeconomic policies played in Korea's economic development and the crisis that erupted in 1997.

ECONOMIC DEVELOPMENT

The 1960s

The Korean government launched a five-year economic develop-ment plan in 1962 in order to cut a vicious circle of poverty.[6] The main strategies of the plan were to foster import-substitution industries, such as basic intermediate materials as cement and fertilizer, and to pro-mote labor-intensive export industries, such as textiles and plywood. To boost the export-led economic growth, the government took exten-sive export-promotion measures. These measures included low interest rate loans to export firms and preferential tax treatment, such as tax exemptions and tariff rebates. As shown in Table 7.1, during the 1960s the real gross domestic product and export growth rate were 8.7 percent and 41.5 percent on average, respectively. However, the annual average growth rate of the consumer price index (CPI) was 11.2 percent. This chronic inflation was due to the large inflow of foreign capital and rapid increase in money supply (36.9%) in order to bridge the serious investment–savings gap.

The 1970s

During the 1970s, the government wanted to upgrade and diversify its exports as well as reduce its import dependence. Therefore, it supported industrial development. In 1973, the government announced the Heavy and Chemical Industry Development Plan, which set forth an accelerated development schedule for technologically sophisticated industries. The Heavy and Chemical Industry Development Plan included iron and steel, shipbuilding, automobiles, machinery, and petrochemicals as the heart of the revitalized Korean economy. Electronics, although not formally part of the plan, received, in fact, similar preferential treatment (Clifford 1994). The process for selecting firms to dominate the new industries specified in the plan was totally under government control. The government used its licensing authority to reward *chaebols* for their loyalty to the government. As a result, *chaebols* established their dominance over the Korean economy: The combined net sales of the top ten *chaebols* rose from 15.1 percent of GNP in 1974 to 30.1 percent in 1978 and 55.7 percent in 1981 (Hart-Landsberg 1993). The government's support of *chaebols* through highly subsidized credit led not only to greatly increased corporate debt-to-equity ratios, leaving *chaebols* increasingly vulnerable to economic instability, but also to overinvestment and excess capacity in a number of industries (Hart-Landsberg 1993). More will be said about this later.

Another factor contributing to the rapid growth of *chaebols* was the General Trading Company (GTC) system, which was introduced in 1975 to boost exports. Trading companies with GTC status received substantial privileges, including access to bank loans at extremely low interest rates (Hart-Landsberg 1993). The share of exports handled by the ten largest general trading companies increased from 13.6 percent in 1976 to 51.3 percent in 1983 (Song 1990). Only *chaebols* had the resources to launch trading companies able to win GTC status. Employing the added financial benefits associated with GTC status to strengthen the economic position of the entire business group, *chaebols* were able to rapidly outperform their non-*chaebol* competitors (Hart-Landsberg 1993).

During the 1970s, real GDP and export grew at 8.8 percent and 36.4 percent on average. Chronic inflation, which was one of the unfortunate by-products of rapid industrialization, was becoming an increasing problem. The annual growth rate of the CPI was 15.12 percent on average during this decade (see Table 7.1).

The 1980s

During the early 1980s, the side effects of the growth-oriented development strategy became more serious, and the second oil crisis hit the economy. The Korean economy suffered from the first ever negative annual growth in real GDP, with a huge current account deficit in 1980.

The government shifted priority in managing the economy from growth to stability, and thus adopted tight monetary and fiscal policies. As a result of these policy changes, the economy rebounded. During the first half of the 1980s, the real GDP growth rate was 6.3 percent on average, and the inflation rate fell into the single digits and remained there (see Table 7.1).

The Korean economy enjoyed remarkable economic performance from 1986 to 1988, owing to both internal and external factors. These include price stability following the structural policy changes implemented in the early 1980s, and three favorable international factors that are called the *three lows*: (1) low oil prices, (2) low international interest rates, and (3) the low value of the U.S. dollar in terms of the Japanese yen. From 1986 to 1988, the economy attained a real GDP growth rate of 11.5 percent on average and a sizable surplus in the current account of the balance of payments. However, the problem of consumer price inflation was rekindled in 1988 (3.1% in 1987 to 7.1% in 1988) following the high economic growth.

In 1989, the Korean economy's growth slowed abruptly (11.3% in 1988 to 6.4% in 1989), and exports turned sluggish (28.4% growth in 1988 to 2.8% growth in 1989) due to wage hikes, vanishing of the favorable three lows, and rapid catch-up growth by late-starter developing countries.

The 1990s

In the early 1990s strong growth was attributable to the construction boom to build two million housing units. One side effect of the growth was an increase in inflation. During the 1990–1991 period, both the real GDP growth rate and inflation accelerated to more than 9 percent.

From 1993 to 1995, the strong yen, low international interest rates, and low international commodity prices bolstered the economy. GDP growth rose to 8.9 percent in 1995 due to exports and investments in

Table 7.1
Major Economic Indicators for Korea

Period	Real GDP Growth[a]	Exchange Rate Rate[b]	Exchange Rate Change	Current Account Balance[c]	Export Growth
1962-69	8.70%				41.50%
1970-79	8.80%				36.40%
1980	-2.70%	659.9	36.30%	-8.50%	16.30%
1981	6.20%	700.5	6.20%	-6.60%	21.40%
1982	7.60%	748.8	6.90%	-3.40%	2.80%
1983	11.50%	795.5	6.20%	-1.80%	11.90%
1984	8.70%	827.4	4.00%	-1.40%	19.60%
1985	6.50%	890.2	7.60%	-0.80%	3.60%
1986	11.60%	861.4	-3.20%	4.30%	14.60%
1987	11.50%	792.3	-8.00%	7.40%	36.20%
1988	11.30%	684.1	-13.70%	8.00%	28.40%
1989	6.40%	679.6	-0.70%	2.40%	2.80%
1990	9.50%	716.4	5.40%	-0.80%	4.20%
1991	9.10%	760.8	6.20%	-2.80%	10.50%
1992	5.10%	788.4	3.60%	-1.30%	6.60%
1993	5.80%	808.1	2.50%	0.30%	7.30%
1994	8.60%	788.7	-2.40%	-1.00%	16.80%
1995	8.90%	774.7	-1.80%	-1.90%	30.30%
1996	7.10%	844.2	9.00%	-4.70%	3.70%
1997	5.50%	1415.2	67.60%	-1.90%	5.00%
Jan.		861.3	2.00%		-9.00%
Feb.		863.9	0.30%		-5.30%
Mar.	5.70%	897.1	3.80%		-3.10%
Apr.		892.1	-0.60%		7.20%
May		891.8	0.00%		4.60%
Jun.	6.60%	888.1	-0.40%		9.70%
Jul.		892	0.40%		19.40%
Aug.		902	1.10%		14.20%
Sep.	6.10%	914.8	1.40%		14.60%
Oct.		965.1	5.50%		5.60%
Nov.		1163.8	20.60%		4.90%
Dec.	3.90%	1415.2	21.60%		

Sources: "Statistics of the Korean Economy," Bank of Korea, January 1998; "Statistical Data," Ministry of Finance and Economy (Korea), April 1998.

[a](Real GDP$_t$ – Real GDP$_{t-1}$) / Real GDP$_{t-1}$.

[b]Exchange Rate = Basic Exchange Rate

[c]Current Account Balance = Current Account Balance/GDP

Table 7.1 (*continued*)

Import Growth	External Debt[d]	Interest Rate[e]	Inflation Rate[f]	Money Supply[g]	Stock Price Index
24.70%			11.20%	36.90%	
27.70%			15.10%	30.30%	
9.60%			28.70%	25.80%	-9.80%
17.20%			21.30%	27.40%	16.10%
-7.20%	49.50%		7.10%	28.10%	-3.40%
8.00%	48.80%		3.40%	19.50%	-0.20%
16.90%	47.10%		2.20%	10.70%	8.40%
1.60%	49.60%		2.30%	11.80%	5.30%
1.40%	41.00%		2.80%	16.80%	64.00%
29.90%	26.10%		3.10%	18.80%	83.30%
26.30%	17.10%		7.10%	18.80%	66.00%
18.60%	13.20%		5.70%	18.40%	32.50%
13.60%	12.50%		8.50%	21.20%	-18.70%
16.70%	13.30%	18.98%	9.30%	18.60%	-12.00%
0.30%	13.90%	14.00%	6.30%	18.40%	-10.60%
2.50%	13.20%	12.21%	4.80%	18.60%	24.00%
22.10%	14.90%	14.22%	6.20%	15.60%	32.60%
32.00%	17.20%	11.65%	4.50%	15.50%	-3.20%
11.30%	32.50%	12.57%	4.90%	16.20%	-10.90%
-3.80%	34.80%	24.31%	4.50%	19.20%	-50.90%
3.90%		12.15%	0.80%	1.40%	-3.00%
0.00%		12.17%	0.60%	2.40%	4.30%
7.60%		12.69%	0.40%	0.40%	-5.90%
1.00%		12.50%	0.50%	0.70%	5.70%
-3.20%		12.21%	0.10%	0.50%	2.70%
4.80%		11.65%	0.20%	0.40%	7.30%
-0.70%		11.86%	0.20%	1.70%	-1.70%
-11.20%		12.11%	0.70%	1.80%	-1.60%
1.30%		12.36%	0.50%	3.70%	-8.60%
-7.00%		12.53%	0.00%	-0.80%	-13.70%
-12.50%		14.08%	0.10%	2.00%	-15.40%
		24.31%	2.50%	5.20%	-21.00%

[d]External Debt = External Debt/GDP

[e]Yield on Corporate Bonds (O.T.C.)

[f]Changes in Consumer Price Index

[g]Money Supply = Change in M2 ("End of" before 1980 and "Averages" after 1980) from previous period.

equipment. However, fortunes were reversed in the next two years. The Korean economy had a current account deficit of $23.7 billion in 1996 due to the fall in international prices of major export items, especially a fall in the prices of semiconductors. Economic growth slowed due to lackluster exports and investments in equipment.

ECONOMIC CRISIS IN LATE 1997

The economic crisis in Southeast Asia began when Thailand unpegged the Thai baht from the dollar in July 1997. It was followed by a currency crisis and falling stock prices. The crisis in Thailand affected other countries. In South Korea, which was already having economic problems, stock prices fell sharply, the Korean won against the U.S. dollar plunged, and interest rates soared (Bae 1998).

The major causes of the economic crisis can be divided into internal and external factors. There are two internal factors: sales-volume-oriented growth by companies, especially *chaebols*, and the underdeveloped financial sector. Two major external factors are the financial crisis in Southeast Asia and the Hong Kong stock market crash.

Internal Factors

Chaebols

The legacy of government-directed investments and political interference was an inefficient financial sector and a highly leveraged corporate sector that lacked effective market discipline (IMF 1997). Typically, *chaebols* attempted to maximize sales rather than shareholder value, and they were too heavily leveraged (Yoo 1998). The debt-to-equity ratio of the top thirty *chaebols* was up to 387 percent. Because they crossguarantee debts but the guarantees are not shown in their financial statements, the 387 percent may understate their financial leverage. The average debt-to-equity ratio of Korean manufacturing firms is 317.1 percent. This is in sharp contrast to the average debt-to-equity ratios of manufacturing firms in the United States, Japan, and Taiwan, 159.7 percent, 206.3 percent, and 85.7 percent as of 1995, respectively (Bae 1998).

Both *chaebols* and banks were considered too big to fail. However, this myth of too big to fail was shattered in 1997, when eight large *chaebols* went bankrupt; they had combined debts of $21 billion ("Bankruptcy in Asia: The Living Dead" 1998). These and other *chaebols* had overinvested in plants and equipment, resulting in excess capacity.

The semiconductor industry was the first industry in Korea to feel the effects of worldwide overcapacity. Japan, Korea, and Taiwan account for more than half of the world's computer-chip revenues.[7] Korea's semiconductor exports increased from $13 billion in 1994 to $22.1 billion in 1995 (Chang 1996). It was their leading export. The growth in computer chips was spurred by the introduction of Microsoft's Windows 95, Intel's developments in motherboards, and new programs. The rapid growth of this industry led to excess capacity and lower chip prices. The price of the sixteen-megabit DRAM (dynamic random access memory) chip declined from $53 in 1995 to $12 in 1996 (Thorton 1996). The weaker Japanese yen against the U.S. dollar adversely affected Korean exporting firms (Yoo 1998).

Bankruptcy

In 1997, 17,168 Korean firms went bankrupt. On average, about 50 firms per day went bankrupt. In December 1997, more than 100 firms in a day went bankrupt ("Soaring Bankruptcy and Unemployment Disturbance" 1998). In the past, the number of bankrupt firms was 30 on daily average (Lee 1997).

Bankruptcy procedures in Korea are affected by political considerations. Thus, the lack of market discipline has been a major obstacle to the efficiency of the Korean economy. There are three laws concerning the resolution of insolvent companies in Korea: the Corporate Reorganization Act, the Composition Act, and the Bankruptcy Act. Firms that declare bankruptcy are supposed to develop business plans to be submitted to the creditors and to the court. However, with only four bankruptcy judges, the Seoul district court is in no position to move cases quickly. Filing bankruptcy papers is easy, but months of inaction inevitably follow under the current legal structure ("Bankruptcy in Asia: The Living Dead" 1998).

Financial Sector

Structural weaknesses of financial institutions were exacerbated by a sharp increase in nonperforming loans due to a series of bankruptcies of firms, the crash of the Korean stock market, and the downgraded international credit ratings of Korean financial institutions. In addition, a credit crunch was brought about by the vicious cycle of bankruptcies. Insolvent firms caused related financial institutions to get insolvent, and then the institutions called in loans, causing solvent but illiquid firms to go bankrupt. Finally, the sharp decline in stock prices cut the value of banks' portfolios and further reduced their net worth. All these factors led to successive downgrades of Korean financial institutions by international credit rating agencies and a sharp tightening in the availability of external finance.

External Factors

In October 1997, the Hong Kong stock market crashed. It was affected by the economic crisis that began in Thailand and problems in Indonesia, Malaysia, and elsewhere earlier that year. Foreign investors' fears concerning stock markets all over Asia peaked after the Hong Kong crash, and the Korean stock market was the next to tumble. There were great concerns that there would be massive outflows of capital from Korea. The demand for the U.S. dollar soared as a result ("Impact on Financial Markets in Korea" 1997).

The values of the currencies of Korea's major competitors sharply declined. The sharp depreciation of the Taiwanese dollar and the currencies of the Southeast Asian countries heightened the depreciatory pressure on the Korean won. During the October–November 1997 period, the won plunged from 950 won/dollar to 1,150 won/dollar. Korea could not realize any real gain in price competitiveness over Taiwan or such Southeast Asian countries as Indonesia, Malaysia, and Thailand. As shown in Table 7.2, Southeast Asia accounted for 15.6 percent of Korea's total exports in 1996 and is the only region where Korea has enjoyed a trade surplus. Korea's overall exports were in danger of flattening or even declining ("Impact on Financial Markets in Korea" 1997).

Although Korea experienced a current account deficit in 1996 as a result of problems in the semiconductor industry, it was a temporary problem, unlike the problems in Indonesia and Thailand.

Table 7.2
Korea's Trade with ASEAN (Brunei, Indonesia, Malaysia, Philippines, Singapore, Thailand, and Vietnam) in 1996

	Korea's total trade	Trade with ASEAN	Percentage of Trade with ASEAN
Exports	$129.7 billion	$20.2 billion	15.6
Imports	$150.3 billion	$12.1 billion	8.1
Trade volume	$280.0 billion	$32.3 billion	11.5
Trade balance	-$20.6 billion	$8.1 billion	-

Source: "Impact on Financial Markets in Korea," *Korean Economic Trends* (Samsung Economic Research Institute, Korea), 15 November 1997.

THE IMF PROGRAM

As of December 1997, the IMF rescue package was worth about $55 billion.[8] Of that total, $21 billion was from the IMF, $10 billion from the World Bank, $4 billion from the Asian Development Bank, and the remaining $20 billion from the United States, Japan, the United Kingdom, Germany, France, and Italy (Schuman and Davis 1997). The amount of the international financial commitment was increased to $58.2 billion.[9] While $58.2 billion is no trivial sum, Korea's offshore borrowing was estimated to be in excess of $153 billion, and most of it was short-term debt to foreign banks (Glain, Schuman, and McDermott 1997; "Banking on Korea" 1998). It was hoped that the short-term private debt could be converted into long-term sovereign debt. In either case, it was the biggest rescue package that the IMF had ever engineered.

The IMF rescue package did not come without strings attached. The IMF wanted a series of reforms to take place. The principal macroeconomic objectives of the IMF's economic program were to narrow the external current account deficit from 4.7 percent in 1996 to below 1 percent of GDP in 1998 and 1999, to contain inflation at or below 5 percent, and to limit the deceleration in real GDP growth to about 3 percent in 1998 followed by a recovery toward potential in 1999 (see Table 7.1). The program includes reform measures in six areas.

Macroeconomic Policies

A strong macroeconomic framework is needed to continue orderly adjustment in the external current account and contain inflationary pressures, involving a tighter monetary stance and substantial fiscal adjustment. This includes increasing the call rate; limiting money growth; maintaining a flexible exchange rate policy; increasing VAT coverage and removing exemptions; widening the corporate and income tax bases; increasing excises, luxury taxes, and transportation taxes; reducing current expenditures, particularly support to the corporate sector; and reducing low-priority capital expenditures.

Financial-Sector Restructuring

This requires a comprehensive strategy to restructure and recapitalize the financial sector and make it more transparent, market oriented, better supervised, and free from political interference in business decisions; revising the Bank of Korea Act to provide for central bank independence; enacting a bill to consolidate supervision of all banks; enacting a bill requiring that corporate financial statements be prepared on a consolidated basis and be certified by external auditors;

closing troubled financial institutions; accelerating the disposal of nonperforming loans; and replacing current blanket guarantees with a limited deposit insurance scheme.

Trade and Capital Account Liberalization

This involves further trade liberalization and accelerated liberalization of capital account transactions, including eliminating trade-related subsidies; eliminating restrictive import licensing; eliminating the import-diversification program; streamlining and improving the transparency of the import certification procedure; liberalizing foreign investment in the Korean equity market by increasing the ceiling on aggregate and individual foreign ownership; allowing foreign banks to acquire equity in Korean domestic banks in excess of the 4-percent limit under certain conditions; allowing foreign investors to purchase domestic money market instruments without restriction; allowing foreign investment in the domestic corporate bond market without restriction; further reducing restrictions on foreign direct investment through simplifying procedures; and eliminating restrictions on foreign borrowings by corporations.

Corporate Governance and Structures

Measures are needed to improve corporate governance, including improving the transparency of corporate balance sheets, including profit and loss accounts, by enforcing accounting standards in line with generally accepted accounting practices (independent external audits, full disclosure, and provision of consolidated statements for business conglomerates); removing government intervention in bank management and lending decisions; eliminating directed lending; eliminating government support to bail out individual corporations and allowing bankruptcy provisions to operate without government interference; maintaining the real-name system in financial transactions; implementing measures to reduce the high debt-to-equity ratios of corporations; developing capital markets to reduce the share of bank financing by corporations; and implementing measures to change the system of mutual guarantees within conglomerates.

Labor Market Reform

Measures are needed to improve labor market flexibility and strengthen the capacity of the new Employment Insurance System to facilitate the redeployment of labor.

Information Provision

This involves improvement of the transparency and timely reporting of economic data, including regularly publishing data on foreign exchange reserves; biannually publishing data on financial institutions, including nonperforming loans, capital adequacy, and ownership structures and affiliations; and publishing quarterly data on short-term external debt.

Feldstein (1998) argues that the IMF's interference with national sovereignty with its long list of fundamental reforms is inappropriate. They should insist only on those policies that are necessary to restore a country's access to international financial markets. Moreover, the conditionality of the funds based on fundamental reforms is incompatible with their role as a lender of last resort. In addition, using IMF funds to pay off private investors creates a moral hazard problem.

CONCLUSION

The Korean government's growth initiatives worked well for decades. The basic strategy was that the government used debt-laden *chaebols* and banks that were controlled or influenced by the government to invest in particular sectors of the economy. The strategy worked well for over three decades, and the economy prospered. Over time, however, the *chaebols* focused on sales instead of adding value. The result was excess capacity in a number of industries.

The first sign of trouble was in the semiconductor industry, where there was worldwide overcapacity. Semiconductors were Korea's leading export, and when prices of semiconductors declined sharply in 1996, exports fell. There was excess capacity in other industries as well. In 1997, Thailand unpegged the baht from the dollar and the exchange rate fell sharply. Exchange rates of other Southeast Asian countries came under pressure, and they too declined. In Korea, Hanbo Steel and some highly leveraged *chaebols* collapsed.

After the bubble burst, there was a cascading effect of temporary government bailouts and bankruptcies, and the Korean economy was in serious trouble. It was so serious that the IMF was called to the rescue. The IMF extended credit and demanded structural reforms to halt the collapse of Korea's economy, currency, and stock market.

Only time will tell if the Korean culture of *chaebols* and government-directed investments supported by complacent banks will adapt to the IMF's conditions and make the reforms that are required as a condition for aid. In mid-1997, however, the high hopes for a quick turnaround after the election of President Kim Dae Jung faded as political opposition hampered his ability to reform banks and *chaebols* (Engarido et al. 1998). In late May 1997, Korean stock prices fell to an eleven-year low as a result of labor unrest and the slow pace of economic reforms (Cho 1998). The IMF's lack of success in stemming falling stock and currency values in Indonesia and the inability of the Japanese government to turn its economy around does not bode well for Korea.

NOTES

The authors are indebted to Tae-Yeong Choi for his helpful comments and suggestions.

1. The Commercial Bank of Korea was privatized in 1973 and the remaining four banks were privatized in the early 1980s.

2. There were sixteen nationwide commercial banks, ten regional banks, sixty-eight branches of fifty-two foreign banks, and four specialized banks as of the end of August 1997.

3. This section is based on "Banking Supervision in Korea" (1997) and "Financial System in Korea" (1997).

4. There are three development institutions, which are the Korea Development Bank, the Export–Import Bank of Korea, and the Korea Long-Term Credit Bank. The savings institutions include 49 trust accounts of banks, 234 mutual savings and finance companies, 1,664 credit unions, 1,765 mutual credit facilities, 2,814 community credit cooperatives, and one postal savings. The investment institutions are thirty merchant banking corporations, twenty-six securities investment trust companies, and the Korea Securities Finance Corporation. The life insurance institutions include twenty-one domestic life insurance companies, seven joint ventures, two foreign life insurance company branches, and three subsidiaries, and postal life insurance.

5. The exchange rate is determined by the weighted average of the interbank exchange rates applied in interbank spot transactions of the previous business day.

6. This section is based on "The Korean Economy" (1998).

7. As of 1995, the market shares for semiconductors were United States 39.8 percent, Japan 39.5 percent, Korea 10.3 percent, and Taiwan 5 percent.

8. The contents of this section are from "IMF Stand-By Arrangement: Summary of the Economic Program" (1997).

9. As of April 10, 1989, only $15.1 billion had been disbursed by the IMF (IMF 1998).

REFERENCES

Bae, Hyun-Kee. 1998. "IMF Program on Structural Reforms and 1998 Business Prospects" (in Korean). *1998 Economic Outlook* (Korea Long-Term Credit Bank Economic Research Institute), 21 January.
"Banking on Korea." 1998. *Wall Street Journal*, 27 January, p. A22.
"Banking Supervision in Korea." 1997. Report, Bank of Korea.

"Bankruptcy in Asia: The Living Dead." 1998. *The Economist*, 24 January, pp. 71–72.

Branscomb, Lewis M., and Young-Hwan Choi, eds. 1996. *Innovation-Based Strategies for Development*. Westport, Conn.: Praeger.

Chang, S. W. 1996. "Impact of Semi-Conductor Slum and Measures" (in Korean). *Weekly CEO Information* (Samsung Economic Research Institute, Korea), 18 September.

Cho, N. 1998. "South Korean Stocks Plummet Further on Worry Over Stalled Economy and Threat of Strike." *Wall Street Journal*, 27 May, pp. A14, A17.

Clifford, Mark L. 1994. *Troubled Tiger: Businessmen, Bureaucrats, and Generals in South Korea*. Armonk, N.Y.: M. E. Sharpe.

Engardio, P., B. Bremmer, M. McNamee, and M. I. Hwan. 1998. "Asia: The Global Impact." *Business Week*, 1 June, pp. 52–54.

Feldstein, M. 1998. "Trying to Do Too Much." *Financial Times*, 5 March, p. 12.

"Financial System in Korea." 1997. Report, Bank of Korea.

Gilbert, A., and P. W. Wilson. 1998. "Effects of Deregulation on the Productivity of Korean Banks." *Journal of Economics and Business* 50: 133–55.

Glain, Steve, Michael Schuman, and Darren McDermott. 1997. "Seoul, Sinking, May Need Stronger Rescue Pact." *Wall Street Journal*, 12 December, p. A12.

Goldstein, Morris. 1998. "The Asian Financial Crisis." In *Policy Brief 98-1*. Washington, D.C.: Institute for International Economics.

Hart-Landsberg, Martin. 1993. *The Rush to Development: Economic Change and Political Struggle in South Korea*. New York: Monthly Review Press.

"IMF Stand-By Arrangement: Summary of the Economic Program." 1997. Korea Institute for International Economic Policy, 5 December.

"Impact on Financial Market in Korea." 1997. *Korean Economic Trends* (Samsung Economic Research Institute, Korea), 15 November.

"Implementation Measures for Corporate Structural Adjustment." 1998. Ministry of Finance and Economy (Korea), 16 February.

International Monetary Fund (IMF). 1997. *Korea–Memorandum on the Economic Program*. Washington, D.C.: IMF.

International Monetary Fund (IMF). 1998. *The IMF's Response to the Asian Crisis*. Washington, D.C.: IMF.

Jones, Leroy P. 1994. "Big Business Groups in South Korea: Causation, Growth, and Policies." In *Korea's Political Economy: An Institutional Perspective*, edited by Lee-Jay Cho and Yoon Hyung Kim. Boulder, Colo.: Westview Press.

"The Korean Economy." 1998. Report, Bank of Korea, January.

Lee, Hyung-Koo. 1996. *The Korean Economy: Perspectives for the Twenty-First Century*. Albany: State University of New York Press.

Lee, Min-Koo. 1997. "Bankruptcy Protection of Kia Group and Prospect of Interest Rates" (in Korean). Korea Long-Term Credit Bank Economic Research Institute, 22 July.

Noland, Marcus. 1996. "Restructuring Korea's Financial Sector for Greater Competitiveness." APEC Working Paper 96-14, Institute for International Economics, Washington, D.C.

"Quaking in Seoul." 1997. *Business Week*, 4 August, pp. 46–47.

Schuman, Michael, and Bob Davis. 1997. "South Korea Agrees to IMF's Bailout Terms." *Wall Street Journal*, 4 December, p. A14.

"Soaring Bankruptcy and Unemployment Disturbance" (in Korean). 1998. *Weekly Economic Trend Brief* (Samsung Economic Research Institute, Korea), 3 March.

Song, Byung-Nak. 1990. *The Rise of the Korean Economy*. New York: Oxford University Press.

Thornton, E. 1996. "Bitter Pill: Will Asia Ever See Another Electronic Boom." *Far Eastern Economic Review*, 31 October, pp. 58–59.

Yoo, Joon-Yeol. 1998. "Outlook for Exchange Rate of Won and Dollar" (in Korean). *1998 Economic Outlook* (Korea Long-Term Credit Bank Economic Research Institute), 21 January.

8

Russia's Financial Debacle

Benton E. Gup and Doowoo Nam

On August 17, 1998, the Russian government announced a 33.7-percent de facto devaluation of the Russian ruble against the U.S. dollar by widening the exchange rate intervention band. It also declared a ninety-day moratorium on the repayment of $40 billion of foreign debts in its banks, and restructured domestic treasury bills, known as GKOs, that come due before the end of 1999 (Higgins 1998).[1] These actions sent shock waves around the world that resulted in flight to quality in terms of investments. The flight to quality led to large trading losses at banks, hedge funds, and investment banking firms. BankAmerica, Bankers Trust, Citigroup, UBS, and other banks and investment banking firms had large losses from their trading activities (Serwer 1998; Brooks and Pachelle 1998). Five hedge funds filed for bankruptcy in August, and the Federal Reserve helped organize a bailout for Long-Term Capital Management ("Hedge Funds Win and Lose" 1998; U.S. House 1998). What caused the problems in Russia, and why did the markets react like that?

   A simplified answer to the first part of that question is the subject of this chapter. In general terms, a continued, rapid increase in the central government's fiscal deficit and unsustainable foreign debt made the Russian economy vulnerable to the Asian economic turmoil that began when Thailand devalued the baht in July 1997. Russia's GDP had declined 45 percent between 1989 and 1997; in that same period its real capital investment fell 92 percent, real wages had fallen, and it was in distress (Koretz 1998). Russia inherited large debts from the former

Soviet Union, which added to their own debts that were coming due. New IMF aid was not forthcoming in 1998, and the government had to cover a deficit of about $3.9 billion in the fourth quarter. They did not have sufficient funds to repay those debts (McKay 1998a). Their solution of devaluation of the ruble, defaulting on domestic debts, and printing more money may have created more problems than it solved.

The answer to the second part of the question dealing with the markets' reaction to events is that investors lost their confidence in Russia and became risk averse. However, they could not sell the defaulted Russian securities in their portfolios. It was rumored that Russian GKOs were worth only 10 cents on the dollar. Therefore, they liquidated stocks, bonds, and currency contracts. Another factor contributing to investors unloading their positions was that they feared that other emerging-market nations might default on their debts or impose exchange controls. Malaysia, for example, had already imposed some controls. Securities markets that were thought to be liquid in good times proved to be illiquid when everyone wanted to sell at the same time. Stock prices in Russia had already fallen sharply. In the United States, stock prices were overvalued, the market was ripe for a correction, and stock prices plunged. In addition, the prices of lower-quality debt securities declined sharply. Because of the flight to quality investments, the prices of short-term U.S. government securities increased. Hedge funds and other investors had to meet margin calls. Some hedge funds were unable to do so, and they failed or were bailed out by banks and investment banks.

Since the devaluation in August 1998, Russia has experienced the typical pattern associated with an economic crisis: a sharp decline in the value of its currency, plunging stock prices, and soaring interest rates (see Table 8.1). The exchange rate of the ruble against the dollar reached its highest level of 20.2 on September 8, 1998, which implied that the value of the ruble plummeted by 210.8 percent from 6.5 rubles per dollar on August 17, 1998. The RTS (Russian Trading System) stock index, which is Russia's principal stock price index introduced on September 1, 1995, fell 83.5 percent, from 396.86 at the beginning of 1998 to 65.61 on August 31, 1998 (RTS 1998). The yield on GKOs rose sharply, from below 100 percent to above 200 percent. Table 8.1 shows the tumult in the foreign exchange market, the stock market, and the credit market.

RUSSIAN ECONOMY

The Soviet Union collapsed at the end of 1991. Price reforms and privatization were used to stimulate economic growth. However, the former Soviet firms that were privatized languished because they were run by managers who did not know how to operate in a market sys-

Table 8.1
Crises in the Russian Financial Markets

	Exchange Rate		Stock Index		Interest Rate	
	Ruble/$*	% Change	RTS**	% Change	GKO***	% Change
1992	0.42	–	–	–	–	–
1993	1.25	200.4	–	–	–	–
1994	3.55	184.7	–	–	–	–
1995	4.64	30.7	82.92	–	168.0	–
1996	5.56	19.8	200.50	141.8	85.8	-48.9
1997	5.96	7.2	396.86	97.9	26.0	-69.7
Oct.	5.89		422.26	15.3	19.8	
Nov.	5.92	0.5	328.49	22.2	22.6	14.1
Dec.	5.96	0.7	396.86	20.8	36.6	61.9
1998						
Jan.	6.03	1.1	284.35	-28.4	33.4	-8.7
Feb.	6.07	0.8	309.56	8.9	29.6	-11.4
Mar.	6.11	0.6	325.50	5.1	24.4	-17.6
Apr.	6.13	0.4	312.37	-4.0	27.8	13.9
May	6.16	0.5	191.29	-38.8	54.8	97.1
Jun.	6.20	0.6	151.35	-20.9	65.1	18.8
Jul.	6.28	1.3	149.65	-1.1	81.0	24.4
Aug.	9.70	54.5	65.61	-56.2	200.0	

Sources: IMF, *International Financial Statistics* (Washington, D.C.: IMF, 1998); Russian Trading System, *RTS Statistics*, at http://www.rtsnet.ru, last visited September 1998.

*Official exchange rate at the end of period.

**Composite stock price index of the RTS.

***The GKO yield represents a treasury bill rate with maturities under ninety days.

tem (Bayer 1998). In contrast, new start-up companies in high-tech industries did well.

Russia is the world's largest country in terms of geography, spanning eleven time zones. It has a population of about 148 million. Nevertheless, it is small in terms of global economic activity. Russia accounts for less than 1 percent of the world's gross domestic product, but the expectation of economic growth and riches lured investors to this market that had large reserves of natural resources. The natural resources include gold, diamonds, crude oil, and natural gas, particularly in Western and Eastern Siberia and the Russian Far East (Bank Austria Economics Department 1997). The development of these natural resources requires large-scale foreign investment because the existing plants and equipment are obsolete. Although many companies have been privatized in recent years, their efficiency has not improved significantly due to the shortage of new capital and new management capable of dealing in a market system (Bank Austria Economics Department 1997).

Russia exports a large part of its commodities and other products. As of 1995, its main trading partner was the European Union, accounting for 33 percent of exports and 38 percent of imports (Bank Austria Economics Department 1997). However, oil exports fell in recent years because Russia lacked the infrastructure (pipelines, etc.) necessary to exploit its oil reserves. In addition, the price of crude oil (West Texas crude) fell from about $21 per barrel to $12 per barrel. About 24 percent of its oil output is exported (Thornhill and Corzine 1998). The decline in oil exports had a serious impact on the Russian budget.

The new Russian economy took several years to achieve positive growth in real GDP and a lower rate of inflation (see Table 8.2). These statistics were interpreted as a signal that the recession was bottoming out and that the economy was consolidating (Afanasyev 1997). However, arrears in the payment of pensions and salaries as well as taxpayer tax avoidance coupled with the government's inability to collect taxes undermined the stability of Russian society (Bank Austria Economics Department 1997). In May 1998, miners blocked rail lines that cross the country in an effort to force the government to pay back wages that in some cases were two years in arrears (McKay, Brzezinsky, and Davis 1998). One estimate is that unpaid wages amounted to more than $10 billion in September 1998 (Liesman and Higgins 1998). If workers do not receive wages, they cannot pay taxes. Tax receipts dropped 50 percent from July to September 1998 (Matlack 1998).

The Banking System

Russian banks differ from Western style banks. Russia's biggest banks used government funds to make large bets on the ruble and bond markets rather than making loans to productive businesses that would help the economy expand (Liesman and Higgins 1998). They lost those bets. Of those investments that they did make, about one-third are estimated to be nonperforming assets (Bernstam and Rabuskha 1998). As a consequence, most Russian banks are insolvent. The government has closed a few of them. The Russian banking system has been characterized by "spectacular looting" by bankers ("The Undead" 1998). Manipulation of the thinly traded ruble to avoid paying their foreign debts and the prospects that the Russian government wants to print new money provide lucrative opportunities and incentives for Russian bankers to stay in business.

The Russian government is expected to expand its monetary base by more than 50 percent to meet its current obligations and to finance the deficit (McKay 1998b). This amounts to printing about $1.2 billion

Table 8.2
Principal Economic Indicators of Russia

	GDP Growth Rate	Fiscal Deficit (% of GDP)	Inflation	Current Account Balance Billions	Exports Growth Rate
1992	-14.5%	–	1,500.0%	–	–
1993	-8.7%	–	874.6%	–	5.4%
1994	-12.6%	–	307.4%	$9.3	52.5%
1995	-4.0%	4.39	197.4%	$7.9	20.1%
1996	-6.0%	6.71	47.6%	$12.1	9.9%
1997	3.0%	5.78	14.6%	$3.3	-2.0%
1998					
Jan.			1.5%		-37.4%
Feb.			0.9%		-1.8%
Mar.			0.7%		12.7%
Apr.			0.4%		-17.7%
May					19.6%
Jun.					1.6%
Jul.					
Aug.					

Sources: IMF, *International Financial Statistics* (Washington, D.C.: IMF, 1998); Dmitry Afanasyev, "World Economic Analysis: Russia," *Euromoney*, September 1997.

to help the bankers. The expansion of the money supply may also rekindle inflation. In September 1998, the inflation rate was 28 percent, the highest level in several years.

Foreign Exchange Rate System

The ruble corridor is a band with upper and lower limits, called the maximum and minimum corridors. It was introduced in July 1995. The currency is allowed to fluctuate within the band. Initially, the band was set between 4.30 and 4.90 rubles to the dollar. About six months later, the band was moved upward to between 4.55 and 5.15 rubles, although the width of the band remained at 0.6 rubles to the dollar (Chase Manhattan International 1997).

In July 1996, the Central Bank of Russia adopted a crawling band. This allowed the Central Bank to make daily adjustments to its upper and lower limits. However, they maintained the same width of 0.6 rubles to the dollar as before (Bank Austria Economics Department 1997). The ruble corridor significantly contributed to the stabilization of inflation in the Russian economy by strengthening confidence in its currency—until the ruble was devalued.

Security Markets

The Russian Trading System is a computerized stock trading system that was introduced in 1995 (UNEXIM-ICFI Financial Group 1997). It is the principal market for trading corporate securities. The RTS index and the Moscow Times Index (MTI) are the two leading stock indices. The RTS index is based on twenty-four stocks, while the MTI index consists of fifty stocks (Troika Dialog 1997). The RTS index peaked at 571.66 on October 6, 1997, and reached its lowest level of 50.12 on September 18, 1998 (RTS 1998).

Government securities, such as GKOs and OFZs, are traded mainly on the Moscow Interbank Currency Exchange (MICEX) trading system. GKOs, which were introduced in May 1993 as noninflationary instruments for financing the fiscal deficit have maturities of three, six, and twelve months. OFZs, introduced in June 1995 as a complement to GKOs, are coupon-bearing federal loan bonds with maturities of one and a half through three years (ING Bank Eurasia 1997). Foreign investors were not allowed access to these government security markets until February 1996. As of January 1, 1997, nonresident investors held 17 percent of these securities (ING Bank Eurasia 1997).

ECONOMIC CRISIS

Fiscal Deficit

The fundamental problem of the Russian economy was the central government's fiscal deficit and the inability to repay debts as they became due. The deficit of about $30 billion amounted to 6.7 percent of GDP in 1996 and 5.78 percent the following year (see Table 8.2). These percentages are high compared to no deficit in Korea, 0.9 percent in Indonesia, and 1.4 percent in Thailand in 1997 (IMF 1998a).

Russia financed the deficits by issuing government bonds at high interest rates to attract foreign investors ("Russia's Economic Bear" 1998). In order to support the ruble, the Central Bank increased interest rates in one day from 100 percent to 150 percent (Chase Manhattan International 1997; McKay, Brzezinski, and Davis 1998). One investment manager said, "Interest rates were so high it was almost as if they were giving money away" ("How Russia Set Off Wave That Swamped Markets Around the World" 1998).

Finally, the Russian government is unable to collect taxes because of widespread avoidance of tax payments and corruption. This is due, in part, to an outdated tax system, and corruption by the Russian mafia is widespread ("Russia's Economic Bear" 1998).

External Debt

Russia inherited about $130 billion in debt from the former Soviet Union (Oh 1998). According to the Fitch IBCA, a bank credit-rating agency, the total foreign debt of Russia currently amounts to $213.8 billion, of which $159.6 billion is public debt and $54.2 billion is private-sector debt (Liesman 1998).[2] The private-sector debt is composed of $25 billion owed by Russian companies and $29.2 billion owed by Russian commercial banks. As noted, the Russian banks are insolvent.

A group of German banks are major creditors that have $65.6 billion in claims, which constitutes 30.7 percent of the total foreign debt of Russia. Russia reached debt rescheduling agreements with the London Club (procedures for resolving sovereign debts to public creditors) for about $33 billion in 1995 and with the Paris Club (procedures for resolving sovereign debts to private banks) for $40 billion in 1996 (Bank Austria Economics Department 1997).

In 1999, Russia has to repay about $17 billion, but only has about $12 billion in reserves. Therein lies the problem. President Boris Yeltsin signed an austerity program in May 1998 to cut the central government's fiscal deficit, and the Russian government requested a loan of at least $10 billion from the IMF in June 1998 to keep its economy from collapsing. The IMF agreed to coordinate a $22.6 billion loan from international lenders on July 13, 1998, for the following two years. However, this was not enough to restore confidence in the Russian economy.

Russia's exports have subsided, mainly due to the sharp fall in oil prices. Considering that Russia is one of the world's largest oil producers, the price declines adversely affected the current account balance, which had already suffered from the unbearable interest payment on foreign debt.

CONCLUSION

On September 8, 1998, the headline of a *Wall Street Journal* article read "IMF Aide Calls Russia's Plans 'Destructive'" (Davis 1998). The IMF aide was Stanley Fisher, the IMF's deputy managing director. He went to say that some plans to jump-start economies make matters worse. The devaluation and defaulting on debts undermined the confidence of foreign investors and shocked financial markets around the world. In late October 1998, the Western banks cut off talks with the Russians ("Russians, Western Banks Cut Off Talks to Restructure Ruble Debt" 1998). The foreign banks wanted 20 percent of the ruble-denominated debts owed to them to be paid in cash. The Russians wanted to swap the GKOs for seventeen-year dollar-denominated bonds with an eight-year grace period, during which time no interest would be paid. Analysts feared that Russia might default on some of the $140 billion of its foreign currency debts that were coming due shortly. The Russian government was expected to print more rubles to cover some of its debts, and to dip into its foreign reserves (McKay 1998b; Matlack 1998).

NOTES

1. GKOs (*Gosudarstvennye Kratkosrchnye Obyazatelstva*) are ruble-denominated short-term zero-coupon Russian government treasury bills.

2. Estimates of the size of the foreign debt vary widely. Another source states that it is $180 billion (Higgins and Liesman 1998).

REFERENCES

Afanasyev, Dmitry. 1997. "World Economic Analysis: Russia." *Euromoney*, September.

Bank Austria Economics Department. 1997. "The 1997 Guide to the Russian Financial Markets: Economic Overview." *Euromoney Research Guides*, March.

Bayer, Alexei. 1998. "Russia Needs to Create Wealth." *Wall Street Journal*, 8 June, p. A22.

Bernstam, Michael S., and Alvin Rabushka. 1998. "Russia's Banks Need to Be Reformed, Not Rescued." *Wall Street Journal*, 15 July, p. A14.

Brooks, Rick, and Mitchell Pachelle. 1998. "BankAmerica Knew in August of Trading Woes." *Wall Street Journal*, 16 October, p. A3.

Chase Manhattan International. 1997. "The 1997 Guide to Emerging Currencies: Russia." *Euromoney Research Guides*, July.

Davis, Bob. 1998. "IMF Aide Calls Russia's Plans 'Destructive.'" *Wall Street Journal*, 8 September, p. A30.

"Hedge Funds Win and Lose." 1998. Http://cnnfn.com/quickenonfn/investing/9809/16/q_hedgefunds/.

Higgins, Andrew. 1998. "In a Financial Gamble, Russia Lets Ruble Fall, Stalls Debt Repayment." *Wall Street Journal*, 18 August, pp. A1, A16.

Higgins, Andrew, and Steve Liesman. 1998. "Signs in Russia Point Away from Free Market." *Wall Street Journal*, 14 September, p. A24.

"How Russia Set Off Wave That Swamped Markets Around the World." 1998. *Wall Street Journal*, 22 September, pp. A1, A8.

ING Bank Eurasia. 1997. "The 1997 Guide to the Russian Financial Markets: Bonds." *Euromoney Research Guides*, March.

International Monetary Fund (IMF). 1998a. *The IMF's Response to the Asian Crisis*. Washington, D.C.: IMF.

International Monetary Fund (IMF). 1998b. *International Financial Statistics*. Washington, D.C.: IMF.

Koretz, Gene. 1998. "How Sick Is the Russian Bear?" *Business Week*, 5 October, p. 30.

Liesman, Steve. 1998. "Missteps by Moscow, New Asian Turmoil Set Off Russian Crisis." *Wall Street Journal*, 5 June, pp. A1, A8.

Liesman, Steve, and Andrew Higgins. 1998. "The Crunch Points: How Russia Staggered from Here to There." *Wall Street Journal*, 23 September, pp. A1, A12.

Matlack, Carol. 1998. "What Disasters Lie Ahead in Moscow?" *Business Week*, 19 October, p. 62.

McKay, Betsy. 1998a. "Russia Gives Up on New IMF Aid for This Year, Central Banker Says." *Wall Street Journal*, 27 October, p. A15.

McKay, Betsy. 1998b. "Russia's Financing of Projected Deficit Likely to Involve Printing More Rubles." *Wall Street Journal*, 21 October, p. A17.

McKay, Betsy, Matthew Brzezinski, and Bob Davis. 1998. "Russia Triples Key Rates to Defend Ruble: Talk of IMF Aid Grows as Stocks Plummet." *Wall Street Journal*, 28 May, p. A17.

Oh, Seungkoo. 1998. "Russia: The Announcement of Moratorium and Its Impact." *Research Paper of Samsung Economic Research Institute*, August.

Russian Trading System (RTS). 1998. *RTS Statistics*. Http://www.rtsnet.ru. Last visited September 1998.

"Russians, Western Banks Cut Off Talks to Restructure Ruble Debt." 1998. *Wall Street Journal*, 23 October, p. A13.

"Russia's Economic Bear." 1998. BBC Online Network, 14 September.

Serwer, Andy. 1998. "Frank Newman Feels the Heat." *Fortune*, 26 October, pp. 121–26.

Thornhill, John, and Robert Corzine. 1998. "Oil Price Collapse Threatens Russian Economy." *Financial Times*, 19 March, p. 2.

Troika Dialog. 1997. "The 1997 Guide to the Russian Financial Markets: Equities." *Euromoney Research Guides*, March.

"The Undead." 1998. *The Economist*, 19 September, pp. 89–90.

UNEXIM-ICFI Financial Group. 1997. "The 1997 Guide to the Russian Financial Markets: Custody and Settlement." *Euromoney Research Guides*, March.

U.S. House. 1998. Committee on Banking and Financial Services. *Statement by William McDonough before the Committee on Banking and Financial Services*. 1 October.

9

The Tequila Banking Crisis in Argentina

Marcelo Dabós and Laura Gómez Mera

This chapter studies the main consequences that the Mexican crisis of December 1994 had on Argentina's financial system. It describes the development of events, the institutional and structural characteristics of the Argentine financial system at the moment of the Mexican devaluation, and the extent to which these factors contributed to increasing or reducing the impact of the shock. The measures adopted in response to the crisis and their effectiveness are also considered. A summary of other scholarships analyzing the banking crisis which began in Argentina due to the "Tequila" effect is included as well.

THE MEXICAN CRISIS

The Events in Mexico

Several different factors seem to have contributed to the outbreak of the Mexican crisis. Political turmoil during 1994, the bad shape of Mexican macroeconomic fundamentals, and external factors such as the rise in international interest rates had been affecting the behavior of financial markets during 1994 (Folkerts-Landau and Ito 1995). According to Garrido (1996), the institutional design of the financial system and its regulatory framework (which added to its vulnerability to external pressures and its limited development) were the main determinants of the December 1994 Mexican crisis.

On December 20, 1994, the Mexican Central Bank established the widening of the exchange rate bands, which resulted in an immediate 15-percent devaluation of the Mexican currency. The devaluation of the Mexican peso continued, and the fall in international reserves deepened, leading the authorities to announce the floating of the peso two days later. The growing selling pressures observed during the following days were exacerbated by two factors: on one hand, the value of the Mexican debt in *tesobonos*, short-term securities denominated in pesos but indexed to the dollar, grew quickly as the peso devaluated, and, on the other hand, the growth in domestic interest rates increased the proportion of nonperforming loans in the banking system, mainly because most of the loans had floating interest rates which promptly reflected the increased market rates (Folkerts-Landau and Ito 1995).

The recovery of confidence only began when a package of multilateral aid was agreed to with the United States. The Mexican government was also forced to launch a new adjustment and stabilization program, which included cuts in public expenditures and substantial increases in fiscal revenues. On January 2, an $18 billion loan agreement was announced, half of which would be granted by the American government. The rest of the package would be provided by the Canadian government and the BIS. Although on January 12, President Clinton had proposed a program guaranteeing the Mexican debt, opposition in the U.S. Congress led to the replacement of this plan with a $50 billion package of direct assistance.[1] This new external aid package was approved by the IMF on February 1, although negotiations between the Mexican and American governments did not end until later that month. On March 9, the Mexican authorities announced the new stabilization plan, and the Clinton administration authorized the release of the first $3 billion of the agreed credit.

Spillover Effects of the Mexican Crisis

The confidence triggered by the Mexican devaluation reached the emerging markets. Argentine and Brazilian stock exchange indexes fell substantially, although other Latin American economies were not as significantly affected. On the other hand, the Asian and the industrialized Western countries' stock markets evolved favorably after the Mexican peso devaluation (Folkerts-Landau and Ito 1995).

Brady bonds prices fell in most Latin American countries. The spreads on these bonds over comparable American treasury securities grew, increasing country risk. Brady bonds return correlation between the Latin American emerging economies grew substantially after the crisis (Folkerts-Landau and Ito 1995). Ganapolsky and Schmukler (1998) found empirical evidence of the increase in the co-movement among these and other financial variables in those countries affected by the Mexican shock. These authors analyzed, more specifically, how changes in external factors impacted Argentine financial markets. The close integration of Latin American capital markets and the developed markets, probably explained by a more intense participation of international investors in emerging economies, determined a high correlation among the main financial variables in these countries. According to Ganapolsky and Schmukler, this tends to increase the extent to which an external shock such as the Mexican devaluation affects other economies. In particular, bonds and stock prices in Mexico, Argentina, Chile, and Brazil moved together in response to the Mexican crisis.[2] Furthermore, the correlation among these variables increased drastically during this period relative to pre-crisis levels. This could be explained by common fundamentals, similarities in institutional design, or the reaction of investors who could have perceived resemblances between these markets. However, the study also shows that the correlation among Argentinean, Mexican, and American interest rates was not too significant, probably due to differences in the monetary policies adopted by each country. Apart from this, it was found that North American and Latin American capital markets were not affected by the same factors.

THE TEQUILA CRISIS IN ARGENTINA

Part of the existing literature on the impact of the Mexican devaluation on Argentina's financial markets has tried to link the main structural and institutional features of the financial system at the time of the events with the characteristics of the crisis and its evolution. Bleger and Rosenwurcel (1995), for example, argue that the reforms introduced by the Convertibility Plan in 1991, in spite of being successful in reducing inflation, had other less favorable consequences, such as augmenting the vulnerability of the Argentine economy to external shocks. Fernández and Schumacher (1996), on the other hand, admit that the limitations set on the Central Bank's abilities to act as a lender of last resort and to provide liquidity to the system could be seen as a weakness of the implemented reforms. However, this general framework was effective in creating enough market discipline and in minimizing the moral hazard fostered by the previous design of the system. The Convertibility Plan regulatory framework constituted the most efficient way of achieving these ultimate objectives.

Argentina's Financial System:
Pre-Crisis Institutional Characteristics

The Convertibility Plan was introduced in 1991 with the purpose of putting an end to several decades of inflation, fiscal deficits, and mismanagement of the economy. Its main objective was to achieve price stability, fixing full convertibility of the domestic currency into American dollars, and setting limitations on the ability of the Central Bank to employ the dangerous instrument of money printing. Due to the failure of the previous fixed exchange rate programs implemented in Argentina, policymakers thought this plan had to be accompanied by a strict legal framework in order to keep monetary authorities from using discretional powers. Only a regime with these characteristics, it was believed, would enjoy the needed credibility (Kiguel 1995; Arnaudo 1996). The monetary measures established the convertibility of one peso for one dollar, binding the Central Bank to back up the whole monetary base with international reserves.[3] Up to 20 percent of this backup could be constituted by public securities from the Argentine government, denominated in dollars and valued at market prices.

Apart from this, in 1992, the Central Bank Charter and the Law of Financial Institutions were modified. As a consequence, the Central Bank was banned from conducting active monetary policy. The former deposit insurance system was abolished and new rules of procedure for closure and liquidation of institutions with problems were implemented. Other reforms introduced at the time increased reserve requirements and minimum required capital to assets ratios, which were established according to the risk undertaken by each financial institution.[4] The high reserve requirements had the objective of creating a liquidity mass which could be released in case of a run. The severe minimum capital regulations, apart from constituting an alternative liquidity source, tried to penalize banks according to the risk undertaken.

Between 1991 and 1994, Argentina's financial system was characterized by the lack of a security network or deposits insurance system, which kept the Central Bank from having to bear the consequences of the excessive risk undertaken by financial institutions; high reserve requirements as a prudential regulation in case of liquidity problems arising; severe capital regulations; and the lack of a lender of last resort, given the limitations imposed by the convertibility regime on the Central Bank. In this way, Argentine policymakers had tried to create enough incentives to discipline financial agents. Furthermore, in the event that the market discipline achieved was insufficient, financial institutions would be prepared to face the consequences of the risk undertaken (Fernández and Schumacher 1996). The new monetary and financial regime tried to make bankers aware that the government would not rescue them in case of trouble (Schumacher 1996). We will see how this was put aside once the crisis started, and how the Central Bank took an active role.

The Convertibility Plan was highly effective in stopping hyperinflation. At the same time, a favorable external situation determined a high rate of capital inflow since 1991. During the four years before the outbreak of the Mexican currency crisis, both peso and dollar deposits grew significantly: Total deposits increased 350 percent between March 1991 and November 1994. The Mexican shock, however, interrupted this process of expansion.

Evolution of the Crisis

The reversion of capital inflows had a strong impact on Argentina. The confidence crisis translated into an important deposit and international-reserves withdrawal, posing a threat to the convertibility commitment and to the banking system and having a negative impact over investors' credibility. The fall in deposits started by affecting only a group of banks and reaching only peso deposits before it was generalized to the whole financial system and to deposits in all denominations. The crisis was also evidenced by an increase in country risk, which translated into a fall in Argentine bond and stock prices. Furthermore, liquidity problems were responsible for an abrupt increase in nominal interest rates.

The Tequila effect also had negative consequences over the level of economic activity. The GDP, which had grown 7.1 percent during 1994, fell 4.4 percent in 1995. Unemployment reached 18.6 percent in April 1995, 6 percent higher than in October 1994 (Kiguel 1995). Consumption and domestic investment were also affected. While in 1994 gross domestic investment represented 19.9 percent of GDP, in 1995 this proportion fell to 18.1 percent (Bleger and Rozenwurcel 1995). In 1995, total consumption, which had grown 6.16 percent in 1994, went down 5.5 percent. Exports, on the other hand, were the only component of aggregate demand which increased, from $15.8 billion in 1994, to $21 billion in 1995.

There are four phases into which the study of the evolution of the Tequila crisis in Argentina is often divided. During the first phase, which started the day the Mexican peso was devaluated (December 20, 1994) and finished at the end of February 1995, there was an important process of peso deposit withdrawal and a reallocation of deposits among financial institutions. During the second phase, the month of March, the fall in deposits became a true bank run, affecting both peso and dollar deposits and extending to all groups of financial institutions. At the same time, interest rates reached their highest levels. During the third stage of the crisis, from April until the middle of May, the deposit withdrawal slowed down, until it was reversed on May 14, when the fourth and last period, recovery, began. On this day, President Menem was elected for a second term.

Phase 1: Flight to Quality (December 20, 1994 to February 28, 1995)

During this phase, there was a reallocation of deposits, from pesos to dollars. Total deposits came down during the whole initial phase of the crisis by 8 percent. The observed fall in total deposits, which was equal to $3.694 billion, can be explained by an important drop in peso deposits, which decreased by 16 percent. Dollar deposits, on the other hand, grew 1.4 percent during this period (see Figure 9.1).

At the same time, a reallocation of funds from the smallest to the biggest institutions, and in particular to foreign banks, was observed. Figure 9.2 shows the monthly evolution of deposits for each group of institutions in the financial system. Foreign banks saw their deposits grow $368 million (almost 5% relative to the level registered in November 1994), while the deposits of national private and public banks decreased $2.462 billion (10% and 3%, respectively) during the first period of the crisis. On the other hand, the evolution of the biggest banks' deposits (the ten biggest private banks and the Nación, Provincia, Ciudad, and Hipotecario banks) showed an increase of $1.073 billion, or 4.2 percent.

A subgroup of banks, the wholesale banks, were strongly affected during this period due to the fall in Argentine public securities' prices caused by the increase in country risk as this group was very active in capital markets (their portfolios were mainly composed by govern-

Figure 9.1
Peso and Dollar Deposits: Daily Evolution

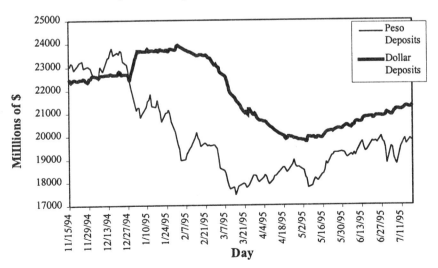

Figure 9.2
Monthly Evolution of Total Deposits (November 1994 = 100)

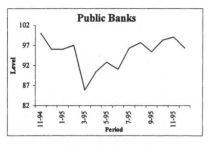

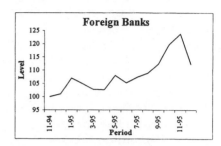

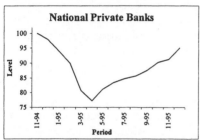

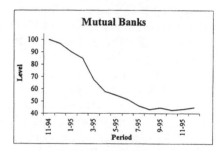

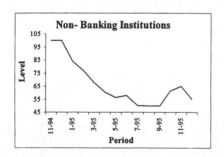

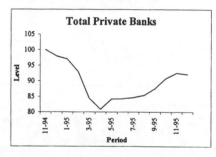

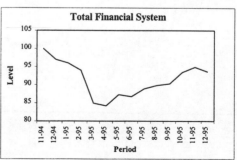

ment bonds). The suspension of two wholesale banks, Extrader on December 28, and Finansur on January 9, contributed to the increase in uncertainty and to the deepening of the problems which by now had extended to the entire financial system.

Another indicator of the confidence crisis initiated by the Tequila effect was the great increase observed in country risk premium. A measure of this is constituted by the spread on Argentinean FRB bonds over comparable American treasury bonds. Figure 9.3 shows that this spread grew 103 basis points the day after the Mexican devaluation. In all, throughout this first phase, the country risk premium increased 374 basis points, from 925 on December 20, 1994, to 1,299 on the last day of February 1995.

Furthermore, liquidity problems caused by the important deposit withdrawal determined a marked increase in interest rates. Nominal interest rates, both in pesos and in dollars, grew significantly after the Mexican devaluation. The annual interest rate on term peso deposits (thirty days), which was equal to 8.7 percent in November 1994, reached almost 13 percent at the end of February 1995. The annual rate on this same type of dollar deposits grew from 6 percent to 7.3 percent during this phase. An increase in the difference between nominal rates in pesos and dollars was also verified over this period, as shown in Figure 9.4.

The behavior of deposits also affected the evolution of monetary aggregates and international reserves. M3 (currency in pesos plus to-

Figure 9.3
Daily Evolution of Country Risk: Spread of Argentine FRB Bonds over Thirty-Year American Treasury Bonds

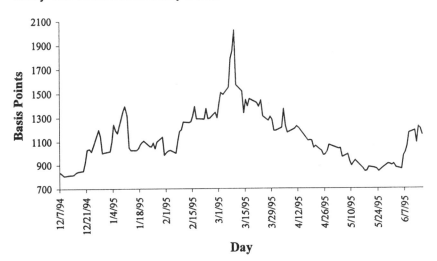

Figure 9.4
Monthly Evolution of Annual Interest Rates on Peso and Dollar Term Deposits

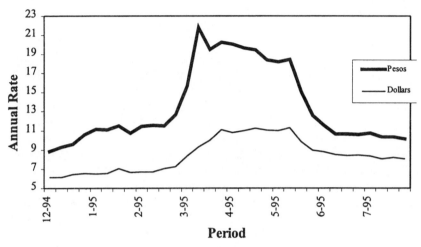

tal deposits in pesos and in dollars) decreased from $55.223 billion on December 20, 1994, to $51.613 billion at the end of February 1995 (6.5%), while the Central Bank's international reserves fell by 15 percent during this period (see Figure 9.5).

The initial effects of the crisis also reached the stock market. A marked fall in the Merval stock index (Buenos Aires Stock Exchange), which decreased from 538 points in November 1994 to 378 in February 1995 (30%) can be seen in Figure 9.6.

Confronting this serious situation, the authorities decided to act. The first measures taken, however, did not seem to have significant success (Arnaudo 1996). On December 28, reserve requirements on dollar deposits were reduced in order to provide liquidity to the system. By mid-January, requirements on peso deposits were also lowered and set equal to those on dollar deposits, with the objective of reducing pressures on the banks. At the same time, the dollarization of bank deposits in the Central Bank was resolved.[5]

Due to the restrictions that the reforms had imposed on the role of the Central Bank as the lender of last resort, a special security fund integrated by five private institutions and two public banks was constituted with the purpose of assisting those institutions which had suffered higher deposit withdrawal rates. It was managed by Banco Nación and financed with reserve requirements. However, all these measures were received with uncertainty by the markets. The fall in deposits, far from being reversed, was accentuated.

Figure 9.5
Evolution of Convertibility Backup: Central Bank International Reserves and Monetary Liabilities

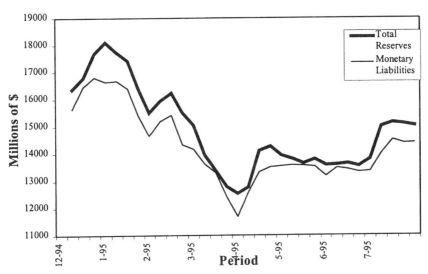

During February, total deposits came down by 2.6 percent ($1.142 billion) relative to the month before. On February 27, the national government announced a series of fiscal and financial measures. The Central Bank Charter was also modified in order to allow for greater flexibility in the assistance of troubled institutions through the use of repos and rediscounts. The reforms included the extension of the suspension term applied to banks with problems and the constitution of the Trust Fund for Provincial Development.[6] This fund was created with the objective of assisting provincial banks in their process of privatization by giving them additional credit and helping them with liquidity problems. These measures, however, were unable to stop the crisis.

Phase 2: Generalized Deposit Loss (March 1995)

The set of measures announced on February 27, far from improving the situation, seemed to give negative signs to the markets, which reacted promptly, accelerating the deposit withdrawal. Total deposits decreased in March more than $4 billion, which represents a higher drop than that verified over the whole first phase. Furthermore, the decreasing trend extended to dollar deposits. During March, the fall in dollar deposits was higher than the drop in peso deposits: They decreased by 10 percent and 8 percent, respectively. Furthermore, all

Figure 9.6
Monthly Evolution of Merval Stock Exchange Index

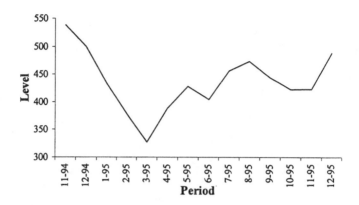

groups of financial institutions suffered deposit losses during this second phase.

The deepening of the financial crisis and of the liquidity problems caused by the important deposit loss was reflected not only in interest rates but also in monetary aggregates. Nominal interest rates on both peso and dollar term deposits reached their highest levels in March: Peso annual interest rates reached 21 percent in the second week of March, while dollar annual interest rates grew to 11 percent. The rates increased 70 percent and 54 percent, respectively, in relation to their values from the previous phase. Country risk also worsened significantly during this month, reaching 2,023 basis points on March 9.

M3 fell $4.378 billion (8.5%) (see Figure 9.7), while the Central Bank lost $2.508 billion in international reserves (16%). The Merval stock index also suffered its deepest fall in March: It decreased 51 points, 13 percent relative to its value in February, reaching a minimum of 328 points.

When, in mid-March, the reserves that had been left aside to support the system had been depleted, the Central Bank was compelled to launch a new program to obtain foreign financing. On March 15, an agreement with the IMF was announced. This included the renewal and extension of the Extended Facilities Program, which would generate $2.4 billion. Loans from the World Bank and the IBD were also arranged in the amount of $2.6 billion. At the same time, the subscription of a new $2-billion public bond was decided. These funds were used to increase international reserves and to the constitution of the trust funds. As will be seen, these measures were important for the resolution of the bank run in Argentina, although their effects were not immediate.

Figure 9.7
Monthly Evolution of M3

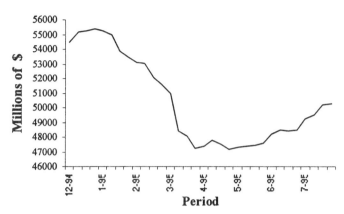

Other significant measures were the constitution, at the end of March, of another fund, the Trust Fund for Bank Capitalization, and the establishment of a deposit insurance network.[7] The Trust Fund for Bank Capitalization tried to aid those banks with liquidity problems and to assist them in their process of merger with those institutions which had emerged from the crisis in a better shape. It was financed with a transference from the National Treasury and part of the funds provided by the World Bank. Among its functions were the subscription and integration of capital, the purchase and sale of stock from troubled institutions, and the granting of loans and credits.

The new limited deposit insurance system granted investors a guarantee over part of their funds. Financial institutions were obliged to contribute monthly with a proportion of the daily balances of their total deposits, in addition to another contribution established according to the risk undertaken by the bank.[8] The insurance covered up to $10 thousand for each person who held money in a checking account, savings account, or time deposit up to ninety days, and up to $20 thousand for deposits of terms longer than ninety days.[9] However, it did not cover deposits paying interest rates higher than two percentage points of a deposit rate calculated by the Central Bank.

Phase 3: Slowing Down of the Run (April 1 to May 14)

The measures adopted in March, more effective than those implemented in the first phase, contributed to slowing down the bank run (BCRA 1995). The announcement of the agreed external aid had important consequences over investor's expectations. During the third stage, deposit withdrawal slowed down significantly, and the dollarization process was reversed. Although dollar deposits went on falling, a slight improvement in peso deposits, which increased $600 million, was verified during this phase. Total deposits fell 1.2 percent, while dollar deposits came down by 3.7 percent.

During this third phase, the nominal interest rate on peso term deposits dropped by 1.6 percent, although the interest rate on dollar deposits continued its ascent until May 15. This interest rate reached 11 percent annual on the second week of May. Country risk also improved by 305 basis points (going from 1,190 on March 31 to 885 on May 15). On the other hand, M3 remained almost constant relative to the level reached during the previous phase. Central Bank reserves, however, grew $878 million (7%).

Phase 4: Crisis Resolution (from May 14, 1995)

In spite of the measures taken, political uncertainty predominating at this time determined that only after the presidential reelection did the return of deposit begin. The outcome of the elections held on May 14, where President Menem won a second mandate, contributed to reinforcing policy commitments and restoring investors' credibility.

May 15 is generally considered as the date the bank run ended. On this date, a turning point in total deposit levels was observed (see Tables 9.1 and 9.2). During the second fortnight of March, total deposits increased by 4 percent. Between May and December 1995, both peso and dollar deposits continued returning to the financial system. By June 15, peso and dollar deposits had increased 6.4 percent and 4.4 percent, respectively, relative to their previous levels (May 14).

Annual interest rates paid on peso deposits continued falling, while annual dollar rates started going down after May 15. M3 and international reserves also increased significantly, while capital markets evolved favorably during this period. Both bonds and stock prices increased. The Merval index reached 428 points in May, growing 30 percent relative to its value in March. This evolution was influenced by the positive effects the presidential elections had on political uncertainty.

According to Central Bank estimations, more than 70 percent of the deposit fall was financed with liquidity instruments available to the monetary authorities, such as liquidity rediscounts, repos, and reserve requirements reductions. The remaining 30 percent was covered with external credit lines and with private credit cuts (Kiguel 1995; Schumacher 1996).

Table 9.3 shows exactly how the total deposit fall registered between December 1994 and May 1995 was financed. Evidently, the commit-

Table 9.1
Percentage Change in Deposits

Period	Peso Deposits	Dollar Deposits	Total Deposits
12/20 – 2/28	-17.2	1.8	-7.8
3/1 – 3/31	-7.9	-10.4	-9.0
4/1 – 5/14	1.75	-3.7	-1.1
5/15 – 6/15	5.5	4.3	5.1
Total Fall			
12/20 – 5/14	-22.4	-10.4	-17.5

Table 9.2
Absolute Change in Deposits (in millions of pesos)

Period	Peso Deposits	Dollar Deposits	Total Deposits
12/20 – 2/28	-4,066	430	-3,637
3/1 – 3/31	-1,548	-2,399	-3,946
4/1 – 5/14	316	-769	-457
5/15 – 6/15	1,016	868	1,954

ment to not intervening was abandoned. Although the monetary and financial regime constrained the assistance of banks, there was massive intervention due to the panic. The Central Bank relied heavily on reserve requirements reductions, which generated about $3.4 billion. Other sources of liquidity were loans to banks for $1.537 billion and repos for $820 million (Table 9.3).

Table 9.3 shows an important Central Bank intervention. Not only the current liquidity instruments were used, as Central Bank authori-

Table 9.3
Financing of Total Deposit Withdrawal (in millions of pesos)

	Change in Total Deposits	Change in Private Credit	Central Bank Creation of New Liquidity				Other Sources	Creation of Liquidity / Change in Deposits	Change in Private Credit / Change in Deposits	Other Source/ Change in Deposits
			Repos	Loans to Banks	Reserve Requirement Reduction	Total				
12/20/94 to 2/28/95	-3,637	304	369	256	2,400	3,025	916	83.17%	-8.35%	25.18%
3/1/95 to 3/31/95	-3,946	-1,424	436	842	1,000	2,278	244	57.72%	36.08%	6.20%
4/1/95 to 5/14/95	-457	9	15	439	0	454	12	99.34%	-1.96%	2.62%
12/20/94 to 5/14/95	-8,040	-1,111	820	1,537	3,400	5,757	1,172	71.60%	13.81%	14.59%

Sources: Liliana Schumacher, "Bubble or Depositors Discipline: A Study of the Argentine Banking Panic (December 1994–May 1995)" (Ph.D. diss., University of Chicago, 1996); Miguel Kiguel, "Convertibilidad: Una Historia de Tango y Tequila" (Banco Central del la República Argentina, 1995, mimeographed).

ties argue (Kiguel 1995), but the rules were also changed in order to increase their ability to intervene. An example of this is the reimplementation of the deposit insurance system. Arnaudo (1996) argues about the difficulties in combining a state guarantee of this type with a convertibility regime, mainly because of the fiscal constraints imposed on the Central Bank. Even though in theory the security network had been designed to minimize the extent to which fiscal resources were jeopardized, empirical evidence suggests that the monetary authorities were involved in the bail-out of a number of troubled financial institutions.

The agreed external aid was essential to restore the system's credibility and to help financial institutions overcome their difficulties. Ganapolsky and Schmukler (1998) argue that this was one of the most significant measures received by financial markets. Its announcement had a positive impact on country risk, leading to an increase in Brady bond prices and in the stock market index. However, empirical evidence has shown that this measure also contributed to raising short-term interest rates. According to Ganapolsky and Schmukler, this suggests that although financial markets perceived the agreement with the IMF as positive in the long run, it was also believed to constrain credit opportunities in the short run. On the other hand, these negotiations not only implied an additional source of financing but also provided support to the way the panic was being handled by Argentine authorities.

Consequences of the Crisis on the Financial System

The evolution of financial system indicators shows the negative effects of the crisis. The indicators analyzed include the main variables considered by the CAMEL system (capitalization, assets, management, earnings, liquidity). Indicators 1 and 2 (equity over assets, and liabilities over equity) are capitalization indicators; indicator 3 (immediate liquidity, defined as cash plus public securities over liabilities) constitutes a measure of the institution liquidity position; indicator 4 (operating expenses over liabilities) tries to measure banks management efficiency; indicator 5 (nonperforming loans net of provisions over equity) shows asset quality and provides a measure of the credit risk undertaken by financial institutions; indicator 6, ROE, shows the financial system returns over its equity.

While the value of total assets decreased by 7.2 percent between November 1994 and April 1995, total liabilities dropped by $6.939 billion (9%). Thus, the value of the financial system equity increased by $393 million (3%). Apart from a reduction in total value, liabilities suffered a change in composition. By November 1994, before the crisis, deposits represented 63 percent of total liabilities, while by April 1995 this participation had fallen to 57 percent. Instead, an increase in Central Bank and foreign credits can be observed.

The drastic reduction in total deposit explains the behavior of capitalization indicators. Indicator 1 (equity/assets) grew from 14.8 percent in November 1994 to 16.5 percent in May 1995 (see Figure 9.8). It can thus be seen that capital integration was above the required levels (11.5%) even before the crisis had begun. The leverage indicator (indicator 2, defined as liabilities/equity in times of equity) also fell during this period, reaching a minimum level of five times in March, and reflecting the important deposit withdrawal (see Figure 9.9).

Indicator 3 shows a prompt impact of the crisis over the financial institutions liquidity position. The immediate liquidity indicator fell

Figure 9.8
Evolution of Indicator 1

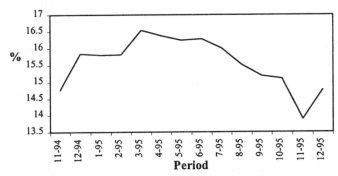

Figure 9.9
Evolution of Indicator 2

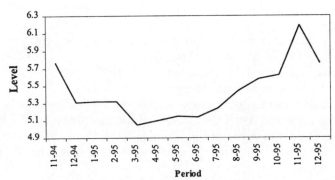

by more than 7 percent between December 1994 and March 1995. After March, however, it started improving (see Figure 9.10).

The evolution of indicator 4 (operating expenses/liabilities) shows that the system also suffered in terms of efficiency due to the bank run. Indicator 4 grew from 8.5 percent in November 1994 until it reached its maximum value of 9.7 percent in March 1995 (see Figure 9.11).

The damage to the quality of the financial system's portfolio of loans was another negative consequence of the Tequila crisis, as can be seen by the evolution of indicator 5, which increased from 51.2 percent to 71 percent between November 1994 and July 1995 (see Figure 9.12).

Financial institution returns were severely harmed by the Tequila effect. In January 1995, the ROE indicator had a negative value (–1.12%), and although a slight improvement can be observed in March (0.7%), return deterioration continued after April (see Figure 9.13).

Figure 9.10
Evolution of Indicator 3

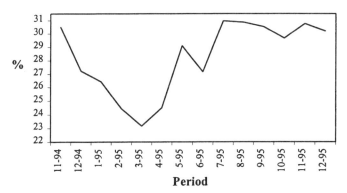

Figure 9.11
Evolution of Indicator 4

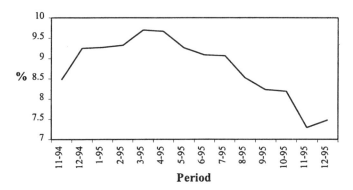

Figure 9.12
Evolution of Indicator 5

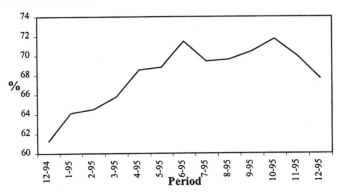

Figure 9.13
Evolution of Indicator 6

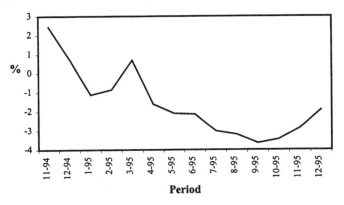

To sum up, Argentina's financial system was affected by the Mexican crisis. Liquidity positions, asset quality, and returns were significantly reduced. Structurally, there were two main effects generated by the bank run: a higher concentration of the financial system and a deposit reallocation among the different groups of institutions.

The Argentine financial system was characterized over the last decades by its heterogeneity: The total number of institutions can be classified as public, national private, foreign, mutual banks, and nonbanking institutions. Table 9.4 presents the total number of banks, as classified in November 1994. This table also shows the concentration process initiated after the Tequila crisis. Out of the 169 banks existing in December 1994, before the bank run 9 private banks disappeared before the end of the crisis (between December 20, 1994 and May 15, 1995),

Table 9.4
Evolution of the Number of Banks in Argentina

Classification	Existing by 12/20/94	Disappearing before 5/15/95	Disappearing between 5/15/95 and 12/20/95	Disappearing between 12/20/95 and 12/20/96	Disappearing between 12/20/96 and 9/25/97	Existing by 9/25/97
Public	36	-	-	-	-	36*
National Private	64	3	11	8	2	40
Foreign	31	-	-	-	-	31
Mutual	38	6	23	2	1	6
Total Banking System	169	9	34	10	3	113

*Ten public provincial banks were privatized between December 1995 and December 1996.

while 47 disappeared during the succeeding months, after being severely affected by the panic. In all, the number of banks dropped by
33 percent between December 1994 and September 1997, as shown in
the following list:

Classification	Disappeared
Public	0
National Private	24
Foreign	0
Mutual	32
Total Banking System	56

The different groups of banks were unevenly affected by the run.
Mutual banks were the most affected: They suffered the highest rate
of deposit withdrawal (45.1% between December 1994 and May 1995)
(see Tables 9.5 and 9.6). Also, this was the group with the higher number of troubled banks: Six mutual banks disappeared during these five
months. Foreign banks not only gained both peso and dollar deposits
during the first phase of the crisis, but also, once the crisis resolved, saw
their participation in total deposits grow (see Figures 9.14 and 9.15).
These figures show the difference between total deposits distribution
before and after the bank run and reveal a certain reallocation of deposits between the different groups of financial institutions. The proportion of total deposits held by foreign banks, for example, grew from
16 to 20 percent, while that of public banks, which was 35 percent in November 1994, increased to 37 percent by May 1995. Both national private
and mutual banks saw their share in total deposits reduced. In particular, the proportion of total deposits held by mutual banks dropped
from 9 to 6 percent between November 1994 and May 1995, reflecting
the disappearance of six banks of this type during this period.

A certain reallocation from peso to dollar deposits was also verified. While by November 1994 peso deposits represented 49.5 percent
of total deposits, Table 9.7 shows that by November 1995, the proportion of peso deposits fell to 44 percent of total deposits in the system.

OTHER SCHOLARSHIPS ANALYZING THE TEQUILA
BANKING CRISIS IN ARGENTINA

Many of the authors dedicated to studying the consequences of the
Tequila effect in Argentina link the intensity of the impact suffered by
this economy with the institutional features of the financial system at
the time of events. The extent to which the convertibility regime and
the reforms introduced in the system's design helped in reducing its

Table 9.5
Percentage Change in Deposits between November 1994 and May 1995 (by bank type)

Classification	Peso Deposits	Dollar Deposits	Total Deposits
Public	-13.2	2.1	-7.2
National Private	-18.6	-18.9	-18.8
Foreign	7.3	8.4	8.0
Mutual	-49.1	-41.1	-45.1
Total Banking System	-16.1	-9.5	-12.7

Table 9.6
Evolution of Total Deposits between November 1994 and May 1995 (by bank type)

Classification	Total Deposits (Nov-94)	Total Deposits (May-95)
Public	100	92.8
National Private	100	81.2
Foreign	100	108
Mutual	100	54.9
Total Banking System	100	87.3

Figure 9.14
Change in Deposit Market Share among Groups of Financial Institutions

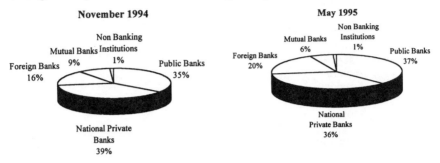

Figure 9.15
Change in Total Deposits by Bank Type (November 1994 = 100)

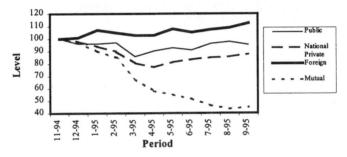

ability to react to shocks is often analyzed. Bleger and Rosenwurcel (1995) blame the structural and institutional reforms implemented in the banking system in 1991 for accentuating the negative effects of the Mexican crisis on Argentina. They argue that the convertibility regime, by reducing the Central Bank's power over monetary policy and by limiting almost completely its role as a lender of last resort, had the effect of augmenting the system's vulnerability to external shocks. According to Arnaudo (1996), the Mexican crisis put in evidence the fragility of the financial system and the weaknesses of the monetary regime to react favorably to external disturbances.

Other authors, such as Fernández and Schumacher (1996), consider that the consequences of the Mexican devaluation would have been more serious without the strict regulatory framework imposed by the Convertibility Plan, which established high reserve requirements, limited the risk undertaken by financial institutions before the crisis, and constrained the Central Bank's ability to rescue troubled institutions.

Table 9.7
Evolution of Total Deposits Distribution (%)

Deposits	Nov. 1994	May 1995	Nov. 1995
In Pesos	49.5	47.4	44
In Dollars	50.5	52.6	56

Kiguel (1995) also argues that in spite of the rigidities introduced by the convertibility regime, the severe prudential regulations helped overcoming the adverse situation triggered by the Mexican crisis.

Another type of analysis studies whether there was market discipline or contagion during the crisis. The relevance of this question lies in its implications in terms of preventive policy to be implemented. In particular, evidence in favor of market discipline would reduce the relative relevance of a deposit insurance system. In that case, a scheme for information disclosure would be more efficient. This would allow depositors to know and distinguish among the different types of institutions.

Schumacher (1996, 1997) shows that depositors used the available information to discriminate between healthy banks and those which presented weaker fundamentals (lower capitalization level, higher proportion of nonperforming loans, and fewer returns). These banks appeared as less fit to overcome the crisis and were therefore punished with higher deposit withdrawal rates. However, the results show that the possibility of contagion cannot be ruled out. Given the obtained results, the existence of considerable discipline imposed by depositors on the financial system is proved, although some elements of contagion among institutions are also verified.

Fernández and Schumacher (1996) analyzed the characteristics of the legal framework introduced by the Convertibility Plan and its links with the evolution of the crisis in Argentina. Once again, the authors try to see if the number of failures and mergers of financial institutions observed since December 1994 was a consequence of market discipline, or if, instead, there was contagion among them. Contagion would have caused healthy and sound institutions to be equally seriously damaged by the bank run. Empirical evidence suggests that the problems suffered by the banks could be explained by specific features of their portfolios and by their consequent inability to react to such an extreme situation. Because Fernández and Schumacher show, as well, that troubled banks suffered a higher deposit withdrawal than the banks surviving the crisis, it can be inferred that the differences among these types of institutions was somehow known to depositors, who decided to reallocate their funds in favor of those institutions perceived as healthier.

Dabós (1995), focusing on the group of mutual banks, measured the relative default risk among financial institutions, using public information. The study shows the existence of differential characteristics among the banks which had problems once the crisis began and those which survived without being severely harmed. Mutual banks that disappeared after the crisis presented lower capitalization levels, weaker liquidity positions, and higher leverage. The existing differences in terms of these characteristics by November 1994 determined that some of them had a lower level of resistance to the effects of the bank run.

D'Amato, Grubisic, and Powell (1997), following this line of analysis, included a third factor as one of the possible determinants of the run: macroeconomic variables. The objective of their work was to separate the individual effects of three types of factors: bank fundamentals, macroeconomic effects of the crisis affecting the entire financial system, and a contagion component among the different groups of banks. They found empirical evidence of the presence of contagion effects, particularly among provincial, mutual, and small national retail banks. The study also presents evidence suggesting that not only the institutions' specific characteristics but also the macroeconomic effects of the shock were highly significant in the evolution of deposits. Evidence in favor of contagion effects provides justification for the establishment of a deposit insurance system.

In an empirical study comparing the performance of financial institutions during the run originated by the Tequila effect, Catena (1996) showed that those banks presenting a higher solvency position were able to face and overcome the panic more easily.

Ganapolsky and Schmukler (1998) studied the impact of the measures implemented by the authorities in response to the crisis on the short- and long-term behavior of the main financial variables: Brady bonds prices, the stock exchange index, and interest rates on peso deposits. The objective of this study was to observe the reaction of capital markets to the announcement of each measure taken by the government or the Central Bank. They concluded that those announcements which reflected the adoption of credible policies and which demonstrated a strong commitment from the regime were well received by the markets. The results showed that, in particular, the agreement with the IMF was one of the most significant and better perceived measures.

CONCLUSION

The Argentine financial system between 1991 and 1994 was characterized by the lack of a security network which kept the Central Bank from having to rescue troubled institutions, high reserve requirements as a prudential regulation in case of liquidity problems arising, high minimum capital requirements, and the lack of a lender of last resort given the limitations imposed by the convertibility regime on the Central Bank.

The new monetary and financial regime tried to make financial agents aware that the government would not be willing to rescue institutions with problems. However, the facts of the crisis led to a substantial amount of intervention.

Between December 20, 1994 and May 14, 1995, the deposits in the financial system fell by $8.040 billion. Of this fall, 71.6 percent was financed with liquidity creation in the form of reserve requirement reductions (42.28%), loans from the Central Bank to financial institutions (19.12%), and repos from the monetary authority (10.2%). The Central Bank relied to a greater extent on reserve requirement reductions for liquidity creation, which reveals that the prudential measure of maintaining high reserve requirements (with its costs) provided relief to the crisis. Thus, only 13.81 percent of the deposit withdrawal was financed by private credit cuts. The reduction in credit to the private sector would have been higher if there had not been high reserve requirements, and probably the level of economic activity would have been more seriously affected. However, not only were the current liquidity instruments used, but also the authorities modified the initial rules in order to increase their ability to intervene.

The external aid agreed between the Argentine government and the IMF was important to restore credibility. This foreign assistance negotiation not only implied an additional source of financing but also reflected the support of the international community for the way in which the crisis was being handled.

Finally, President Menem's reelection put an end to political uncertainty and reinforced the commitment to the economic plan. Only then did the return of deposits begin.

As a sequel to the crisis, a process of banking concentration was triggered. The number of banks fell 33 percent between December 1994 and September 1997. A number of public provincial banks were privatized and recently a process of purchase of national banks by international institutions can be verified. The crisis also had real effects, impacting negatively on the growth of GDP, which fell 4.4 percent during 1995. In spite of the bank run and the speculation against the peso, the convertibility regime was maintained.

NOTES

1. This package included $20 billion from the United States, $18 billion from the IMF, $10 billion from the BIS, and $2 billion from commercial banks.

2. Ganapolsky and Schmukler (1998) studied the impact of the Mexican crisis on Latin American capital markets using two different techniques: the correlation matrix and factor analysis.

3. This exchange rate prevails over the entire period of analysis until 1998.

4. Reserve requirements could be seen as a tax on the financial system. The structure established a 43-percent rate on the most inelastic deposits (checking accounts) and a 3-percent tax rate on term deposits. Minimum capital requirements were set at 11.5 percent.

5. Central Bank Communication "A" 2293 (December 28, 1994) established the reduction of reserve requirements on dollar deposits, setting them at 35 percent for checking accounts and 1 percent for term deposits. Communication "A" 2298 (January 12, 1995) resolved the lowering of reserve requirements on peso deposits and the dollarization of bank deposits in the Central Bank.

6. Modifications were also intended to facilitate the transfer of assets between those institutions that were more severely affected by deposit withdrawals and those that were not as harmed by the effects of the run. Constraints on rediscount use were relieved, and the Central Bank was allowed to grant rediscounts exceeding the net worth of the assisted institutions. These reforms were introduced by Decree 290/95 of February 27, 1995. The Trust Fund for Provincial Development was created by Decree 286/95 of February 27, 1995.

7. The Trust Fund for Bank Capitalization was created by Decree 445/95 of March 28, 1995. The establishment of the deposit insurance system was disposed by Law 24.485, which was passed on April 12, 1995, and which also created an Oversight Committee for the Trust Fund for Provincial Development (Decree 286/95) and for the Trust Fund for Bank Capitalization.

8. This was intended to avoid the moral hazard of financial institutions; that is, to keep banks from undertaking higher risk due to the existence of a Central Bank guarantee for their deposits. It was with the objective of reducing this probability that the contribution of each financial institution was established in direct relation to its level of risk. On the other hand, the fact that the insurance did not guarantee those deposits receiving high rates was an attempt to alleviate another type of moral hazard, that exercised by depositors who, when aware of the existence of a deposit insurance system guaranteeing their funds, lose incentives to behave with discipline.

9. The deposit insurance was managed by a private institution (SEDESA), whose board was integrated with the Ministry of Economy and representatives from the Central Bank and the commercial banks. Financial institutions were supposed to face the cost of the funds. Each bank had to contribute with 0.03 to 0.06 percent of its deposits, according to the risk undertaken.

REFERENCES

Arnaudo, Aldo. 1996. "La Crisis Mexicana y el Sistema Financiero Argentino." In *La Macroeconomía de los Mercados Emergentes*, edited by Gonzalo Rodríguez Prada. Madrid: Universidad de Alcalá.

Banco Central de la República Argentina (BRCA). 1995. *Boletín Monetario y Financiero*, June–July.

Bleger, Leonardo, and Guillermo Rozenwurcel. 1995. "Argentina's Banking Sector in the Nineties: From Financial Deepening to Systemic Crisis." Instituto y Universidad Torcuato Di Tella, Buenos Aires, Argentina. Mimeographed.

Catena, Marcelo. 1996. "The Argentine Banking Crisis of 1995: A Micro-Economic Analysis." Ph.D. Program, UCLA. Mimeographed.

Dabós, Marcelo. 1995. "Crisis Bancaria y Medición del Riesgo de Default: Métodos y el caso de los Bancos Cooperativos en Argentina." Universidad de San Andrés, Buenos Aires, Argentina. Mimeographed.

D'Amato, Laura, Elena Grubisic, and Andrew Powell. 1997. "Contagion, Banks Fundamentals or Macroeconomic Shock? An Empirical Analysis of the Argentine 1995 Banking Problems." Banco Central de la República Argentina, Documento de Trabajo, July.

Fernández, Roque, and Liliana Schumacher. 1996. "The Argentine Panic After the Mexican Devaluation: Did 'Convertibility' Help or Hurt?" In *Banking Crisis in Regional Blocks*. Washington, D.C.: George Washington University.

Folkerts-Landau, David, and Takatoschi Ito. 1995. "Evolution of the Mexican Crisis." In *International Capital Markets: Developments, Prospects and Policy Issues*. Washington, D.C.: IMF.

Ganapolsky, Eduardo, and Sergio Schmukler. 1998. "The Impact of Announcements and News on Capital Markets: Crisis Management in Argentina During the Tequila Effect." Working document, Banco Central de la República Argentina.

Garrido, Celso. 1996. "El Sistema Financiero en México a Principio de los Noventa: Crisis de una Reforma Contradictoria." In *La Macroeconomía de los Mercados Emergentes*, edited by Gonzalo Rodríguez Prada. Madrid: Universidad de Alcalá.

Kiguel, Miguel. 1995. "Convertibilidad: Una Historia de Tango y Tequila." Banco Central de la República Argentina. Mimeographed.

Schumacher, Liliana. 1996. "Bubble or Depositors Discipline: A Study of the Argentine Banking Panic (December 1994–May 1995)." Ph.D. diss., University of Chicago.

Schumacher, Liliana. 1997. "Information and Bank Runs—Evidence from a Contemporary System Without a Safety Net: Argentine After the 'Tequila' Shock." George Washington University, Washington, D.C.

Sotelsek, Daniel. 1995. "La Crisis Bancaria en la República Argentina en un Contexto de Tipo de Cambio Fijo." In *La Macroeconomía de los Mercados Emergentes*, edited by Gonzalo Rodríguez Prada. Madrid: Universidad de Alcalá.

10

Measuring the Default Risk of Banks: The Case of Mutual Banks in Argentina during the Tequila Banking Crisis

Marcelo Dabós

When evaluating financial entities' relative default risk, analysts often obtain information which is not of public knowledge. It is thus possible to make a different, deeper evaluation of the institution, more informed and more detailed than the evaluation made with public information. In a complete evaluation, information such as statements of sources and uses of funds, cash-flow, and so on is considered and in critical situations with short periods (weekly or even daily). The evaluations take into consideration property and management characteristics, the financial entity's competitive position in the industry, capitalization and liquidity indicators, duration mismatching, profit levels and structure indicators, efficiency indicators, composition of assets and currency mismatching indicators, portfolio concentration by debtors and by economic activity, debtors' arrears indicators, fulfillment analysis of authority norms, sensibility to macroeconomic environment, and industry situations and perspectives. All this information is reduced, according to established procedures and to the judgement of professional and experienced analysts, to a relative default risk ranking.

However, the only information available to the analyst of each and every one of the existing financial entities is, in practice, public information. A relative default risk ranking of financial entities can be built based on public information, with all the limitations implied by this.

In this chapter it is assumed that only public information is available. This public information is contained in the banks' financial statements published with a three-to-four-month lag by the Central Bank of the Argentine Republic. It includes balance sheets, income statements, contingent assets and liabilities, and statements of debtors' arrears for all the financial entities month to month.

Information about the situation of entities which have been liquidated (although, in the case of the mutual banks, there were no liquidations by May 1995), suspended, placed in the rescue trust fund, absorbed, or merged is also available. The information on the balance sheets, income statements, and statements of debtors' arrears published by the Central Bank plus the information about banks "with problems" is the only information considered in the present work.

Measuring the relative default risk of financial entities when only public information is available by using one of the proposed methods is the main motivation of this article. However, it is not the only one. The second motivation is the banking crisis which affected Argentina's financial system between December 1994 and May 1995. This crisis left a series of banks with problems (defined as those liquidated, suspended, placed in the rescue trust fund and absorbed). Those merged, at this first exploratory stage, were not considered to have problems, although that could have been the case for some of them. Several related questions are posed:

- Was there a series of characteristics already manifest before the crisis which would make a group of banks especially vulnerable to the macroeconomic shock given by the withdrawal of deposits which happened afterward?
- On the other hand, was the homogeneity of the financial institutions such before the crisis so that the financial institutions had their problems in a more or less random way?
- Are there any differential characteristics shared by those institutions which seemed to have a lower degree of resistance to the stress generated by the crisis?

PRELIMINARY ANALYSIS

The mutual banks were seriously affected by the crisis.[1] The following is a list of banks which were suspended, placed in the rescue trust fund, or absorbed by May 1995. Until this date and during the crisis concerned no mutual bank was liquidated:

Bank's Name	Problem
Aciso	Absorbed by Integrado Departamental Bank
Cooperativo del Este	Absorbed by Entre Ríos Bank
Caseros	Rescue Trust Fund
De la Ribera	Absorbed by Integrado Departamental Bank

Noroeste	Absorbed by Caseros Bank
Institucional	Absorbed by Entre Ríos Bank
Integrado Departamental	Suspended
NOAR	Absorbed by Mayo Bank
Nueva Era	Absorbed by Patricios Bank

These nine banks with problems represent 29.2 percent of the total deposits of the mutual banks by November 1994 and 24 percent of the total number of mutual banks by that date. There were thirty-eight mutual banks by November 1994.

The following coefficients were considered as indicators of the banks' situation (by November 1994):

1. equity/assets (indicator 1)
2. liabilities/equity (indicator 2)
3. immediate liquidity = (cash + public securities)/deposits (indicator 3)
4. structural liquidity = (equity – fixed assets)/liabilities (indicator 4)
5. operating expenses/liabilities (indicator 5)
6. arrears portfolio[2] – losses provisions/equity (indicator 6)
7. return on equity (indicator 7)

This selection of indicators follows traditional wisdom in the analysis of financial institutions' default risk, including the main variables considered by the CAMEL system. Indicators 1 and 2 are capitalization indicators (C), indicator 6 is an assets' quality indicator (A), indicator 7 is an earnings indicator (E), and indicators 3 and 4 are liquidity indicators (L). A preliminary approximation for management (M) in this quantitative evaluation would be given by the efficiency indicator introduced by indicator 5. The different indicators' averages for the group of mutual banks with future problems and for the rest of the mutual banks by November 1994 (that is, before the problems began the following month) are shown in Table 10.1.

The differences in indicators' averages between both groups are revealing of the pre-crisis characteristics of the mutual banks that had problems. Average capitalization is smaller for those banks who had problems. As a matter of fact, the equity/assets indicator is 6.1 percent smaller for the first group relative to the second. Conventional wisdom establishes that a smaller capitalization level is translated into a weaker solvency level. This measure (weighted by the assets' risk) has been chosen by the Basilea Agreement as the main characteristic to be considered by the regulators of a financial system. The second indicator measures the leverage level of the institution. A higher aver-

Table 10.1
Indicators' Averages for Two Groups of Mutual Banks (November 1994)

Indicator	Mutual Banks with Future Problems (9 Banks)	Rest of Mutual Banks (29 Banks)
Equity/Assets	12.5%	18.6%
Liabilities/Equity	7.3x	5.3x
Immediate Liquidity	19.1%	23.4%
Structural Liquidity	6.1%	13.1%
Operating Expenses/Liabilities	12.7%	17.5%
(Arrears Portfolio- Losses Provisions)/Equity	81.9%	62.3%
ROE	10.6%	-1.6%

age leverage is observed in those banks which had problems. As far as immediate liquidity is concerned, its average is smaller for the mutual banks with problems. Average structural liquidity is also smaller for these banks. The banks with problems present higher arrears net of losses provisions as a percentage of equity than the banks without problems. If the banks with problems were to make losses provisions for their total arrears portfolio, they would find their equity consumed by 82 percent. According to this first analysis, the banks with problems had a lighter structure relative to their liabilities. This is shown by the efficiency indicators' values.

The banks with problems, by November 1994, were more leveraged, had a higher average arrears portfolio net of losses provisions, and had a lighter operating structure. By assuming more risk and having less capital and fewer expenses relative to their operations, they managed to achieve a substantially higher ROE than the banks without problems. It should be remarked that a high profit level does not always reflect financial soundness. It could be the consequence of policies privileging short-term return over the viability of the institution in the long run. Those banks which just before the crisis enjoyed a good profit level were the ones which because of it, or in spite of it, were not able to maintain their names in the market.

Statistical Tests

To complete the analysis it is necessary to introduce statistical procedures in order to test our results in a rigorous way. We seek to establish if the distribution of the characteristics of the mutual banks measured by their indicators by November 1994 differs between the banks which later on encountered problems and the banks which did not have problems. We try to find a statistical procedure to establish if the differences observed in the characteristics between the two groups of banks are significant. Are the distributions of characteristics of the banks which had problems (using pre-crisis information) intrinsically different to those of the rest of the mutual banks, or on the other hand is it possible to declare that the distribution of characteristics of the banks which had problems was in the pre-crisis similar to the distribution of characteristics of the rest of the mutual banks?

The statistical tests frequently used to account for the heterogeneity or homogeneity we are interested in are the following:

1. Chi-squared test of homogeneity between samples
2. Kolmogorov–Smirnov test for two samples
3. Wilcoxon–Mann–Whitney ranking test

The Wilcoxon–Mann–Whitney ranking test was chosen to answer the questions given that it ranks the banks according to their indicators. These rankings are useful in the building of scores for these banks.

Wilcoxon–Mann–Whitney Ranking Test Computation

The intuitive idea is that there are two groups (or samples), one containing banks with problems (1) and one with the rest of the banks (0). Both groups have a size, in this case there are nine banks classified as 1 and twenty-nine banks classified as 0. Each group has a distribution for each of the seven indicators considered. The test is conducted on one indicator at a time. Therefore, seven tests will be performed. The idea is to test if the distribution of values of, for example, the leverage level measured as liabilities/equity is equal or not between the two groups. The null hypothesis (H_0) is that they are equal, and the alternative (H_1) is that they are not (that they differ by a constant). No assumptions about the functional form of the distributions of the indicators' values are made.

We start by arranging all the observations (the 1s and the 0s) in a sequence, from the smallest to the highest value of the indicator. Each observation is assigned a ranking according to its position in the order. The smallest is assigned number 1 and the highest number 38. Table 10.2 presents the thirty-eight mutual banks ranked according to their leverage levels, from lower to higher levels of their leverage indicators by November 1994. It also presents the classifier: 1 if it corresponds to a mutual bank with future problems or 0 if it belongs to the rest of the mutual banks.

The Wilcoxon–Mann–Whitney test is based on the property that if the null hypothesis were true (no differences between groups), then the observations in group 1 would tend to be dispersed all through the ranking, instead of being concentrated among those with smaller or higher values. Our calculations show how the observations in group 1 tend to be concentrated among the higher values for the leverage variables. To see this, the sum (S) of the rankings of the observations in group 1 is calculated: $S = 9 + 19 + 24 + 29 + 30 + 32 + 34 + 35 + 36 = 248$. After this, the distance (D) between S and the expectation of S relative to the standard deviation of S is measured. In this case, this distance is 2.4897, given that the expectation of S is 175.5 and its standard deviation is 29.12. This means that the observed values of S are 2.4897 standard deviations to the right of (are bigger than) the expected value under H_0. The test rejects H_0 if the distance is large enough. Since the number of observations is big enough, we use a standard normal distribution table to determine, in a two-tailed test, the P-value. In this case it is 1.28 percent. That is, at the usual level of 10 percent, the hypothesis of equality of the distributions is rejected.

This means that the leverage level distribution for the banks in group 1 is different from that for group 0. High leverage is a differential characteristic shared by the banks with future problems. The leverage level of the banks having problems is different from the leverage of the rest of the banks, and this difference is statistically significant. This is therefore a differential characteristic. The same test was performed for the other six indicators. Table 10.3 presents the results of the Wilcoxon–Mann–Whitney test for the seven indicators considered.

The test performed for the first indicator shows that the capitalization level in the group of banks with future problems, given pre-crisis information, was smaller than the value which would have been expected had its distribution been equal to that of the rest of the mutual banks. Given the negative distance, capitalization appears to be lower for the banks in group 1. The test clearly rejects the equality in capitalization between the two groups. Group 1 is relatively undercapitalized.

The test performed for the second indicator rejects the equality in the distribution of the leverage indicators between the two groups. The banks with future problems were significantly more leveraged.

The third test indicates that immediate liquidity for the group of banks with future problems was smaller than what it would have been if the distribution of this indicator were the same for the two groups. The test rejects the equality. Group 1 is relatively illiquid.

Table 10.2
Ranking Derived from the Computation of the Test

Ranking (liabilities/equity)	Value of liabilities/equity (in times of equity)	Group
1	0.99298	0
2	2.20214	0
3	2.40446	0
4	2.55694	0
5	2.55963	0
6	2.84982	0
7	2.89791	0
8	3.35688	0
9	4.62988	1
10	4.66703	0
11	4.96563	0
12	4.97650	0
13	5.07207	0
14	5.12420	0
15	5.19737	0
16	5.33713	0
17	5.40988	0
18	5.41872	0
19	5.50585	1
20	5.60210	0
21	5.64045	0
22	5.79582	0
23	6.29322	0
24	6.59362	1
25	6.70733	0
26	6.71025	0
27	6.98865	0
28	7.22214	0
29	7.22759	1
30	7.42975	1
31	7.45133	0
32	7.84435	1
33	7.91479	0
34	8.56320	1
35	8.69391	1
36	8.90568	1
37	9.60423	0
38	10.93480	0

Table 10.3
Inferences Based on the Test

Indicator	D	P-Value	Decision at 10%
Equity/assets	-2.4897	1.28%	Rejects equality
Liabilities/equity	2.4897	1.28%	Rejects equality
Immediate Liquidity	-1.6999	8.92%	Rejects equality
Structural Liquidity	-1.8029	7.18%	Rejects equality
Administrative expenses./Liabilities	-2.3523	1.88%	Rejects equality
(Arrears Portfolio- Losses Provisions)/Equity.	1.4251	15.28%	Accepts equality
ROE	2.4897	1.28%	Rejects equality

The test applied to the forth indicator confirms the relative low structural liquidity suffered by banks in group 1. The test rejects the equality, showing these banks had a relatively low structural liquidity level.

The test performed for indicator 5 reveals the relative lightness in the administrative structures of the banks with future problems. The test rejects the hypothesis that the distribution of this indicator is equal for the two groups of mutual banks.

The test performed for indicator 6 reveals that although the banks with problems had a higher average arrears value, the distance is not so large. It is thus accepted that the distribution of the arrears portfolio indicator is not significantly different between the two groups. This is the only indicator for which the test accepts equality.

The test performed for the ROE indicator rejects equality. However, this is not because the distance is very negative, as would have been the case had the returns of the banks with future problems been very low. The rejection is explained by the fact that these banks' returns were much higher than the returns of the rest of the banks. By November 1994, the banks with future problems presented a higher distribution of returns than expected.

There are two distances that do not have the expected sign. This is the case for indicators 5 and 7. This reveals that, although the mutual banks defined here as having problems were relatively undercapitalized, relatively overleveraged, and had relatively low liquidity and a portfolio situation not significantly different from the rest of the banks' portfolio situations (measured by indicator 6), they also differed in their operating structure and in their returns. These were banks with relatively low operating expenses relative to their liabilities. As a result, they presented a relatively high return on equity.

The tests show the high degree of heterogeneity present among mutual banks when they are analyzed using pre-crisis information. The situation and characteristics of mutual banks before the crisis were obviously not equal for all of them. There is a distribution of characteristics and situations among the banks which determines that each one of them has a different probability of having problems in the face of unfavorable changes in the environment. In confronting a stress situation, each bank has a defined tolerance. Those with a lower level of tolerance would be, on average, the first ones to fail.

MUTUAL BANKS' RELATIVE RISK QUANTITATIVE ESTIMATION

Quantitative methods are a rigorous way of putting information in order and then applying professional criteria and clarifying the assumptions implicit in the analysis. The quantitative models used to analyze banks have two main objectives. The first is to provide the researcher with a quantitative description of the banks' relative risk in order to obtain a classification of these banks based on public information. This is useful in providing numerical answers to those questions referred to banks' relative risk in a limited-information context. The second is to help monitoring entities in a context where only limited public information is available.

In order to obtain a relative risk classification and to analyze the empirical importance of the different indicators used in the model, given a context where limited public information is available, it is possible to employ five main methods:

1. the score method
2. discriminant analysis
3. linear probability model
4. logit or logistic regression
5. probit

The score method corresponds to a linear combination of the different indicators utilized. This method gives a score based on which different classified banks are ranked. Alternatively, a ranking of all the banks according to each one of the indicators can be produced and then all the rankings can be combined, in order to obtain a final ranking as a function of the partial rankings previously obtained. The discriminant analysis, linear probability model, logit, and probit differ in the specification and adjustment criteria but all have one point in common. The rule to find banks with a determined default probability (or banks with a determined probability of having problems, banks with a determined failure probability, or banks with a determined probability of bankruptcy) can in each case (with the exception of a quadratic discriminating model) be written in the following way:

$$Z = C_0 + C_1 X_1 + \ldots + C_k X_k \text{ bigger than T}$$

where the C are the estimated parameters, the X are variables (the indicators), and T is a limit value of classification. The Z in a linear probability model is the estimated default probability. The Z in a probit model is the estimated default probability which follows a normal distribution. The Z in a logit model is the estimated failure probability which follows a logistic distribution. The dependent variable assumes a value of 1 for the banks with problems and 0 for the rest.

The model can estimate a failure probability for a bank such that it would determine that it belongs to group 0 (without problems) in spite of being in group 1 (with problems). On the other hand, a bank without problems could see its probability of failure increased as new information is used and could be placed in a high default-probability status. This is the early warning property in these models.

These models are also useful to classify each of the institutions considered in the analysis in a relative risk ranking according to its estimated default probabilities. In this framework, careful analysis helps to discover peculiarities and characteristics of the institutions.

Selection of the Methods to be Employed

The score method is immediate and intuitive; however, it does not take into account in a direct way all the potential information referring to suspensions, trust fund rescues, and absorption of banks (that is, the variability produced by the crisis). The score method does not have an interpretation in terms of failure probabilities. It only provides a relative ranking. It is considered an interesting method to evaluate in a second stage due to its relative simplicity and easy computation. It can provide a very useful first approach to the problem.

Between the discriminating analysis, a linear probability model, a logit, and a probit, the most attractive choice is the probit because of its statistical properties. This chapter uses a probit model because it presents some advantages over the other alternatives. A linear probability model can produce estimated probabilities outside the 0 to 1 range, though the other three models do not have that inconvenience. The probit and logit do not depend on the assumption of multivariate normality of the independent variables as the discriminant analysis does. Finally, the Z normal scores estimated with a probit model are somewhat easier to interpret than those provided by a logit model.

Probit Model

A probit model was estimated using the dependent variable formed by the nine values (1) of banks with problems and the twenty-nine values (0) of the rest of the banks. The X variables are the seven indicators already explained, here indicated as IND1, IND2, IND3, IND4, IND5, IND6, and IND7, with values at November 1994:

Indicator	Definition
IND1	equity/assets, in %
IND2	liabilities/equity in times of equity
IND3	immediate liquidity = cash + public securities/deposits, in %
IND4	structural liquidity = equity – fixed assets/liabilities, in %
IND5	operating expenses/liabilities, in %
IND6	arrears portfolio – losses provisions/equity, in %
IND7	annualized return/equity (ROE), in %

The estimation of the probit model provides the following results:

Variable	Coefficient	Standard Error	Statist. T	P-Value
Constant	–3.644509	9.877928	–0.368955	0.7148
IND1	0.151973	0.430951	0.352647	0.7268
IND2	0.491972	0.873165	0.563435	0.5773
IND3	–0.065878	0.061411	–1.072734	0.2919
IND4	–0.075850	0.176513	–0.429714	0.6705
IND5	–0.107943	0.079987	–1.349502	0.1873
IND6	0.011726	0.016388	0.715536	0.4798
IND7	0.093530	0.047545	1.967190	0.0585
Log likelihood	–9.858895			

The model estimates failure probabilities for each bank. Based on these estimated values it can be determined if the model correctly classifies the observations in 1 and 0. The classification error of the model can thus be estimated. The T value is situated at 50 percent. If the estimated default probability is less than 50 percent, the bank is placed in 0, if it is higher, it is placed in 1. There can be two types of errors: The first type classifies a bank as 0 when it is actually 1, the second type classifies a bank as 1 when it is actually 0. The cost of each type of error (a loss function) depends on the type of application being performed.

If our main objective is the detection of banks 0 which could become 1, then the error of the second type has a lower cost. This would be indicating that a bank is 1 when it is really 0. Therefore, the model provides a warning, presenting the opportunity for a closer examination of the institution and the detection of problems. It would be worse if it did not give a warning, an error of the first type. The following is a list of correct and incorrect classifications based on pre-crisis information:

Correct classification

The estimated default probability classifies the bank as 1. The bank has serious problems in the future. It is 1.

7 cases

Error of the second type

The estimated default probability classifies the bank as 1. The bank did not have serious problems in the future. It is 0.

2 cases

Error of the first type

The estimated default probability classifies the bank as 0. The bank has serious problems in the future. It is 1.

2 cases

Correct classification

The estimated default probability classifies the bank as 0. The bank did not have serious problems in the future. It is 0.

27 cases

The percentage of correct classifications is $(27+7)/38 = 89$ percent. The percentage of incorrect classifications is $(2+2)/38 = 11$ percent. The percentage of errors is 11 percent of the total classifications done.

The low classification error provides some reassurance about the model's classification ability. To illustrate this point, a ranking with the estimated default probabilities (calculated as the value of the estimated probability based on the sample indicators' values and the estimated coefficients) can be built. This ranking is a relative risk ranking which arranges cooperative banks from less risky to riskiest, using limited information. The values of the seven indicators here considered were calculated using this limited public information by November 1994 and the coefficients estimated by the model. The rankings shown in Table 10.4 are an approximation of mutual banks' relative risk.

Table 10.4
Mutual Banks Ranking

Ranking	G	Mutual Banks	Default Probability
1	0	Local Coop. Lmtdo.	3.4E-09
2	0	Empresario de Tucumán Coop. Lmtdo.	7E-09
3	0	Vallemar Coop. Lmtdo.	2.8E-06
4	0	Nicolas Levalle Coop. Lmtdo.	0.00012
5	0	De las Comunidades Coop. Lmtdo.	0.00013
6	0	Aliancoop Coop. Lmtdo.	0.00045
7	0	C.E.S. Coop. Lmtdo.	0,00195
8	0	San José Coop. Lmtdo.	0.00434
9	0	De Balcarse Coop. Lmtdo.	0.00508
10	0	Horizonte Coop. Lmtdo.	0.00957
11	0	Credicoop Coop. Lmtdo.	0.01264
12	0	Meridional Coop. Lmtdo.	0.02628
13	1	Cooperativo de Caseros	0.02638
14	0	Nordecoop Coop. Lmtdo.	0.03623
15	0	Independencia Coop. Lmtdo.	0.04007
16	0	Carlos Pellegrini Coop. Lmtdo.	0.04167
17	0	Núcleo Coop. Lmtdo.	0.04759
18	0	Mayo Coop. Lmtdo.	0.04966
19	0	De Río Tercero Coop. Lmtdo.	0.07036
20	0	De los Arroyos Coop. Lmtdo.	0.08517
21	0	Vaf Coop. Lmtdo.	0.09855
22	0	Rural de Sunchales Coop. Lmtdo.	0.10540
23	0	Cooperativo de La Plata	0.10755
24	0	Sudecor Coop. Lmtdo.	0.13121
25	0	Coopesur Coop. Lmtdo.	0.16301
26	0	Unión Comercial e Ind. Coop. Lmtdo.	0.19212
27	0	El Hogar de Parque Patricios Coop. Lmtdo.	0.36209
28	0	Coinag Coop. Lmtdo.	0.39536
29	1	Nueva Era Coop. Lmtdo.	0.40798
30	0	Bica Coop. Lmtdo.	0.54336
31	0	Almafuerte Coop. Lmtdo.	0.54474
32	1	Cooperativo del Este Argentino Lmtdo.	0.62010
33	1	Del Noroeste Coop. Lmtdo.	0.64623
34	1	Institucional Coop. Lmtdo.	0.70076
35	1	Aciso Banco Coop. Lmtdo.	0.88017
36	1	Integrado Departamental Coop. Lmtdo.	0.92314
37	1	De La Ribera Coop. Lmtdo.	0.98786
38	1	Noar Coop. Lmtdo.	0.99018

There are seven banks which, because of their estimated default probability based on public information by November 1994, enter the problematic zone. The fact that it is possible to make such a classification with pre-crisis information is remarkable. On the other hand, within the estimated statistical error of 11 percent, neither Caseros Bank nor Nueva Era Bank were classified as problematic. However, banks such as Cooperativo del Este, Del Noroeste, Institucional, Aciso, De la Ribera, and Noar, which later on had problems, did show signs leading them to be classified as 1 according to pre-crisis information. Integrado Departamental Bank also showed a 92-percent probability of becoming problematic. A more detailed analysis of these and other groups of banks' situations leading to a more complete model than the present could be built with these quantitative methods.

CONCLUSION

The classification error obtained in this study (11%) is reasonable, especially since pre-crisis information was used. As of November 1994, of the existing mutual banks, none had really serious problems.

The analysis shows that there was a group of characteristics, manifest before the crisis, which made a group of entities especially vulnerable to the macroeconomic shock of deposit withdrawal which happened afterward. The analysis also reveals that there was a low homogeneity among mutual banks before the crisis, and therefore problems did not happen randomly to the different banks. There seemed to be some differential characteristics, measurable with public information, which caused some banks to have lower degrees of resistance to the stress generated by the crisis.

We can rely on a preliminary relative risk ranking based on which a deeper analysis of the origin of financial institutions' weaknesses can be conducted. This makes numerical sensibility or stress exercises possible.

It is possible to pinpoint the banks for which the probability of failure is increasing. Their characteristics will possibly become closer to those of the failed banks. Those institutions can be specially monitored by the banking authorities. It is thus possible to rely on a quantitative warning indicating which banks could be entering the problematic zone and to therefore adopt anticipated corrective measures. An "early warning system" could be implemented. Some of these methods can also be applied, in principle, to the measurement of bonds, companies, mutual funds, and insurance companies' relative default risk.

STATISTICAL APPENDIX

Tables 10.5 and 10.6 give more detailed information about the banks studied. The measure of bias used is defined as the third moment respect to the average of the variable divided by the standard deviation raised to the cube. The measure of bias is negative, zero, or positive for the different distributions if these are biased to the left, not biased, or biased to the right, respectively. The bias of the normal distribution is zero.

Table 10.5
Data of the Variables Used in the Analysis (by November 1994)

Bank	Depen	IND1	IND2	IND3	IND4	IND5	IND6	IND7
Aciso	1	11.31	7.84	15.13	5.42	14.83	71.7	15.1
Aliancoop	0	16.14	5.20	26.76	10.28	25.55	29.6	2.9
Almafuerte	0	15.78	5.34	30.39	4.82	9.01	96.6	10.1
Bica	0	12.97	6.71	18.95	9.53	13.28	33.3	16.0
C.E.S.	0	22.95	3.36	26.41	14.22	25.30	73.4	3.3
Carlos Pellegrini	0	14.71	5.80	29.53	9.47	13.49	17.4	7.9
Coinag	0	16.47	5.07	22.59	12.20	13.16	50.4	17.4
Cooperativo del Este	1	12.15	7.23	16.17	8.04	13.39	57.1	10.7
Nicolas Levalle	0	28.09	2.56	34.37	10.85	22.59	50.2	-6.6
Caseros	1	17.76	4.63	22.80	10.28	20.00	48.6	6.4
Coop. De la Plata	0	11.83	7.45	8.62	0.15	9.84	135.3	-32.1
Coopesur	0	12.52	6.99	22.88	4.88	20.39	60.3	7.4
Credicoop	0	15.06	5.64	31.73	9.27	20.12	8.3	12.9
De Balcarse	0	25.65	2.90	23.98	15.42	11.99	23.7	-5.2
De la Ribera	1	10.46	8.56	17.89	0.85	14.01	178.4	8.1
De las Comunidades	0	29.37	2.40	22.53	25.40	25.12	38.6	0.2
De los Arroyos	0	15.58	5.42	22.55	10.24	14.95	36.6	7.3
De Río Tercero	0	25.98	2.85	11.84	21.45	20.18	46.3	9.2
Del Noroeste	1	10.09	8.91	32.78	4.85	9.10	139.0	-0.2
Patricios	0	11.22	7.91	20.19	2.36	22.06	71.7	7.9
Emp. De Tucumán	0	50.18	0.99	55.17	91.24	9.77	44.0	10.2
Horizonte	0	16.73	4.98	17.43	7.93	22.55	77.1	-4.4
Independencia	0	16.76	4.97	20.39	9.76	13.47	43.8	-0.8
Institucional	1	13.17	6.59	14.82	9.44	13.57	35.2	17.9
Integrado Depart.	1	11.86	7.43	13.31	6.00	11.63	48.3	17.5
Local	0	9.43	9.60	22.31	1.19	27.78	177.2	-62.3
Mayo	0	12.97	6.71	31.54	3.30	13.87	38.6	1.0
Meridional	0	17.65	4.67	19.41	9.04	17.26	80.9	-4.2
Noar	1	10.32	8.69	17.10	4.21	10.10	98.0	16.2
Nordecoop	0	16.33	5.12	14.63	11.80	18.36	34.2	3.05
Núcleo	0	31.23	2.20	17.89	31.38	16.12	93.5	3.72
Nueva Era	1	15.37	5.51	22.11	6.08	7.57	61.3	4.10
Rural de Sunchales	0	13.71	6.29	18.95	6.68	13.25	87.6	-6.7
San José	0	28.11	2.56	26.69	22.14	16.50	17.3	5.4
Sudecor	0	15.15	5.60	17.02	8.42	14.07	11.2	6.6
B.U.C.I.	0	15.60	5.41	16.12	12.07	16.24	37.3	11.1
Vaf	0	12.16	7.22	26.60	4.08	19.03	132.5	-5.2
Vallemar	0	8.38	10.93	20.57	1.04	20.86	158.8	-61.2

The measure of kurtosis used is defined as the fourth moment respect to the average of the variable divided by the standard deviation raised to the fourth potency. The measure of kurtosis of the normal distribution is 3. A distribution with longer tails than the normal distribution has a measure of kurtosis greater than 3.

For example, a variable such as indicator 2 (leverage) has a measure of bias and kurtosis approximately compatible with a normal distribution (-0.003 and 2.59, respectively). The median of this variable (5.55) is approximately equal to the average (5.74).

Table 10.6
Variables' Descriptive Statistics

	IND1	IND2	IND3	IND4	IND5	IND6	IND7
Average	17.14	5.74	22.37	11.47	16.33	66.93	1.33
Median	15.26	5.55	21.34	9.15	14.89	50.31	5.91
Maximum	50.18	10.93	55.17	91.24	27.78	178.37	17.86
Min	8.38	0.99	8.62	0.15	7.57	8.29	-62.33
Stand. Dev.	8.09	2.24	8.19	14.90	5.21	44.96	17.72
Bias	2.11	-0.003	1.67	418	0.39	1.06	-2.49
Kurtosis	8.28	2.59	7.69	22.35	2.21	3.24	9.16
Obs.	38	38	38	38	38	38	38

The variable indicating profitability, indicator 7, is biased to the left with long tails, as shown by its measures of bias and kurtosis (–2.49 and 9.16, respectively). The median of the IND7 (5.91) is 4.4 times higher than its average (1.33). There are some observations with important negative values which cause the average to be smaller than the median.

NOTES

The author would like to thank Lic. Fabian Abadie, Lic. Enrique Folcini, Dr. Rolf Mantel, Dr. Pedro Pou, Dr. Liliana Schumacher, Lic. Luis Secco, Dr. Mariano Tommasi, Dr. Edgardo Zablotzky, and the participants in Segundas Jornadas de Investigación en Economía and in the seminaries dictated at the Central Bank of the Argentine Republic and at the Universidad de San Andrés for their comments. Any mistakes are exclusive responsibility of the author.

1. By December 1994, there were thirty-eight mutual banks that owned 10.1 percent of the total deposits in the system. By November 1995, there were eleven mutual banks that owned only 5.5 percent of the total deposits in the Argentinean financial system.

2. Arrears portfolio represents nonperforming loans.

BIBLIOGRAPHY

Altman, Edward I. 1968. "Financial Ratios, Discriminant Analysis and the Prediction of Corporate Bankruptcy." *Journal of Finance* September, pp. 589–609.
Altman, Edward I. 1983. *Corporate Financial Distress: A Complete Guide to Predicting, Avoiding and Dealing with Bankruptcy.* New York: John Wiley and Sons.

Altman, Edward I. 1984. "The Success of Business Failure Prediction Models: An International Survey." *Journal of Banking and Finance* 8: 171–98.

Altman, Edward I., Robert Avery, Robert A. Eisenbeis, and Joseph F. Sinkey Jr. 1981. *Application of Classification Technique in Business Banking and Finance.* Vol. 3 of *Contemporary Studies in Economic and Financial Analysis.* Greenwich, Conn.: JAI Press.

Altman, Edward I., T. Baidya, and L. M. Ribero-Dias. 1979. "Assessing Potential Financial Problems of Firms in Brazil." *Journal of International Business Studies*: Fall.

Altman, Edward I., R. Haldeman, and P. Narayanan. 1977. "ZETA Analysis: A New Model for Bankruptcy Identification." *Journal of Banking and Finance* 1: June.

Altman, Edward I., and Arnold W. Sametz. 1977. *Financial Crises: Institutions and Markets in a Fragile Environment.* New York: John Wiley and Sons.

Aziz, Abdul, and Gerald H. Lawson. 1989. "Cash Flow Reporting and Financial Distress Models: Testing of Hypotheses." *Financial Management* 18: 55–63.

Beaver, W. H. 1966. "Financial Ratios as Predictions of Failure." *Journal of Accounting Research* 4: 71–127.

Beaver, W. H. 1968. "Market Prices, Financial Ratios and the Prediction of Failure." *Journal of Accounting Research*: Autumn.

Benston, George. 1975. "How We Can Learn from Past Bank Failures." *Bankers Magazine* 158.

Bovenzi, John, James A. Marino, and Frank E. McFadden. 1983. "Commercial Bank Failure Prediction Models." *Economic Review* (Federal Reserve Bank of Atlanta) 68 (November): 14–26.

Castagna, A. D., and Z. P. Matolcsy. 1981. "The Prediction of Corporate Failure: Testing the Australian Experience." *Australian Journal of Management*: June.

Collins, Robert A., and Richmond D. Green. 1982. "Statistical Models for Bankruptcy Forecasting." *Journal of Economics and Business* 34: 349–54.

Cosslett, Stephen R. 1981. "Efficient Estimation of Discrete Choice Models." In *Structural Analysis of Discrete Data with Econometric Applications*, edited by C. Manski and D. McFadden. Cambridge: MIT Press.

Deakin, E. 1972. "A Discriminant Analysis of Predictors of Business Failure." *Journal of Accounting Research* 10.

De Groot, Morris H. 1975. *Probability and Statistics.* Reading, Mass.: Addison-Wesley.

Duff & Phelps and MCM Investment Research. 1993. *Banking Comparative Statistics.* Chicago: Duff & Phelps and MCM Investment Research. Aplican método de scoring para hacer un ránking de todos los bancos de Estados Unidos que tienen sus depósitos asegurados por la F.D.I.C.

Eisenbeis, Robert A. 1977. "Financial Early Warning Systems: Status and Future Directions." *Issues in Bank Regulation* 1: 8–12.

Eisenbeis, Robert A., Gary G. Gilbert, and Robert B. Avery. 1973. "Investigating the Relative Importance of Individual Variables and Variable Subsets in Discriminant Analysis." *Communications in Statistics* 2: 205–19.

Federal Reserve Bank of Atlanta. 1983. "Warning Lights for Bank Soundness, Special Issue on Commercial Bank Surveillance." *Economic Review* 68 (November).

Fischer, R. A. 1936. "The Use of Multiple Measurements in Taxonomic Problems." *Annals of Eugenics.*

Flannery, Mark J., and Jack M. Guttentag. 1979. "Identifying Problem Banks." Paper presented at the Conference on Bank Structure and Competition, Federal Reserve Bank of Chicago, 3–4 May, Chicago.

Gahlon, James M., and Robert L. Vigeland. 1988. "Early Warning Signs of Bankruptcy Using Cash Flow Analysis." *Journal of Commercial Bank Lending* 71 (December): 4–15.

Gheva, David, and Meir Sokoler. 1982. "An Alternative Approach to the Problem of Classification: The Case of Bank Failures in Israel." *Journal of Bank Research* 12: 228–38.

Hanweck, Gerald A. 1977. "Predicting Bank Failures." Research paper in Banking and Financial Economics, Financial Studies Section, Board of Governors of the Federal Reserve System.

Ho, Thomas, and Anthony Saunders. 1980. "A Catastrophe Model of Bank Failure." *Journal of Finance* (December): 1189–207.

Joy, O. Maurice, and John O. Tollefson. 1975. "On the Financial Applications of Discriminant Analysis." *Journal of Financial and Quantitative Analysis* 10: 723–39.

Korobow, Leon. 1983. "Measuring and Managing Bank Risk: Some Recent History." Paper presented to the Third International Symposium on Forecasting, sponsored by the Wharton School, 5 June, Philadelphia.

Korobow, Leon, and David Stuhr. 1975. "Toward Early Warning of Changes in Bank's Financial Condition: A Progress Report." *Monthly Review* (Federal Reserve Bank of New York), July, pp. 157–65.

Korobow, Leon, David Stuhr, and Daniel Martin. 1976. "A Probabilistic Approach to Early Warning Changes in Bank Financial Condition." *Monthly Review* (Federal Reserve Bank of New York), July, pp. 187–94.

Korobow, Leon, David Stuhr, and Daniel Martin. 1977. "A Nationwide Test of Early Warning Research in Banking." *Quarterly Review* (Federal Reserve Bank of New York), Autumn.

Maddala, G. S. 1983. *Limited-Dependent and Qualitative Variables in Econometrics.* Cambridge: Cambridge University Press.

Manski, Charles F., and Steven R. Lerman. 1977. "The Estimation of Choice Probabilities from Choice Based Samples." *Econometrics* 45: 1977–88.

Martin, Daniel. 1977a. "Early Warning of Bank Failure." *Journal of Finance*, 1st Quarter.

Martin, Daniel. 1977b. "Early Warning of Bank Failure: A Logit Regression Approach." *Journal of Banking and Finance* 1.

Meyer, P. A., and H. W. Pifer. 1970. "Prediction of Bank Failure." *Journal of Finance* (September): 853–68.

Ohlson, J. A. 1980. "Financial Ratios and the Probabilistic Prediction of Bankruptcy." *Journal of Accounting Research* 18: 109–31.

Pany, Kurt, and Lawrence F. Sherman. 1979. "Information Analysis of Several Large Failed Banks." *Journal of Bank Research* (Autumn): 145–51.

Pettway, Richard H., and Joseph Sinkey Jr. 1980. "Establishing On-Site Bank Examination Priorities: An Early Warning System Using Accounting and Market Information." *Journal of Finance* (March).

Pettway, Richard H. 1980. "Potencial Insolvency, Market Efficiency, and Bank Regulation of Large Commercial Banks." *Journal of Finance and Quantitative Analysis* 15: 219–36.

Putnam, Barron. 1981. "Computer Screening Methods Employed by the Five Financial Regulatory Institutions to Identify Banks Having Actual or Potential Financial Problems."

Putnam, Barron. 1983. "An Empirical Model of Financial Soundness: A Case Study for Bank Holding Companies." Ph.D. diss., George Washington University, Washington, D.C.

Rose, Peter S., and William L. Scott. 1978. "Risk in Commercial Banking: Evidence from Postwar Failures." *Southern Economic Journal* 45: 90–106.

Santomero, Anthony M., and Joseph D. Vinso. 1977. "Estimating the Probability of Failure for Commercial Banks and the Banking System." *Journal of Banking and Finance* 1: 185–205.

Sharpe, William F., and Gordon J. Alexander. 1990. *Investments.* 4th ed. Englewood Cliffs, N.J.: Prentice Hall.

Shick, Richard A., and Lawrence F. Sherman. 1980. "Bank Stock Prices as an Early Warning System for Changes in Condition." *Journal of Bank Research* 11: 136–46.

Simon, Carol Jean. 1980. "Predicting the Failure of Credit Unions: An Application of Multivariate Logit Analysis." Master's thesis, Massachusetts Institute of Technology.

Sinkey, Joseph. 1975a. "The Failure of United States National Bank of San Diego: A Portfolio and Performance Analysis." *Journal of Bank Research* 6: 8–24.

Sinkey, Joseph. 1975b. "A Multivariate Statistical Analysis of the Characteristics of Problem Banks." *Journal of Finance* (March): 21–38.

Sinkey, Joseph. 1977. "Identifying Large Problem/Failed Banks: The Case of Franklin National Bank of New York." *Journal of Financial and Quantitative Analysis,* pp. 779–800.

Sinkey, Joseph. 1978. "Identifying Problem Banks: How Do the Banking Authorities Measure a Bank's Risk Exposure?" *Journal of Money, Credit and Banking* 10: 184–93.

Sinkey, Joseph. 1979. *Problem and Failed Institutions in the Commercial Bank Industry.* Vol. 4 of *Contemporary Studies in Economic and Financial Analysis.* Greenwich, Conn.: JAI Press.

Sinkey, Joseph, and David A. Walker. 1975. "Problem Banks: Identification and Characteristics." *Journal of Bank Research* 5: 208–17.

Stuhr, David P., and Robert Van Wicklen. 1974. "Rating and Financial Condition of Banks: A Statistical Approach to Aid Bank Supervision." *Monthly Review* (Federal Reserve Bank of New York), September, pp. 233–38.

Sundararajan, V., and Tomás J. T. Baliño, eds. 1991. *Banking Crises: Cases and Issues.* Washington, D.C.: International Monetary Fund.

PART III

BANK REGULATORY ISSUES

11

Is Prudential Bank Regulation Effective?

Benton E. Gup

Bank regulators throughout the world must deal with banking crises, changing financial technologies, consolidation, contagion, deregulation, globalization, nonbank providers of financial services, and more. To a large extent, innovations in information and financial technology have linked financial markets together, so a financial crisis that began in Thailand in July 1997 was quickly transmitted to other countries throughout the world (Moreno 1998). Consequently, the safety and soundness of banks in other Asian countries, Russia, the United States, and elsewhere were adversely affected. In general terms, prudential regulation deals with the safety and soundness of financial institutions. It also provides bank depositors protection against fraud and malpractice. This chapter presents an overview of bank regulation in various countries and questions whether prudential bank regulation is effective.

PURPOSES OF REGULATION

Stigler's (1971) seminal article, "The Theory of Economic Regulation," declared that the state has one basic resource that is not shared by even the mightiest of its citizens: the power to coerce. The power to coerce includes taxation, subsidies, control over entry, laws affecting substitutes and compliments, and price fixing. Given the power to coerce, how does regulation affect banks? Kane (1988, 346–47) provides a starting point for answering that question by pointing out that regulation consists of efforts to monitor, discipline, or coordinate the behavior of financial institutions to achieve some greater good. According to the Organization for Economic Cooperation and Development (OECD) (*Banks Under Stress* 1992, 31), the greater good includes (1) prevention of systemic risk, (2) prevention of individual risk, and (3) promoting systemic efficiency. Fostering an efficient and competitive banking system is another objective of bank regulation (Spong 1990). Dewatripoint and Tirole (1994, 31) claim that regulation is needed to protect small depositors. Freixas and Rochet (1997, 263–64) add that small depositors tend to be uninformed, and that some of their deposits are used as a means of payment. Because small depositors are uninformed, it is unlikely that reducing deposit insurance coverage or limiting systemwide insurance coverage will provide depositor discipline on bank risk taking.[1]

Edwards (1988, 115–16) states that regulation should be used to interfere with the natural and competitive evolution of the market structure in order to prevent monopoly power. Moreover, if size by itself carries with it undesirable features, then it too should be regulated. In a historical context, American public opinion has always mistrusted large corporations, including banks. It is said that Woodrow Wilson created the Federal Reserve to take power away from J. P. Morgan and his bank, which some believed had become the nation's de facto central bank (Roe 1994, 40).

Benston (1986, 2) claims that most of the historical reasons for regulating banks are no longer relevant. He lists the reasons as taxation of banks as monopoly suppliers of money, the prevention of centralized power, bank failures and effects of failures on the economy, the provision of banking services as a social goal, support of housing to allocate credit as a social goal, and the prevention of invidious discrimination and unfair dealing against persons. Eisenbeis (1986) reached a different conclusion. He stated that the rationale for restricting banking activities suggests that the traditional concerns for economic efficiency, safety and soundness, concentration of power, and conflicts of interest continue to be valid.

There are other purposes of regulation as well. Alan Greenspan (U.S. House 1997), chairman of the Federal Reserve, stated that the Federal Reserve is particularly sensitive to how regulatory and supervisory postures (e.g., capital, liquidity, and loan loss reserves) influence bank behavior, because they directly influence the manner and speed with which monetary policy actions work. In this connection, bank regulation is also an aid in financing government borrowing. In contrast, Goodfriend and King (1988, 219) claim that there is a mainstream professional consensus that monetary policy can be accomplished without supporting financial regulations.

Schwartz (1988, 39) asserts that the main concern with banks is that a widespread failure of banks could lead to a drastic reduction in the money supply with disastrous effects on economic activity. In emerging economies, banks bear the brunt of interest rate increases and they are necessary to defend a currency. Therefore, issues of solvency and liquidity in the banking system "quickly move to the top of the agenda in countries experiencing financial distress" (Folkerts-Laundau and Ito 1995, 8). As increasing numbers of emerging countries are integrated into global capital markets, they will become more vulnerable to external developments, such as cycles changes in industrial countries and shocks in major markets. The 1987 stock market crash and the Mexican peso crisis of December 1994 demonstrate how disturbances in one market may spread to others (Folkerts-Laundau and Ito 1995, 26).

The fact that one incident may trigger another raises concerns about systemic risk. Systemic risk occurs when bank failures are potentially contagious, and then only if the losses exceed a bank's capital by enough to produce losses at creditor banks that exceed their capital, forcing that bank into insolvency, and it cascades on to other creditor banks (Kaufman and Kroszner 1996, 7). Federal Reserve Governor Meyer (1998) argues, "The possibility of a systemic failure of the banking system, and the moral hazard incentives created by the safety net that is designed to contain systemic risk, *require* some government supervision of banks." Robert T. Parry (1997), president of the Federal Reserve Bank of San Francisco, points out the during the 1987 stock market crash, the Fed, fearing systemic risk, provided indirect "lender of last resort" support, but not the regulation of stock brokerage firms. Thus, the possibility of systemic risk may be a necessary but not sufficient condition to justify regulation.

The IMF claims that banking laws and prudential regulation seek to (1) establish policies that allow only viable banks to operate; (2) limit excessive risk taking; (3) establish accounting, valuation, and reporting rules; and (4) provide corrective measures and restrictions for weak institutions (Folkerts-Landau and Lindgren 1998, 11).

Finally, it can be argued that one purpose of prudential regulation is to facilitate and minimize the cost of exit from the banking system when individual banks fail or there is a banking crisis.

It is clear that prudential regulation means different things to different people and organizations. The concept involves a variety of areas ranging from safety and soundness to consumer protection.

THEORIES OF REGULATION

Private Market Regulation

William McDonough (1997, 9), president of the Federal Reserve Bank of New York, has said, "As financial institutions and their activities become more complex, diversified, and global in nature, I believe that market discipline will become an even more important ally of the supervisor than it is now." Market discipline and private market regulation refer to the mechanisms that signal the behavior of firms to holders of debt and equity. A study by Nagarajan and Sealey (1997) found that reliance on market forces to help alleviate the moral hazard problem inherent in deposit insurance was ineffective in lowering bank risk. Boot and Greenbaum (1993) found that when banks raised funds, the cost of funds was related to the bank's reputation. There were lower costs when they invested in safe assets and higher costs when they invested in risky assets. Wall (1989) claims that puttable subordinated debt would add market discipline because the debtholders would be responsible for the solvency and riskiness of the banks that issue those instruments.

Private market regulation is exemplified in stock markets, such as the New York Stock Exchange. Stock market prices are considered efficient because they reflect all available information. This occurs because the listed firms are relatively transparent, and they are monitored continuously by securities analysts, the media, and investors, and changes in stock prices signal managers about what stockholders expect them to do in very general terms. It is worth noting that monitoring firms is not the same as changing management decisions or operations.

There is little evidence that the market for publicly traded corporate debt is as efficient as the stock market, and there is even less evidence that privately placed debt is efficient in controlling the behavior of firms. Consider the Korean *chaebols*, which are large industrial groups of firms. The firms within these groups have crossguarantees of debt that may be five or six times their equity. One would expect the inside debt holders to encourage their related firms to manage their funds prudently. However, that was not the case. In 1997, Hanbo Steel, Kia Motors, and other debt-burdened *chaebols* went bankrupt. Similarly, in the United States most of the firms that go bankrupt have excess debts, and debt holders did not prevent them from going bankrupt. In fact, the high debt levels may have contributed to the bankruptcies.

Nagashima (1997, 210), in an analysis of the banking problems in Japan during the 1990s, stated that "market checks did not function as they should have." He goes on to explain how banks lent imprudently and concentrated their loans in real estate. He states part of the failure of the market to work was due to a lack of transparency and accounting data on the institutions.

Private market regulation works to a degree. Consider the case of Drexel Burnham Lambert Group, Inc. This firm was best known for its junk bonds that were sold to savings and loan associations and others. In the late 1980s, Drexel was in financial trouble. When it was clear that federal bank regulators would not pressure banks to lend to the distressed holding company, Drexel Burnham Lambert Group, Inc. filed for Chapter 11 bankruptcy in 1990 (Layne 1990; Trigaux 1990).

Other firms were not willing to provide funds to support it. Thus, it is clear that private market regulation has limitations.

Accordingly, Shirakawa, Okina, and Shiratsuka (1997) argue that the key issue for bank regulators is to determine what kinds of public intervention are necessary to reinforce the effectiveness of private market regulation. Shirakawa, Okina, and Shiratsuka go on to say that "even if private market regulation in the globalized market gains strength and market discipline plays a core role in maintaining stability of the financial system, we cannot say with confidence that systemic risk which shakes the global financial system will never occur" (p. 48).

Greenspan (1997) examined historical evidence from U.S. history and concluded that in the future, as in the past, we need to place greater reliance on private market regulation. No chartered banks in the United States failed until massive fraud brought down the Farmers Exchange Bank in Rhode Island in 1809. Thereafter, a series of macroeconomic shocks—the War of 1812, the depression of 1819–1820, and the panic of 1837—resulted in large numbers of failures. In the absence of those shocks, the stability of the banking industry reflected private market discipline. With respect to current times, he concluded that rapidly changing technology is rendering much government regulation irrelevant. While it may be irrelevant, the U.S. Treasury (1991, x), in *Modernizing the Financial System*, claims that bank regulation and supervision helps provide a substitute for the market discipline removed by deposit insurance.

Greenspan (1997) said that the self-interest of industry participants generates private market regulation. He used clearinghouses and exchanges as examples of self-regulation. They establish margins and capital requirements to protect the interest of their members. What he failed to say is that there is continuous monitoring by participants because of their daily transactions. Moreover, their debts are cleared at the end of the day or shortly thereafter. This differs significantly from monitoring that is provided by holders of long-term debts.

Recent federal legislation has placed greater emphasis on the role of market regulation. Provisions of the Federal Deposit Insurance Corporation Improvement Act of 1991 impose higher capital standards which shift more risk to shareholders. In addition, changes in depositor preference for payoffs puts creditors and uninsured depositors behind insured depositors if a bank is liquidated. The notion that banks should issue more subordinated debt to the public also has been suggested as a means of establishing market discipline.

Market Failure Theory

Market failure theory argues that regulations are created politically to provide a means to remedy suboptimal equilibrium that would exist in a private, unregulated industry (Garcia 1992). Regulatory bodies are supposed to reduce the inefficiencies caused by market failures. One way to do this is to reduce price competition. The rationale for market restrictions is that if price competition were allowed to prevail, it might undermine the solvency of financial institutions. Limits on interest rates that can be paid on deposits is one example of price controls. By the 1990s, most major countries had eliminated such controls (*Banks Under Stress* 1992, 41). Another technique involves the limitation of powers. Market-restrictive laws lead to segmentation and the development of specialized financial institutions. For example, laws restricting banks from investment banking, such as the Glass–Steagall Act, led to specialized securities firms in the United States and elsewhere (*Banks Under Stress* 1992, 32).

However, such laws per se did not cause fragmentation of the banking system. Fragmentation began in the nineteenth century. Following the destruction of the Second Bank of the United States by Andrew Jackson's veto of the bill to recharter it, each state established its own banking laws, which limited banking activities. According to Roe (1994, 58, 78–79), state banks disliked the Second Bank, which competed with them and could control them. Therefore, the states established unit banking laws that kept institutions small and protected them at that time. When Congress created national banks, they were national in name, but local in operation. The politically strong banks also helped to keep some large New York insurers from becoming the first truly national American financial institutions at the turn of the century. Thus, American federalism contributed to the fragmentation of the financial system.

Regulatory Capture

Regulatory capture means that regulations are created politically to serve some distributional interest. Becker (1983) claims that government corrects market failures with the view that they favor the politically powerful. Regulations, subsidies, and other political instruments are used to create, preserve, and allocate wealth. In this case, the banks have a lot at stake, and they play a significant role in shaping the legislation that affects them. Peltzman (1989) extends that thought and argues that regulation is a way to allocate economic rents. Regulations serve producer's interests, creating cartels which raise prices. Nevertheless, Peltzman points out that regulations that generated rents can be undermined. In the case of financial institutions, they were undermined by product innovations. Thus, money market funds grew at the expense of banks that had limits on the interest that they could pay on deposits.

There is a symbiotic relationship between banks and regulators. Garten (1991, 147) finds that bank regulatory strategies that work best are those that contribute to the profitability of the industry. Bank regulators may be thought of as investors in the banking industry who seek to maximize their own investment. The most significant regulatory reforms in recent years have occurred at the agency level, where there has been a gradual elimination of banking products restrictions.

Deregulation

Peltzman (1989) asserts that regulations create incentives for wealth dissipation, which makes restoration of the preregulation status quo more attractive than continuing regulation and deregulation. The relaxation by the Board of Governors of twenty-eight "firewalls" that separated banks from underwriting activities is a case in point (U.S. Senate 1997). The concept of making laws and then changing them is not limited to the 1990s. Thomas Jefferson, in a letter to Samuel Kercheval in 1816, said, "I am not an advocate for frequent changes in laws and constitutions, but laws and institutions must go hand in hand with the progress of the human mind. As that becomes more developed, more enlightened, . . . with the change of circumstances, institutions must advance to keep pace with the times."

REGULATORY CONCERNS

The U.S. Treasury (1991, x), in *Modernizing the Financial System*, states that there has not always been a satisfactory regulatory mechanism in the United States for the prompt resolution of banking problems. There may be as many as four bank regulators involved in the affairs of a single bank, and no single regulator has either the full information or clear authority and responsibility for decisive, timely action that is required to deal with problem institutions. Garten (1991, viii) points out that the form of regulations is often shaped by practical constraints on agencies' ability to enforce particular policies. Although in theory some regulatory goals may be desirable, in practice they cannot be implemented effectively. Therefore, proponents of changes in banking laws must consider how regulators can implement them.

A key issue in regulation is how regulatory agencies impose their controls on the management actions of privately owned firms that must respond to market forces. Their ability to impose controls is limited by significant costs for both monitoring and enforcement. In the United States, monitoring is provided by on-site examinations, periodic reports provided by the banks, and securities market information for banks with publicly traded securities (typically, large banks). Enforcement takes the form of regulations and the implied threat and use of disciplinary actions for the violators. Thus, Garten (1991, 24) states that the problem of regulation becomes circular: Regulation requires monitoring to detect violations of regulations. However, monitoring requires better enforcement of regulations in order to discourage violations that regulators cannot monitor. Banks have little incentive to aid regulators in their monitoring efforts beyond the minimum required by law.

Risk

Greenspan (1993, 3) has stated that the legislative and regulatory process has not adequately determined how much risk is optimal. Recent banking legislation was a reaction to perceived excesses. He cited the real estate appraisal requirements of FIRREA (Financial Institutions Reform, Recovery, and Enforcement Act 1989), which were designed to eliminate excesses in commercial real estate and development lending, but they also constrained bank lending to small businesses. Stated otherwise, toughened examination standards of the late 1980s were in response to lending excesses of the 1980s, but they also contributed to the credit crunch of the 1990s.

Beyond Regulation

Dick Kovacevich, Chairman of Norwest, said that "banking is dead. . . . Banking is necessary but banks are not" (Nocera 1998). By that he means that banks must offer nonfinanical services if they are to survive. Accordingly, the merger of Travelers and Citicorp is a logical extension of such services. However, it tests the limits of government regulations. Before the Travelers–Citicorp merger was announced in April 1998, the Basle Committee on Banking Supervision recognized that financial conglomerates and complex organizations were blurring the distinctions between banks, insurance companies, and securities companies, and are beyond the scope of a single regulator. The problem is exacerbated when the financial conglomerate's activities are international in scope. In February 1998, the Basle Committee issued *Supervision of Financial Conglomerates* to address some of these issues. Nevertheless, government regulations lag market developments. In the United States, major changes in banking laws were enacted after the Great Depression in the 1930s and after the savings and loan debacle in the 1980s. Following the passage of such legislation, market participants find loopholes in laws to circumvent the laws. By way of illustration, a Bank Administration Institute/McKinsey & Company study, *Building Better Banks* (1996), claims that new banks, such as Merrill Lynch, Fidelity Investments, and GE Capital, are not subject to the same competitive restrictions as old bank holding companies. Likewise, Bell Atlantic and Sears Roebuck gain access to the payments system through the banks they acquire. Moreover, changes in payments technology, such as the Internet and electronic cash, are outpacing regulations. Finally, competition gives rise to substitute products that may not be subject to banking regulations. The growth of money market mutual funds is one example. Thus, government regulations enacted in response to crises may not be suitable to meet changing market conditions.

Role of Government

Eisenbeis (1995, 73) states that there is a substantial body of evidence that government actions have played a significant role in both contributing to crises and mitigating them. Friedman and Schwartz (1963) argued that monetary actions contributed to the duration and magnitude of the Great Depression. The Federal Reserve's failure to provide liquidity to nonmember banks and lending only on sound collateral added to the number of bank failures that occurred. Monetary policy actions to fight inflation in the early 1980s led to a severe recession. Monetary authorities rely on financial institutions to serve as an effective mechanism for the transmission of monetary policy. However, deregulation and the globalization of world financial markets has facilitated the circumvention of domestic credit restrictions. It has also blurred the distinction between banks and other financial institutions.

REGULATORY FAILURES

A former bank regulator said, "Yes, supervisors can help clean up oil spills, but they can't prevent them—only management can do that with the proper controls" (*Building Better Banks* 1996, 71). The cause of most bank failures is loans that went bad. Within that broad category, real estate loans stand out because they have contributed to more bank failures than any other loan category. In this regard, macroeconomic policies have contributed to boom and bust cycles in Japan, South Korea, Thailand, and the United States that resulted in asset value deflation and ultimately in loan losses. Sheng (1996, 15) states, "The deterioration of bank portfolios and their rescue by central banks or the state have large monetary and fiscal implications because of feedback effects that lead to a vicious cycle of macro-economic instability." Thus, macroeconomic shocks caused our most severe banking crises. In discussing the key aspects of a framework for a sound financial system, an IMF report stated, "An unstable macroeconomic environment is the principle source of vulnerability in the financial system" (Folkerts-Landau and Lindgren 1998).

The Basle Committee on Banking Supervision's *Core Principles for Effective Banking Supervision* (1997) recognized the importance of macroeconomic policies. Their preconditions for effective banking supervision state, "Providing sound and sustainable macroeconomic policies are not within the competence of banking supervisors. Supervisors, however, will need to react if they perceive that existing polices are undermining the safety and soundness of the banking system. In the absence of sound macro-economic policies, banking supervisors will be faced with a virtually impossible task." Even if governments attempt to have stable macroeconomic polices, external factors over which they have no control can raise havoc with banks. The impact of oil shocks and speculative attacks on currency such as occurred in the European exchange market in the early 1990s are two examples.[2] The 1997 financial crises in Southeast Asia demonstrate the effects of government-directed investment policies—so called "crony capitalism"—and foreign exchange polices creating conditions that contribute to large-scale failures of banks and other firms.

While one can think of reasons why prudential bank regulation might have contributed to bank failures in developing countries, the following examples are from the United States.

Failure of the Federal Savings and Loan Insurance Corporation (FSLIC), 1989

The success or failure of regulatory agencies is tied to the financial health of the industries that they regulate. So it was that the failure of hundreds of thrift institutions during the 1980s resulted in the 1989 bankruptcy of the Federal Savings and Loan Insurance Corporation that insured those thrifts. Congress reacted to the thrift crises by abolishing the Federal Home Loan Bank Board that regulated thrifts, and it transferred its supervisory authority to the Office of Thrift Supervision (OTS), which now insures thrift deposits (Garten 1991, 33).

Examiner Performance

Regulators need accurate and timely financial information for the early detection of troubled banks. Most information comes from regular on-site safety and soundness examinations. A summary of studies made by the FDIC (Hanc 1996) concerning the effectiveness of CAMEL ratings of 1 to 5 concluded that they identified most banks that required supervisory action well before 1,600 banks failed in the 1980–

1994 period. However, about 16 percent of the banks that failed were not identified at least two years prior to their failure. Of 260 failed banks that were not identified early, fifty-seven were not detected within twelve months of failure and nine were not detected within six months of failure (*History of the Eighties* 1997, 433–37). Another way to look at the data is that only 46 percent of the banks that failed within two years had CAMEL ratings of 4 or 5. This suggests that CAMEL ratings have severe limitations. For example, they are not forward looking, and they do not take into account local economic conditions that may adversely affect the bank.

The GAO reviewed seventy-two banks that had capital adequacy problems in 1988 (U.S. General Accounting Office 1991, 5, 43). They found that examiners often preferred to work informally with bank managers and directors to resolve problems because they lacked a clear mandate and incentives to take more forceful corrective action. While their goal was to close banks as soon as the equity was exhausted, the informal approach did not work. The 1991 failure of the Bank of New England (BNE) is a case in point. In 1992, the "tripwires" which require prompt correct action with respect to capital adequacy were enacted into law.

Bank of New England

Walter J. Connolly (U.S. House 1991), former chairman of the Bank of New England, said that the Bank of New England, created by the merger to two banks in 1985, "was the first superregional bank. . . . A New England Bank for New Englanders, positioned to survive in an increasingly hazardous environment." It failed.

Bank regulators publicly acknowledged that BNE had problems in December 1989, but they were aware of problems as early as 1985. On June 13, 1991, in a hearing before Congress (U.S. House 1991, 179), it was declared that the Office of the Comptroller of the Currency (OCC), BNE's primary federal bank regulator, "failed to accomplish their supervisory responsibilities." Their ability to meet their responsibilities depends on the evaluation of "sufficient relevant, accurate, and timely information." According to the report, the OCC failed to obtain the information necessary to determine the bank's soundness, appraise its management, or identify and follow-up with corrective actions by management necessary to strengthen the bank. In all fairness, bank regulators were not the only ones who did not realize how serious conditions were at BNE. The bank's managers were still buying stock in BNE as late as a year before its failure (Litan 1997, 289).

Equally important, the speed of failure may be increasing. Consider the case of Barings Brothers and Co. Ltd. In a twenty-eight-day period, a rogue trader speculating on Japanese stocks on the Singapore futures exchange brought down the bank. Had examiners been in the bank on day one, it would have looked sound. On day twenty-seven, however, it was too late to save the bank, and it failed in 1995. It had losses of $1.4 billion versus capital of about $500 million (Gup 1998).

THE COST OF REGULATION AND FAILURES

Costs can be measured in terms of failures, resolutions, and cost efficiency at banks. The Federal Financial Institutions Examination Council and the American Bankers Association found that regulatory costs ranged from 6 to 8 percent of noninterest expense. The BAI/ McKinsey report, *Building Better Banks* (1996, 7, 27, 28), estimated FIDICIA added 2 to 3 percent to the previous cost estimates.

A 1992 survey of almost 1 thousand banks that are members of the American Bankers Association estimated that the cost of regulatory compliance, exclusive of deposit insurance premiums, examination fees, and foregone interest on sterile deposits, was at an annual rate of $10.7 billion (*The Burden of Bank Regulation* 1992). Part of these costs are due to the fact that banks are required to perform tasks that were once reserved for government. For example, the Bank Secrecy Act requires banks and other financial institutions to provide reports on large currency transactions in order to deter money laundering. The Community Reinvestment Act (CRA) compels banks to meet social goals that were formerly the purview of government (*Righting the Regulatory Balance* 1992).

In theory, if banks are closed when their net worth is zero, losses should be minimal. However, according to a U.S. General Accounting Office study (1991, 42), from 1985 to 1989, the estimated losses from resolving 896 failed banks was $109 billion, or 16 percent of their assets. James (1991) found that the losses realized in bank failures in the United States from 1982 to 1988 averaged 30 percent of the failed banks' assets, and the direct expense associated with the closures was 10 percent of the assets.

Goldstein and Turner (1996) report the results of an unpublished study by Caprio and Klingebiel (1996a, 1996b) that shows the losses or resolution costs of severe banking crises in industrial countries: Spain (1977–1985) was almost 17 percent of GDP, Finland (1991–1993) was 8 percent of GDP, Sweden (1991) was 6 percent of GDP, Norway (1987– 1989) was 4 percent, and the U.S. savings and loan crisis (1984–1991) was 3 percent. In developing countries, losses were higher: Venezuela (18%), Bulgaria (14%), Mexico (12–15%), Hungary (10%). The most expenses were in Argentina (55%), Chile (40%), and Côte d'Ivoire (25%). Kaminsky and Reinhart (1996) report that the cost of the U.S. savings and loan crisis was about 4 percent of GDP.

As previously noted, one purpose of prudential regulation is to manage the exit policy for banks. Part of this involves the decision as to who is going to bear the cost of failures. Should it be depositors, creditors, or taxpayers? One could even argue that a monetary policy designed to bail out banks, such as occurred in Japan, where short-term interest rates were kept low to facilitate low-cost borrowing, puts the cost on the capital markets. Along that line, one could also consider the marginal cost of regulation—the cost of regulation versus market discipline. The answer to the question of who should pay is beyond the scope of this chapter.

INTERNATIONAL EFFORTS AT REGULATION

Harmonization

International banking regulators have undertaken major efforts to harmonize prudential standards. Harmonization refers to uniform regulations as well as to stemming the divergent standards that are applied to similar activities of different financial institutions. The Basle Committee on Banking Supervision, a committee of national financial supervisors, has led the effort to establish uniform standards. In 1988, the Basle Committee established uniform risk-based capital standards for banks, and later, methods for dealing with trading risks. In the European Union (EU), harmonization is reflected in a number of directives and recommendations. For example, the Second Banking Directive, adopted in 1989, establishes home-country control and mutual recognition of national supervisory regimes. It also established a listing of banking activities subject to mutual recognition. These include leasing, lending, guarantees, investment banks, money brokering, and more. Although the focus here is on the Basle Committee, one should recognize that other international supervisory groups coordinate some of their activities with the Basle Committee.

The EU's Own Funds Directive and Solvency Ratio Directive are generally consistent with the recommendations of the Basle Committee. With respect to services offered by different types of financial institutions, some countries are eliminating the distinctions between banks and nonbank financial institutions for purposes of regulation. For example, in France, the 1984 Bank Law eliminated the distinction between commercial banks, savings banks, and medium- and long-term credit banks. In 1990, the Banking Act in Switzerland was amended to put nonbank financial institutions and underwriters under the same regulations as banks (*Banks Under Stress* 1992, 51–54; U.S. Department of Treasury 1994, 524–32).

Finally, the International Monetary Fund becomes involved in bank regulation during banking crises. In the crises in Southeast Asia, for example, a centerpiece of the IMF programs included closure of financial institutions that were not viable, recapitalization of undercapitalized institutions, close supervision of weak institutions, and more (International Monetary Fund 1998). Feldstein (1998) points out that the IMFs recent emphasis on imposing structural reforms is a major change in policy for an organization that was created to deal with balance-of-payments problems.

Regulatory Capital

In a competitive-market system, private capital cushions debt and equity holders from unexpected losses. The debt holders are cushioned by the firm's equity. The equity holders are cushioned to the extent that substantial equity reduces the likelihood of bankruptcy. Thus, the capital markets "require" a certain amount of capital to maximize the value of a firm. The value of the firm will decline if it has too much or too little capital. The market requirement for bank capital may differ from the regulatory requirements for capital. Regulators generally assume that more bank capital is better than less. Hellmann, Murdock, and Stiglitz (1998, 4) state, "Clearly, once banks have enough of their own capital invested, banks can be induced to invest in the prudent asset." Stockholders, however, favor lower equity capital (higher financial leverage), because it improves the return on equity for a given level of income.[3]

Equity capital-to-asset ratios of banks in the United States declined from a high of over 50 percent in the 1840s to under 10 percent in the 1990s. During the early 1930s, when the United States experienced most of its bank failures, the average capital-to-asset ratio was about 15 percent, substantially higher than at any time since then.

Berger, Herring, and Szego (1995) claim that regulators require capital to protect themselves against the costs of financial distress, agency problems, and the reduction in market discipline caused by the safety net. The capital takes the form of equity and long-term subordinated debt. The safety net includes FDIC insurance as well as the Federal Reserve's discount window and unconditional guarantees of payments over the FedWire. Regulatory capital also insulates the economy from the negative externalities of systemic bank failures. Miller (1995) has pointed out that if the government is insuring banks with a too-big-to-fail policy, it effectively stands as the creditor vis-à-vis the banks' owners. To be socially efficient, its capital requirements should resemble those in a competitive private market.

Garten (1994, 468) points out that public capital and deposit insurance had opposite effects on bank capital structure. Public capital tended to raise the level of equity, while deposit insurance tended to lower it. Another difference is that the high governance cost of public capital encouraged banks to reduce their risks. In contrast, deposit insurance created a moral hazard problem. By shifting the risk from deposits to the FDIC insurance fund, the risk premium paid by banks to attract deposits was reduced. This encouraged the substitution of less costly deposits for higher-cost equity. Hence, banks are highly leveraged.

Uniform International Capital Standards

In 1998, the Basle Committee addressed the issue of capital standards for heterogeneous financial conglomerates. These are conglomerates whose primary business is financial, and whose regulated entities engage to a significant extent in at least two of the activities of banking, insurance and the securities business, which are not subject to uniform capital adequacy requirements (*Supervision of Financial Conglomerates* 1998). The basic objective is to assess capital adequacy on a groupwide basis.

In the European Union, the EU's directive requires banks to hold at least 8 percent of their risk-adjusted assets in the form capital. This method of determining capital adequacy is recognized as a crude first step because it does not take into account differences in loan quality or diversification (Graham 1997). For example, it does not distinguish between loans to a AAA rated company and one with a CCC rating, nor does it distinguish between a portfolio of loans of 100 AAA rated companies versus a portfolio of one loan to a CCC rated company. Simply stated, this method of determining capital is based on simple formulas that are not appropriate for every situation.

Because of these and other deficiencies, quantitative models that can be used to measure risk and determine capital adequacy are being developed by various banking organizations. J. P. Morgan's CreditMetrics is a step in the direction of measuring risk. The Basle Committee on Banking Supervision advocates the use of such value-at-risk (VAR) models and stress testing for measuring exposures to market risks associated with a bank's trading activities, foreign exchange, and commodities risk in connection with market risk capital requirements.

Pre-Commitment Approach

The pre-commitment approach is an attempt to do away with mechanical formulas for determining regulatory capital and replace them with incentive-compatible contracts. In this context, a bank can precommit for a certain level of risk and capital for a quarter or some other time period. If their risk exceeds predicted levels, the bank is penalized. The benefits of this approach are that it is flexible with respect to the amount of capital required, it allows firms to pursue their objects with minimal distortion from regulation, and it reduces the supervisory burden (Estrella 1998). The major drawback is that regulators cannot verify the size of losses associated with "fat-tailed" distributions. Moreover, such schemes have limited ability to resolve information problems for bank regulators (Kupiec and O'Brien 1998). Such information includes knowledge about the banks investment opportunities.

CONCLUSION

Is prudential bank regulation effective? One view is *res ispa loquitur*— the things speak for themselves. During the 1980 to 1996 period, more than 130 IMF member countries, including the United States, had significant banking-sector problems or crises (Lindgren, Garcia, and Saal 1996). In 1997, there were banking crises in several Southeast Asian countries. The large numbers of bank failures and crises suggests that prudential regulation, at least in its present form, has limits, and that it works better in some countries than in others. Systemic causes of bank failures are one of those limits. Hanc (1998, 50) concluded a study of banking crises in the 1980s and early 1990s by saying that "bank regulation can limit the scope and cost of bank failures, but it is unlikely to prevent bank failures that have systemic causes."

Another answer to that question depends on what one thinks prudential regulation is supposed to do. Prudential regulation ranges from safety and soundness to consumer protection. In this context, it may be successful in accomplishing some goals and less successful in other areas. One thing is clear, however. Safety and soundness of the banking system is the primary objective of prudential regulation. If banks fail in large numbers, the other objectives of prudential regulation cannot be met.

Finally, it follows that prudential regulation works best in a stable economic environment. The Basle Committee on Banking Supervision's *Core Principles* (1997, 11) state, "In the absence of sound macroeconomic policies, banking supervisors will be faced with a virtually impossible task." Most banking crises are associated with unstable economic conditions, such as asset price deflation, interest rate shocks, foreign exchange rate shocks, and so on. The flipside of that coin is that prolonged stability and strong economic growth may lead to complacency with respect to risky lending. Birdsall and Gavin (1998) claim that is what happened in Asian countries when stability and rapid economic growth encouraged banks to lend injudiciously, resulting in overspending in the government sector.

Beyond banking crises, the growth of heterogeneous financial conglomerates that cross regulatory and national boundaries, as well as changes in information technology, are testing the limits of prudential banking regulation.

This chapter presented an overview of prudential bank regulation: its purposes, theories, structure, and failures, and international efforts at regulation. This overview provides insights that bank regulators should consider as they change their focus, techniques, and regulations to deal with the dynamic global economic environments in which banks operate today and tomorrow. The changes that are needed are topics for additional research.

NOTES

This chapter was originally presented at a seminar at the Office of the Comptroller of the Currency. The author is indebted to the participants for their helpful comments and suggestions. Additional comments were provided by Catherine Lemieux, Federal Reserve Bank of Chicago.

1. See "Confidence for the Future" (1998, 15–17) for a discussion of limiting deposit insurance coverage.

2. The impact of oil shocks on the economy was a major factor affecting banks in the U.S. Southwest in the 1980s. For a discussion of speculative currency attacks in Europe from 1992 to 1993, see Gerlach and Smets (1994).

3. Return on equity is equal to return on assets times a leverage ratio (LR). ROE is equal to net income NI divided by equity E. ROA is equal to net income divided by total assets A, and LR is equal to the total assets divided by equity.

$$ROE = ROA \times LR$$

$$NI/E = NI/A \times A/E$$

For a given level of net income, ROE can be increased by reducing E.

REFERENCES

Banks Under Stress. 1992. Paris: Organization for Economic Co-Operation and Development.

Becker, G. S. 1983. "A Theory of Competition Among Pressure Groups for Political Influence." *Quarterly Journal of Economics* (August): 371–400.

Bentson, G. J. 1986. "Federal Regulation of Banking: Historical Overview." In *Deregulating Financial Services: Public Policy in Flux,* edited by G. G. Kaufman and R. C. Kormendi. Cambridge, Mass.: Ballinger.

Berger, A. N., R. J. Herring, and G. P. Szego. 1995. "The Role of Capital in Financial Institutions." *Journal of Banking and Finance* 19: 393–440.

Birdsall, N., and M. Gavin. 1998. "False Remedies and Asia's Crisis." *IDBAmerica* (Inter-American Development Bank), April, p. 3.

Boot, A., and S. Greenbaum. 1993. "Bank Regulation, Reputation, and Rents: Theory and Policy Implications." In *Capital Markets and Financial Intermediation*, edited by C. Mayer and X. Vives. Cambridge: Cambridge University Press.

Building Better Banks: The Case for Performance-Based Regulation. 1996. Chicago: Bank Administration Institute, McKinsey & Co.

The Burden of Bank Regulation: Tracing the Costs Imposed by Bank Regulation on the American Public. 1992. Washington, D.C.: The Secura Group.

Caprio, G., Jr., and D. Klingebiel. 1996a. "Bank Insolvency: Bad Luck, Bad Policy, or Bad Banking?" Paper presented at the World Bank Annual Conference on Development Economics, 25–26 April, Washington, D.C.

Caprio, G., Jr., and D. Klingebiel. 1996b. "Bank Insolvencies: Cross-Country Experience." Policy Research Working Paper 1620, the World Bank, Washington, D.C.

"Confidence for the Future." 1998. FDIC Symposium, 29 January, Arlington, Va.

Core Principles for Effective Banking Supervision. 1997. Basle, Switzerland: Basle Committee on Banking Supervision, Bank of International Settlements.

Dewatripoint, M., and J. Tirole. 1994. *The Prudential Regulation of Banks.* Cambridge: MIT Press.

Edwards, F. R. 1988. "The Future Financial Structure: Fears and Policies." In *Restructuring Banking & Financial Services in America*, edited by William S. Haraf and Rose Marie Kushmeider. Washington, D.C.: American Enterprise Institute.

Eisenbeis, R. A. 1986. "Risk as a Criterion for Expanding Banking Activities." In *Deregulating Financial Services: Public Policy in Flux*, edited by G. G. Kaufman and R. C. Kormendi. Cambridge, Mass.: Ballinger.

Eisenbeis, R. A. 1995. "Systemic Risk: Bank Deposits and Credit." In *Research in Financial Services Private and Public Policy.* Vol. 7, edited by G. G. Kaufman. Greenwich, Conn.: JAI Press.

Estrella, A. 1998. "Formulas or Supervision? Remarks on the Future of Regulatory Capital." Presentation at the Conference on Financial Services at the Crossroads: Capital Regulation in the 21st Century, Federal Reserve Bank of New York, 26–27 February.

Feldstein, M. 1998. "Refocusing the IMF." *Foreign Affairs*, March–April.

Folkerts-Landau, D., and C.-J. Lindgren. 1998. *Toward a Framework for Financial Stability.* Washington, D.C.: IMF.

Folkerts-Landau, D., and T. Ito. 1995. *International Capital Markets: Developments, Prospects, and Policy Issues.* Washington, D.C.: IMF.

Freixas, X., and J.-C. Rochet. 1997. *Microeconomics of Banking.* Cambridge: MIT Press.

Friedman, M., and A. J. Schwartz. 1963. *A Monetary History of the United States, 1867–1960.* Princeton, N.J.: Princeton University Press.

Garcia, G. 1992. "Regulatory Theory and Regulatory Reform: A Comment on the Financial Institutions Reform, Recovery, and Enforcement Act." In *Research in International Business: Emerging Challenges for the International Financial Services Industry.* Vol. 9, edited by J. R. Barth and P. Bartholomew. Greenwich, Conn.: JAI Press.

Garten, H. A. 1991. *Why Bank Regulation Failed: Designing a Bank Regulatory Strategy for the 1990s*. Westport, Conn.: Quorum Books.

Garten, H. A. 1994. "Political Analysis of Bank Failure Resolution." *Boston University Law Review* 74: 429–79.

Gerlach, S., and F. Smets. 1994. "1994, Contagious Speculative Attacks." Working Paper no. 23, Bank for International Settlements, Basle, Switzerland.

Goldstein, M., and P. Turner. 1996. *Banking Crises in Emerging Economies: Origins and Policy Options*. BIS Economic Papers no. 46. Basle, Switzerland: Bank for International Settlements.

Goodfriend, M., and R. G. King. 1988. "Financial Deregulation, Monetary Policy, and Central Banking." In *Restructuring Banking & Financial Services in America*, edited by W. S. Haraf and R. M. Kushmeider. Washington, D.C.: American Enterprise Institute.

Graham, G. 1997. "Bankers' Weigh Loss." *Financial Times*, 4 April.

Greenspan, A. 1993. "FDICIA and the Future of Banking Law and Regulation." Presentation to the annual Conference on Bank Structure and Competition, Federal Reserve Bank of Chicago, May 1993.

Greenspan, A. 1997. "Remarks." Presentation to the Annual Conference of the Association of Private Enterprise Education, Arlington, Virginia, 12 April.

Gup, B. 1998. *Bank Failures in the Major Trading Countries of the World: Causes and Remedies*. Westport, Conn.: Quorum Books.

Hanc, G. 1996. *History of the Eighties, Lessons for the Future: A Summary of the Findings*. Washington, D.C.: FDIC.

Hanc, G. 1998. "The Banking Crises of the 1980s and Early 1990s: Summary and Implications." *FDIC Banking Review* 11: 1–55.

Hellmann, T., K. Murdock, and J. Stiglitz. 1998. "Liberalization, Moral Hazard in Banking, and Prudential Regulation: Are Capital Requirements Enough?" Unpublished paper.

History of the Eighties: Lessons for the Future. Vol. 1. 1997. Washington, D.C.: FDIC.

International Monetary Fund (IMF). 1998. *The IMF's Response to the Asian Crisis*. Washington, D.C.: IMF.

James, C. 1991. "The Losses Realized in Bank Failures." *Journal of Finance* 46: 1223–42.

Kaminsky, G. L., and C. M. Reinhart. 1996. "The Twin Crises: The Causes of Banking and Balance-of-Payments Problems." Working Paper, Board of Governors of the Federal Reserve System, September.

Kane, E. J. 1988. "How Market Forces Influence the Structure of Financial Regulation." In *Restructuring Banking & Financial Services in America*, edited by W. S. Haraf and R. M. Kushmeider. Washington, D.C.: American Enterprise Institute.

Kaufman, G., and R. Kroszner. 1996. "How Should Financial Institutions and Markets Be Structured? Analysis and Options for Financial System Design." Working Paper WP-96-20, Federal Reserve Bank of Chicago, December.

Kupiec, P. H., and J. M. O'Brien. 1998. "Deposit Insurance, Bank Incentives, and the Design of Regulatory Policy." Presentation at the Conference on Financial Services at the Crossroads: Capital Regulation in the 21st Century, Federal Reserve Bank of New York, 26–27 February.

Layne, R. 1990. "Banks Crack Drexel Collateral Gridlock." *American Banker*, 26 February, p. 1.

Lindgren, C.-J., G. Garcia, M. I. Saal. 1996. *Bank Soundness and Macroeconomic Policy*. Washington, D.C.: IMF.

Litan, R. E. 1997. "Institutions and Policies for Maintaining Financial Stability." In *Maintaining Financial Stability in a Global Economy*. Kansas City, Mo.: Federal Reserve Bank of Kansas City.

McDonough, W. J. 1997. "The Changing Role of Supervision." In *Annual Report, 1997*. New York: Federal Reserve Bank of New York.

Meyer, L. H. 1998. Remarks before the Spring 1998 Banking and Finance Lecture, Widener University, Pennsylvania, 16 April.

Miller, M. H. 1995. "Do the M&M Propositions Apply to Banks? *Journal of Banking & Finance* 19: 483–89.

Moreno, R. 1998. "What Caused East Asia's Financial Crisis?" *FRBSF Economic Letter* (Federal Reserve Bank of San Francisco), 7 August.

Nagarajan, S., and C. W. Sealey. 1997. "Can Delegating Bank Regulation to Market Forces Really Work?" Presentation at the Eastern Finance Association Meeting, Panama City, Florida, 17 April.

Nagashima, A. 1997. "Role of the Central Bank During Problems of Bank Soundness: Japan's Experience." In *Banking Soundness and Monetary Policy*, edited by C. Enoch and J. H. Green. Washington, D.C.: IMF.

Nocera, J. 1998. "Banking Is Necessary—Banks Are Not." *Fortune*, 11 May, pp. 84–85.

Parry, R. T. 1997. "The October '87 Crash Ten Years Later." *FRBSF Economic Letter* (Federal Reserve Bank of San Francisco), 31 October.

Peltzman, S. 1989. *The Economic Theory of Regulation after a Decade of Deregulation*. Washington, D.C.: Brookings Papers: Microeconomics.

Righting the Regulatory Balance: Reconstructing a Banking System That Works. 1992. Washington, D.C.: Institute for Strategy Development.

Roe, M. J. 1994. *Strong Managers, Weak Owners: The Political Roots of American Corporate Finance*. Princeton, N.J.: Princeton University Press.

Schwartz, A. J. 1988. "Financial Stability and the Federal Safety Net." In *Restructuring Banking & Financial Services in America*, edited by W. S. Haraf and R. M. Kushmeider. Washington, D.C.: American Enterprise Institute.

Sheng, A. 1996. *Bank Restructuring: Lessons from the 1980s*. Washington, D.C.: World Bank.

Shirakawa, M., K. Okina, and S. Shiratsuka. 1997. "Financial Market Globalization: Present and Future." Discussion Paper 97-E-11. Tokyo: Bank of Japan, Institute for Monetary and Economic Studies.

Spong, K. 1990. *Banking Regulation: Its Purposes, Implementation, and Effects*. Kansas City, Mo.: Federal Reserve Bank of Kansas City.

Stigler, G. J. 1971. "The Theory of Economic Regulation." *Bell Journal of Economics and Management Science* 2 (Spring): 3–21.

Supervision of Financial Conglomerates. 1998. Basle, Switzerland: Basle Committee on Banking Supervision, Bank for International Settlements.

Trigaux, R. 1990. "Regulators Put Drexel on Own in Fast Decision." *American Banker*, 16 February, p. 1.

U.S. Department of Treasury. 1991. *Modernizing the Financial System: Recommendations for Safer, More Competitive Banks.* Washington, D.C.: U.S. Treasury.

U.S. Department of Treasury. 1994. *National Treatment Study, 1994.* Washington, D.C.: U.S. Treasury.

U.S. General Accounting Office. 1991. *Deposit Insurance: A Strategy for Reform* (GAO/GGD-91-26). Washington, D.C.: U.S. Treasury.

U.S. House. 1991. Committee on Banking, Finance, and Urban Affairs. *The Failure of the Bank of New England Corporation and Its Affiliate Banks: Hearing before the Committee on Banking, Finance, and Urban Affairs.* 102d Cong., 1st sess., 13 June.

U.S. House. 1997. Subcommittee on Capital Markets, Securities and Government-Sponsored Enterprises of the Committee on Banking and Financial Services. Testimony by A. Greenspan, Chairman, Board of Governors of the Federal Reserve System. 19 March.

U.S. Senate. 1997. Subcommittee on Financial Institutions and Regulatory Relief of the Committee on Banking, Housing, and Urban Affairs. Testimony by S. M. Phillips, Governor of the Federal Reserve. 20 March.

Wall, L. 1989. "A Plan for Reducing Future Deposit Insurance Losses: Puttable Subordinated Debt." *Economic Review* (Federal Reserve Bank of Atlanta), July–August, pp. 2–17.

12

The Decision to Fail Banks: A Global View

Benton E. Gup and Philip F. Bartholomew

The financial crisis that began in Thailand in July 1997 set off a chain of events that contributed to other crises in Asia, South America, and Russia. Some of these crises resulted in bank failures. However, the extent to which banks were allowed to fail depended on government policies and bank regulators. In Russia, following the devaluation of the ruble in August 1998, almost all of the government-owned banks were insolvent, but only a few had been closed ("The Undead" 1998). Before these most recent crises occurred, Lindgren, Garcia, and Saal (1996) reported that over 131 of the 181 countries that are members of the International Monetary Fund had severe banking problems since 1980. However, the new wave of financial crises has brought attention to the role of bank regulators in the process of failure.

Lindgren (1997, 278) asserts, "A strong exit policy for banks (closure and liquidation) is at least as important for an efficient and competitive market system as entry policy, if not more important." The reality of the situation is that bank regulators resolve some problem banks swiftly, whereas it may take years to resolve others. What accounts for the differences in timing?

Research has revealed a variety of factors that influenced failure decisions in U.S. banks, but none of the following studies examined foreign banks. According to Dimergüc-Kunt (1991), a bank's net value (capital plus insurance guarantees) was a good indicator of the likelihood of a failure decision. Thomson (1992) modeled bank regulators' decisions to close banks as a call option whose value depends on the banks' charter, solvency and resolution costs. Mailath and Mester (1994) used dynamic game theory to deal with the issue of when to close a bank that is near failure and invests in risky assets. Thus, solvency appears to be the primary consideration.

Nevertheless, Cole and Gunther (1994) found differences in regulatory treatment helped large banks to avoid failure. In a later study, Cole and Gunther (1995) concluded that the closure of large banks was not delayed relative to the closure of small banks. Freixas and Rochet (1997, 281–87) reviewed a study by R. Repullo that used game theory, and concluded that bank closures should be made by the central bank when depositor withdrawals are small, and by the insurance fund when they are large.

This chapter extends the research on bank closures by examining the principal factors that go into the regulators' decision to fail banks, and by examining the process of failure in an global context. Because of international differences in the definitions of banks and who regulates them, those terms are used in the general sense of the words.

WHAT DOES IT MEAN TO FAIL?

If and when a bank fails is a regulatory or legal decision. Bank regulators fail a bank when they decide that it is unable to operate because it cannot meet its financial obligations, it has violated certain rules (such as inadequate capital) or for other reasons.[1] In France, Crédit Lyonnais (CL) is a state-owned bank that the government bailed out rather than close it. Thus, a government bailout can be considered a de facto failure. In Japan and Korea, it was unthinkable for a bank to fail, until recently. The 1997 banking crises in Southeast Asian countries forced bank regulators in Indonesia, Korea, and Thailand to fail some banks.

In the United States, only state and federal bank chartering agencies have the authority to close a bank, and the FDIC can take control of a failing institution and operate it as a bridge bank. The authority to close or control banks varies from country to country. If or when bank regulators fail a bank is a matter of judgment, which is influenced by the economic condition of the bank and other factors that will be explained.

Financial Stability of the Economy

Crockett (1997) argues that financial stability is an appropriate goal of public policy. Implementation of this policy requires the intervention of bank regulators to prevent runs and contagion, and to reduce the cost of resolution. The treatment of LDC loan losses at the nine largest banks and holding companies in the United States in 1982 is one example. LDC loans were more than 288 percent of their capital and reserves (White 1992, 56). An FDIC study (*History of the Eighties* 1997, 43) states that following the Mexican default on interest payments in 1982, "U.S. banking officials did not require that large reserves be immediately set aside for the restructured LDC loans, apparently believing that some large banks might have been insolvent and that an economic and political crises might have precipitated." It was not until 1987 that the affected banks began to recognize massive losses on their LDC loans that were carried at par on their books for more than a decade. Had they been required to reflect these losses earlier, the banks might have failed. Accordingly, the regulatory policies toward these banks reflected a preference for financial stability and public polices toward LDCs. It also raises the issue of too-big-to-fail, as will be seen later.

Government Ownership

Government-owned banks get special consideration when they are in financial distress. Some governments, such as Russia in 1998, were unwilling or unable to close insolvent government-owned banks during their financial crisis. Crédit Lyonnais was incorporated as a private bank in 1863 in France, and it was nationalized in 1946. It is the largest bank in France. Despite large loan losses in the early 1990s, Crédit Lyonnais was not allowed to fail because it is government owned. Instead, the French government bailed it out ("Commission Decision" 1995). The bailout and restructuring of the state-owned bank was still being debated in 1998, and is expected to continue through the year 2000 (Jack and Tucker 1997). The ultimate goal is to privatize the bank.

International Subsidiaries

Corrigan (1995) addressed the issue of how central banks manage a financial crisis. One point that he made concerned the size, financial condition, and complexity of troubled banks with foreign branches and subsidiaries. If the foreign establishments encounter large-scale deposit outflows, the complexities of managing the situation rise geometrically. The problem is exacerbated when internationally active corporations are made up of dozens of legal entities, many of which are subject to different regulatory and bankruptcy processes. This raises the issues that some banks or organizations may be too-big-to-fail or too-big-to-regulate.

Too-Big-to-Fail

An FDIC study, *History of the Eighties* (1997, 42), concluded, "At various times and for various reasons, regulators generally concluded that good public policy required that big banks in trouble be shielded from the full impact of market forces and that their uninsured depositors be protected." The first time that occurred in the United States was in 1984, when bank regulators intervened in the case of Continental Illinois National Bank and Trust Company of Chicago because they feared that its failure might cause a systemic crisis. Comptroller of the Currency Todd Conover announced that the government will not let the eleven largest banks fail (Carrington 1984). As applied to U.S. banks, the too-big-to-fail doctrine means that the organization may continue to exist, but the stockholders, subordinated debt holders, managers, and some creditors may suffer financial losses. In the case of Continental Illinois, the FDIC assumed a large portion of the bank's bad assets and responsibility for its Federal Reserve liability in exchange for 80-percent ownership (Robertson 1995, 226).

The issue of too-big-to-fail was raised again in the late 1990s when the megabank mergers of BankAmerica and NationsBank, Chase Manhattan and Chemical, Citicorp and Travelers, First Union and Core States, Nations and Barnett, and Wells Fargo and First Interstate resulted in trillion dollar institutions. Former FDIC chairman L. William Seidman said that he doubts that regulators are ready to supervise Citigroup or the largest institutions (Seiberg 1998). A *Business Week* article (Foust 1998) quotes William Isaac, another former FDIC chairman as saying, "the market place is moving so fast that the government is unable to keep up with it;" and Arthur Rolnick, director of research of the Minneapolis Fed, stated that in the case of Travelers, "with the safety net starting to extend beyond banking, the potential taxpayer exposure has grown."

Principal Agent Problems

According to Kane (1989), there are principal agent problems that may give some bank regulators incentives to delay or not close troubled banks. Agency conflicts between regulators and taxpayers helped to explain why some thrifts were closed and others were not. In contrast to principal agent problems, Kroszner and Strahan (1996) found that regulators lacked the cash to close insolvent thrifts, and they induced private investors to provide capital through mutual-to-stock conversions.

INDUSTRY GROWTH PATTERNS

The Life Cycle

Private banks, like other types of firms, evolve through a life cycle as they develop over time. In a normal life cycle, firms are chartered, they grow, and then they mature.[2] Failure can occur at any time. However, failures are most common among new, small firms. An FDIC study revealed that 16.2 percent of all of the institutions chartered during the 1980 to 1994 period failed, compared with a 7.6 percent failure rate for banks already in existence at the end of 1979 (*History of the Eighties* 1997, 14, 32). The average asset size of the failed banks was $128 million. In general, banks with assets of about $100 million are considered to be small banks.

It can take a long time for banks to fail. Francis Baring & Co. was established in London in 1862. It became Barings Bank (Barings PLC), which failed in 1995. More will be said about it shortly.

Economic Concentration

There is a natural tendency toward increased economic concentration as an industry grows, and banking is no exception. The number of banks has declined from 14,434 in 1980 to 9,308 at the end of 1987. The term "economic concentration" refers to the extent to which an industry assets, sales, or deposits are distributed among the firms in that industry. Economic concentration frequently results in a distribution of assets that is log normal. That is, a few large firms dominate the industry. This is the case in the airline, automotive, oil, steel, and banking industries. For example, during the first half of 1997 there were 9,308 commercial banks in the United States (FDIC 1997, Fourth quarter). The sixty-six largest banks in the United States, with assets greater than $10 billion, controlled 62 percent of total assets.

The log normal distribution has led some observers to conclude that market structure may be determined stochastically. Alchain (1950) provides an excellent background for understanding some of the issues. He postulated that firms use adaptive, imitative, and trial-and-error behavior in pursuit of positive profits. In this process, the opinions of decision makers within firms will differ. Alchain argued that "the aggregate set of actions of the entire group of participants may be indistinguishable from a set of individual actions, each selected at random" (p. 216). Accordingly, economic growth, persistent profits, failures, and log normal distributions may be considered as part of a stochastic process (Gup 1980; Mueller 1986).

WHY BANKS FAIL EN MASSE

The reasons for massive bank failures are not a clear cut, but there appears to be something systematic at work. They typically occur in connection with significant changes in government economic policies or external shocks that were beyond their control. For example, Benston and Kaufman (1997, 3) argue that the savings and loan debacle was caused initially and primarily by government policies: Tight monetary policy in the late 1970s resulted in a sharp increase in interest rates that exacerbated the duration mismatch between S&Ls' assets and liabilities. Other institutional rigidities in the S&L industry included limits on rates that could be paid on deposits, and limits on investments.

Significant changes in government policies or external shocks effect banks more than other firms because of their financial fragility. Financial fragility refers to the extent to which banks' high degree of financial leverage makes them more vulnerable to losses than most other firms. A well-capitalized bank, with an 8-percent equity-capital-to-risk-assets ratio, has $1 of capital supporting $12.5 dollars of risky assets such as loans. In contrast, a typical corporation with 30 percent equity has $1 of capital supporting $3.3 of assets.[3] Because of the relatively high financial leverage, a relatively small dollar volume of loan losses can wipe out a bank's equity capital, and the bank will fail. During economic downturns or other economic shocks, it is not surprising that loan losses occur and that highly leveraged banks may fail.

Another view is that banks control their own destinies. Greenspan (1993) has said, "Banks are in the business of managing risk. If done correctly, the bank will create economic value by attracting savings to finance investment. If done incorrectly, real resources will be misallocated, and the bank may fail." There is ample evidence from around the world that many of the banks that failed were engaged in excessive risk-taking activities that were the proximate cause of their demise. If those banks taking excessive risks have "herd behavior," it is possible that they may fail en masse if and when their loans default or they have insufficient liquidity to meet runs on their deposits.

Both views have merit: Some government policies, external shocks (i.e., oil shocks, speculative currency attacks, etc.), and banks' excessive risk taking contribute to bank failures. Sometimes it is the combination of government policies and banks taking excessive risks that results in failures. Kaminsky and Reinhart (1998a, 1998b) found that the typical financial crises occur when an economy enters a recession following a prolonged economic boom that was fueled by credit creation and capital inflows. The crises involve overvaluation of the currency, falling exports, and the bursting of asset bubbles. In Thailand, for example, government policies encouraged rapid economic growth (Greenwood 1997; Gup 1998; Moreno 1997; Mydans 1997). The government liberalized the financial system and let Thai banks and finance companies borrow in dollars and lend in the local currency (baht). The end result was that government policies encouraged overvaluation of the baht and bank lending. Thai banks and finance companies made real estate loans that contributed to a speculative real estate bubble. In Bangkok, office vacancy rates exceeded 20 percent, and there was about a three-year oversupply of housing. In addition, there was a currency crisis. Following speculative currency attacks and the bursting of the real estate bubble, the Bangkok Bank of Commerce, which had over $3 billion in bad loans, was taken over by the government, and fifty-eight of the country's real estate finance companies were suspended.

In South Korea, government-directed investments and the relationships between banks and *chaebols* helped to produce strong economic growth for about three decades. *Chaebols*, such as Hanbo Steel, Kia Motors, and Halla Shipbuilding, were the largest customers of some banks, and they could not or did not refuse extending additional loans, even though there was excess industry capacity. An editorial in *The Economist* ("Asia and the Abyss" 1997, 15) said that "fast growth had concealed, or encouraged, the existence of many poorly run and poorly regulated banks."

In Indonesia, President Suharto was known for crony capitalism. Government-directed and bank investments were made for the benefit of friends and relatives. Such policies did contribute to economic growth, but they also contributed to speculative bubbles that burst in 1997, and political turmoil in 1998. Indonesia closed sixteen banks, including one owned by President Suharto's son, Bamdang Trihatmojdjo. However, within weeks of the closure, Mr. Bamdang had opened another bank ("Back from the Brink" 1998). The closure of the banks was intended to restore confidence, but it had the opposite effect. There are about 220 banks in Indonesia, and there were runs on those banks. As the value of the rupiah plunged, Indonesians put their money in foreign banks, such as Citicorp and Hong Kong Bank, and they bought foodstuffs and tangibles (Shari 1998).

Failure Takes Time

The process of a bank failing usually takes a long time. Barings Bank was an exception. Barings PLC failed because a rogue trader in a foreign subsidiary speculated more than $1 billion on Japanese stock index futures in the Singapore futures market. In a twenty-eight-day period in 1995, the trader lost $1.4 billion. The bank failed because it only had $500 million in capital (Bhalla 1995; Folkerts-Landau and Ito 1995; Leeson and Whitley 1996).

Most banks fail as a result of loans that default. Many of the loans that default had been performing loans on the bank's books for years. At some point in time, however, borrowers exercised their put options to default on their loans. A large number of banks will fail if the defaults happen en masse. The reasons why borrowers default en masse goes back to the government policies and external shocks that were discussed previously. The reasons include, but are not limited to, asset price deflation, reduced expectations of income, foreign exchange risks (e.g., borrowing in dollars and repaying loans in depreciated Indonesian rupiah or Thai baht), and so on. Thus, foreign exchange risk also contributed to failures in Indonesia and Thailand.

Interest rate risk accounted for a large number of failures in the 1980s S&L crisis in the United States. The S&Ls borrowed short term and lent long term at fixed rates. When market rates of interest spiked in the late 1970s and early 1980s, many S&Ls had negative net interest income. These same factors—borrowing short term, lending long term, and interest rate spikes, as well as foreign exchange risk—also contributed to the suspension of fifty-eight finance companies in Thailand in 1997.

Problems Are Not Transparent

Bank regulators in the United States depend on examinations to provide information about a bank's viability. U.S. bank safety-and-soundness examinations prior to January 1, 1997 focused on capital adequacy, asset quality, management, earnings, and liquidity (CAMEL). Subsequently, sensitivity to market risk was added to the examinations and the new designation is CAMELS. Banks are rated on a scale of 1 to 5, where 1 is the highest rating and 5 is the worst. A CAMELS rating of 4 indicates that serious financial weakness or other problems exist. The high potential for failure is present, but not yet imminent. A CAMELS rating of 5 indicates that the bank has an extremely high probability of failure. The CAMELS system focuses on internal bank data and operations, and it does not take into account external factors that may adversely affect the bank in the future.

In the early 1970s, all banks were annually examined on site. But the policies changed over time, and banking agencies placed increased reliance on off-site monitoring of Call Report data. Therefore, banks with high CAMELS ratings were examined on site less often than those with low ratings.

During the 1980 to 1994 period, 260, or 16 percent of the 1,617 banks that failed were not detected as problem banks by bank regulators two years before their failure (*History of the Eighties* 1997, Chapter 12). Of the 260 banks that failed, 141 were not detected within eighteen months of failure, 57 were not detected within twelve months of failure, and 9 were not detected within six months of failure. Only about 10 percent of the banks that failed had a CAMELS 5 rating. If only CAMELS 4 and 5 rated banks are considered, the supervisors only identified 46 percent of the banks that failed.

Examiners are not the only ones who may not recognize problems. Litan (1997, 289) cites the failure of the Bank of New England in 1991. He states that "not only did the bank fail to report its problems promptly to investors, but even managers *inside the company* bought stock in the bank as late as the year before its failure." They were unaware of the problems and the regulator's concerns about the bank.

Even when the problems are transparent, the question is what to do about them. In Japan, the government has propped up some banks since the early 1990s by failing to recognize large loan losses. Other actions could be taken to resolve the situation.

RESOLUTION

The term "resolution," as used here, refers to the actions taken by bank regulators to deal with existing or potential problem banks. In theory, resolution occurs when a bank is insolvent. It is technically insolvent when the value of its assets is worth less than the value of its liabilities, or if it is unable to meet its matured financial obligations.[4] Most bank assets are recorded at book value on banks' financial statements in accordance with generally accepted accounting practices (GAAP) reporting standards.[5] Book value accounting (BVA) records values at cost (historical or amortized), and it has reserves for expected losses. Market value accounting (MVA) is an alternative method for valuing assets. However, the market values of some bank loans are not transparent. Thus, a bank might be solvent under BVA but insolvent under MVA. In either case, it still might be able to meet its matured obligations if it has sufficient cash flow.

In practice, resolution may be a political decision, and what regulators do is limited by the laws of their respective countries. For example, in 1998 the bankruptcy laws of Thailand were being brought up to date to facilitate foreclosure and debt restructuring (Hartman and Wongchirachai 1998).

Regulatory intervention takes many different forms depending on its purpose. One purpose is to aid distressed organizations and maybe prevent failures. Other purposes include avoiding systemic crisis and reducing the cost of resolution, and protecting deposit insurance funds.[6] In Japan, for example, Hokkaido Takushoku, one of the nation's largest city banks, had about 400 billion yen in bad loans when it was failed in November 1997. For several years it was known that the bank had loan problems. However, regulators delayed closing the bank because they feared that it might break the deposit insurance fund (Sapsford 1997).

The intervention techniques used by bank regulators throughout the world can be grouped into six broad categories.[7] Selected examples of each technique are presented.

Long-Term Investments

Long-term investments in problem banks can take a variety of forms. In the United States, for example, the Source of Strength doctrine requires all commonly controlled banks to be liable for the losses of affiliated banks.[8] Open-bank assistance is another form of long-term investment.[9] Open-bank assistance includes the FDIC net worth certificate program for savings banks, the FDIC capital forbearance and loan amortization programs for agricultural and energy banks, and direct open-bank assistance.

In other countries, long-term investments may take the form of debt-equity swaps, long-term loans by other financial institutions, or equity investments. In Japan stronger companies help weaker ones. This is called the "convoy" method of intervention. For example, the Bank of Japan, commercial banks, and life insurance companies invested capital in the failing Nippon Credit Bank (Martin 1997).

In the United States, a consortium of commercial and investment banks (Goldman Sachs, Merrill Lynch, Morgan Stanley Dean Witter, Travelers Group, UBS Securities, and others) bailed out Long-Term Capital Management (LTCM) of Greenwich, Connecticut, with a $3.5 billion package.[10] LTCM is a hedge fund that had been successful. This limited partnership included well-known Nobel laureates Merton Miller and Myron Scholes, former Federal Reserve Vice Chairman David W. Mullins Jr., and former Salomon Inc. trader John W. Meriwether. In spite of their collective wisdom and insights, they did not foresee the impact of the global market turmoil on financial markets, and their large bets on credit spreads and equity derivatives resulted in huge losses. This fund was very highly leveraged. In September 1998, it had trading positions of $107 billion and capital of only $2.3 billion, giving it an asset to equity ratio of 50 to 1. As noted, banks are considered highly leveraged at 12.5 to 1, and corporations are leveraged at 3 to 1. When LTCM's bets turned sour, the value of its assets plummeted more than 50 percent.

The Federal Reserve Bank of New York played a role in the bailout by pressuring lenders to extend a lifeline to LTCM (Raghavan and Pacelle 1998; "How a Big Hedge Fund" 1998). There was fear that if they failed to do so, the unwinding of LTCM's multibillion-dollar positions quickly could have resulted in large losses for banks and brokers who had extended the hedge fund credit. Nevertheless, some banks did lose money: UBS, the world's largest bank, took a $700 million writedown of the value of its investment in LTCM, and Dresdner Bank of Germany lost $143 million. However, these banks made large profits from the hedge fund in previous years.

Another hedge fund, High Risk Opportunities Fund, affiliated with III Offshore Advisors, suffered losses from investments in Russia, and it filed for liquidation in the Cayman Islands. The banks that lent to this and other hedge funds suffered some losses on loans that were not fully collateralized. Even if they were collateralized, the value of the collateral may have declined. As a result of these collapses, Britain's Financial Service Authority asked fifty-five financial companies to provide information about their exposure to hedge funds.

Nationalization

Nationalization refers to government ownership. In the United States, the Reconstruction Finance Corporation held "preferred stock" in hundreds of banks in the early 1930s. Preferred stock is one form of equity interest. In 1984, the FDIC owned 80 percent of the stock in Continental Illinois Bank.

Payoff

A payoff occurs when the insured depositors and in some cases creditors of the insured failed institution are paid. About 25 percent of the bank failures in the United States involve payoffs.

Sell All or Part of the Assets

All or part of a bank's assets can be sold. In 1997, the Japanese Housing Loan Corporation was created to liquidate seven housing loan companies (*jusen*) that failed. Crédit Lyonnais (France) sold some or all of its retail operations in Argentina, Brazil, Chile, the Netherlands, Peru, the Philippines, and Sweden to help resolve its financial difficulties in the early 1990s.

Short-Term Liquidity

During periods of economic distress, central banks provide short-term liquidity in order to avoid even larger economic problems. For example, when the stock market crashed in October 1987, the Federal Reserve System announced its readiness to provide liquidity to support the financial system in order to avoid a systemic crisis. In Japan, during the 1992 to 1997 period, monetary policy kept short-term interest rates low to stimulate growth and to provide distressed banks with low-cost funds. When Hanbo Steel of South Korea went bankrupt in 1997, the central bank of Korea provided $7 billion in emergency funds to support the firm's creditor banks.

Forbearance

Forbearance means waiting: not enforcing capital or other supervisory standards in banks that are financially troubled but are judged to be viable. The delay in recognizing LDC debt exposure at large commercial banks in the United States in the early 1980s is one example of waiting. The Basle Committee on Banking Supervision's *Core Principles* (1997, 12) warn that forbearance, "whether or not a result of political pressure, normally leads to worsening problems and higher resolution costs."

PROFITS AND LOSSES

According to the FDIC, during the 1934 to 1982 period their losses on failed banks' assets amounted to 6.97 percent (FDIC 1984). The losses are understated because they did not include foregone interest or administrative expenses. James (1991) estimated that losses from bank failures in the mid-1980s were about 30 percent of the failed banks' assets. Perhaps one reason for the losses was that the assets were liquidated relatively quickly. As noted, the private bailout for LTCM was intended, in part, to avoid the problems of unwinding hedge positions too fast, thereby averting losses. Only time will tell if the investors were correct.

Not all failures or bailouts result in losses. In 1984, Continental Illinois National Bank and Trust Company was in financial difficulty and bank regulators considered it too-big-to-fail. As noted, the FDIC assumed 80-percent ownership of the bank. When the FDIC disposed of its stock in the bank in 1991, it had earned a profit of almost $100 million (Robertson 1995, 227).

CONCLUSION

The decision to fail a bank involves both economic and political considerations. It is given that banks have financial fragility and that they play a crucial role in the payments system and financial markets. With that in mind, the failure of a small bank is the type of problem that is easily resolved: Liquidate it or let it be acquired by a stronger institution. The failure or potential failure of a very large financial institution, such as Continental Illinois Bank, Crédit Lyonnais, the banks in Russia following the devaluation of the ruble, or LTCM, can have a much greater impact on financial markets and the economy, and they are dealt with differently than small banks.

The problem of resolution is exacerbated when a large number of financial institutions of all sizes fail. Such failures en masse require government intervention. However, the degree of intervention depends on the politics, legal structure, and economic condition of the country in which it occurs. Accordingly, the resolution of banking problems in Japan in the early 1990s is different than the resolution of banking problems in Thailand in 1997 and Russia in 1998. It is clear that what works in one country at one point in time may not be a "cookie cutter" solution to bank failures in another country at a different time. The decision of when to fail a bank and what to do about it is as much an art as it is a social science.

NOTES

1. For additional discussion of this definition, see Dimergüc-Kunt (1989).
2. For a discussion of the life-cycle concept applied to firms, see Gup and Agrrawal (1996).
3. This figure is for all corporations filing U.S. income tax returns. For additional details, see U.S. Department of Commerce (1997, 541).
4. For additional discussion of this point, see Nakamura (1990). Also see Bartholomew (1993, 12) for a discussion of how to measure insolvency.
5. Securities available for sale are reported at fair (market) value.
6. For a discussion of systemic risk, see Bartholomew and Whalen (1995).
7. Freixas and Rochet (1997, 280) report a 1993 study by C. Goodhart and D. Schoenmaker. They classify resolution techniques in four categories: (1) rescue package, (2) acquisition, (3) special treatment by government or insurance fund, and (4) liquidation.
8. The Source of Strength doctrine was enacted into law in the Financial Institutions Reform Act of 1989.
9. The Garn–St. Germain Depository Institutions Act of 1982 amended section 13 (c) of the Federal Deposit Insurance Act to grant the FDIC authority to provide financial assistance to selected banks.
10. See http://cnnfn.com/hotstories/companies/9809/03/impact/index.htm, last visited 3 September 1998; http://cnnfn.com/quickenonfn/investing/9809/23/longterm/, last visited 23 September 1998; and http://cnnfn/hotstories/companies/9809/28/hedge/, last visited 28 September 1998. For additional details, see Siconolfi, Raghavan, and Pacelle (1998).

REFERENCES

Alchain, A. A. 1950. "Uncertainty, Evolution, and Economic Theory." *Journal of Political Economy* 58: 211–21.
"Asia and the Abyss." 1997. *The Economist*, 20 December, p. 15.
"Back from the Brink." 1998. *The Economist*, 7 March, p. 7.
Bartholomew, P. F. 1993. *Resolving the Thrift Crisis*. Washington, D.C.: Congressional Budget Office.
Bartholomew, P. F., and G. W. Whalen. 1995. "Fundamentals of Systemic Risk." In *Research in Financial Services and Public Policy*, Vol. 7, edited by G. G. Kaufman. Greenwich, Conn.: JAI Press.

Benston, G. J., and G. G. Kaufman. 1997. "FDICIA After Five Years: A Review and Evaluation." Working Paper WP-97-1, Federal Reserve Bank of Chicago, July.

Bhalla, A. S. 1995. "Collapse of Barings Bank, Case Market Failure." *Economic and Political Weekly*, 1 April, pp. 658–62.

Carrington, T. 1984. "U.S. Won't Let 11 Biggest Banks in Nation Fail." *Wall Street Journal*, 20 September.

Cole, R. 1990. "Insolvency versus Closure: Why the Regulatory Delay in Closing Troubled Thrifts." Financial Industry Studies Working Paper no. 2-90, Federal Reserve Bank of Dallas, July.

Cole, R. 1993. "When Are Thrift Institutions Closed? An Agency-Theoretic Model." *Journal of Financial Services Research* 7: 283–307.

Cole, R., and J. W. Gunther. 1994. "When Are Failing Banks Closed?" *Financial Industry Studies* (Federal Reserve Bank of Dallas), December, pp. 1–2.

Cole, R., and J. W. Gunther. 1995. "Separating the Likelihood and Timing of Bank Failure." *Journal of Banking and Finance* 19: 1073–89.

"Commission Decision of 26 July 1995 Giving Conditional Approval to Aid Granted by France to the Bank Crédit Lyonnais." 1995. *Official Journal of the European Communities* (English edition), 21 December.

Core Principles for Effective Banking Supervision. 1997. Basle, Switzerland: Basle Committee on Banking Supervision, Bank of International Settlements.

Corrigan, E. G. 1995. "How Central Banks Manage Financial Crises." An address to Goldman, Sachs & Co., Shanghai, China, 25 October, at http://www2.gs.com/about/speeches/shanghai.html.

Crockett, A. 1997. "Why Is Financial Stability a Goal of Public Policy?" *Economic Review* (Federal Reserve Bank of Kansas City) 82/4: 5–22.

Dimergüc-Kunt, A. 1989. "Deposit-Institution Failures: A Review of Empirical Literature." *Economic Review* (Federal Reserve Bank of Cleveland), fourth quarter, pp. 2–16.

Dimergüc-Kunt, A. 1991. "Principal-Agent Problems in Commercial-Bank Failure Decisions." Working Paper 9106, Federal Reserve Bank of Cleveland, April.

Federal Deposit Insurance Corporation (FDIC). 1984. *The Federal Deposit Insurance Corporation: The First Fifty Years—A History of the FDIC 1933–1983*. Washington, D.C.: FDIC.

FDIC. 1997. *The FDIC Quarterly Banking Profile*. Washington, D.C.: FDIC.

Folkerts-Landau, D., and T. Ito. 1995. *International Capital Markets: Developments, Prospects, and Key Policy Issues*. Washington, D.C.: IMF.

Foust, D. 1998. "If This Safety Net Snaps, Who Pays?" *Business Week*, 27 April, pp. 38–39.

Freixas, X., and J.-C. Rochet. 1997. *Microeconomics of Banking*. Cambridge: MIT Press.

Greenspan, A. 1993. "Remarks." Presentation before the 29th Annual Conference on Bank Structure and Competition, Federal Reserve Bank of Chicago, 6 May.

Greenwood, J. 1997. "The Lessons of Asia's Currency Crises." *Wall Street Journal*, 7 October, p. A22.

Gup, B. 1980. "The Financial Consequences of Corporate Growth." *Journal of Finance* 35: 1257–65.

Gup, B. 1998. *Bank Failures in the Major Trading Countries of the World: Causes and Remedies*. Westport, Conn.: Quorum Books.

Gup, B., and P. Agrrawal. 1996. "The Product Life Cycle: A Paradigm for Understanding Financial Management." *Financial Practice and Education* 6 (Fall–Winter): 41–47.

Hartman, D., and M. Wongchirachai. 1998. "Thailand: Laying the Foundation for Financial Recovery." Salomon Smith Barney, New York, 22 September.

History of the Eighties: Lessons for the Future. Vol. 1. 1997. Washington, D.C.: FDIC.

"How a Big Hedge Fund Marketed Its Expertise and Shrouded Its Risks." 1998. *Wall Street Journal*, 25 September, p. A1.

Jack, A., and E. Tucker. 1997. "Paris Pressed on Crédit Lyonnais." *Financial Times*, 14 November, p. 2.

James, C. 1991. "The Losses Realized in Bank Failures." *Journal of Finance* 46: 1223–42.

Kaminsky, G. L., and C. M. Reinhart. 1998a. "Financial Crises in Asia and Latin America: Then and Now." *American Economic Review Papers and Proceedings*.

Kaminsky, G. L., and C. M. Reinhart. 1998b. "The Twin Crises: The Causes of Banking and Balance-of-Payments Problems." Working Paper, Board of Governors of the Federal Reserve System, 4 February.

Kane, E. J. 1989. *The S&L Insurance Mess: How Did It Happen?* Washington, D.C.: Urban Institute.

Kroszner, R. S., and P. E. Strahan. 1996. "Regulatory Incentives and the Thrift Crises: Dividend, Mutual-to-Stock Conversions, and Financial Distress." *Journal of Finance* 51: 1285–319.

Leeson, N., and E. Whitley. 1996. *Rogue Trader: How I Brought Down Barings Bank and Shook the Financial World*. Boston: Little, Brown.

Lindgren, C.-J. 1997. "How to Keep the Banking System Sound in a Period of Change." In *Banking Soundness and Monetary Policy*, edited by C. Enoch and J. H. Green. Washington, D.C.: IMF.

Lindgren, C.-J., G. Garcia, and M. I. Saal. 1996. *Bank Soundness and Macroeconomic Policy*. Washington, D.C.: IMF.

Litan, R. E. 1997. "Institutions and Policies for Maintaining Financial Stability." In *Maintaining Financial Stability in a Global Economy*. Kansas City, Mo.: Federal Reserve Bank of Kansas City.

Mailath, G., and L. Mester. 1994. "A Positive Analysis of Bank Closure." *Journal of Financial Intermediation* 3: 272–99.

Martin, N. A. 1997. "Japan's Turn." *Barrons*, 14 April, pp. 18–20.

Moreno, R. 1997. "Lessons from Thailand." *FRBSF Economic Letter* (Federal Reserve Bank of San Francisco), no. 97-33, 7 November.

Mueller, D. C. 1986. *Profits in the Long Run*. Cambridge: Cambridge University Press.

Mydans, S. 1997. "56 Troubled Lenders Closed by Thailand." *New York Times*, 9 December, p. D10.

Nakamura, L. I. 1990. "Closing Troubled Financial Institutions: What Are the Issues?" *Business Review* (Federal Reserve Bank of Philadelphia), May–June, pp. 15–24.

Raghavan, A., and M. Pacelle. 1998. "A Hedge Fund Falters, and Big Banks Agree to Ante Up $3.5 Billion." *Wall Street Journal*, 24 September, p. A1.

Robertson, R. M. 1995. *The Comptroller and Bank Supervision: A Historical Appraisal*. Washington, D.C.: Office of the Comptroller the Currency.

Sapsford, J. 1997. "Fears Grow That Japan's Bank Woes Could Bust Its Deposit-Insurance Fund." *Wall Street Journal*, 3 December.

Seiberg, J. 1998. "In an Era of New Megabanks, Oversight Efforts Debated." *American Banker*, 14 April, p. 2.

Shari, M. 1998. "Up in Smoke: How the IMF's Rescue Plan for Indonesia Exploded." *Business Week*, 1 June, pp. 60–66.

Siconolfi, M., A. Raghavan, and M. Pacelle. 1998. "How Salesmanship and Brainpower Failed at Long-Term Capital." *Wall Street Journal*, 16 November, pp. A1, A18, A19.

Steindl, J. 1965. *Random Process and the Growth of Firms*. London: Charles Griffin.

Thomson, J. B. 1992. "Modeling the Bank Regulator's Closure Option: A Two-Step Logit Regression Approach." *Journal of Financial Services Research* 6: 5–23.

"The Undead." 1998. *The Economist*, 19 September, p. 89.

U.S. Department of Commerce. 1997. *Statistical Abstract of the United States, 1997*. Washington, D.C.: U.S. Government Printing Office.

White, E. N. 1992. *The Comptroller and the Transformation of American Banking, 1960–1990*. Washington, D.C.: Office of the Comptroller of the Currency.

13

What Basle Forgot

D. Johannes Jüttner and Benton E. Gup

Financial institutions face a multitude of risks in financial markets. Traditionally, the risks of particular concern were credit risk (the risk of bad loans or that the issuer of securities defaults), liquidity risk (the risk associated with differences in the maturity of banks' assets and liabilities), funding risk (the risk caused by unexpected withdrawals of deposits or drying up of other sources of bank funds), interest rate risk (the risk arising from differences in the structure of interest rates on banks' assets and liabilities; for instance, when short-term rates at which the bank borrows rise and long-term rates at which the bank lends falls, losses result), and operational risk (risk of systems failure, error, and fraud). In recent years, financial institutions and their supervisors have become aware of market or position risk, which arises out of their trading books. The large trading losses reported by major U.S. banks as a result of the Asian financial crisis and Russian default is one example. It reflects that changes in the market prices of securities and derivatives in which the institution has taken a short-term position will cause a loss.

In this chapter we focus on one important risk element in banks' balance sheets that has been ignored by the Basle Supervisors, namely the market risk associated with banks' commercial loan portfolios.[1] The Basle Committee on Banking Supervision (Bank for International Settlements 1996) does include in its global supervisory approach market (or position) risk. Market risk is confined to the trading book of banks, which arises when changes in the market prices or rates of securities and derivatives in which the bank has taken a short-term position (ten days or shorter) or in on- and off-balance-sheet positions, will cause a loss. However, a large measure of market risk is omitted from the banking book, which is deemed to be subject only to credit risk. Loans are part of the banking book and their values appear to fluctuate over the business cycle, expanding often disproportionately during an upturn and contracting severely during a cyclical downturn. The recent crises in Asian economies bear testimony to the faulty risk-measurement and -management approach. For example, many Thai and Indonesian banks funded their loans to companies through U.S. dollar borrowings at pegged exchange rates. In addition, corporations directly borrowed dollar funds or their loans were tied to the U.S. dollar exchange rates. When this quasifixed exchange rate system collapsed and the baht, the rupiah, and other Asian currencies tumbled, the pervasive nature of exchange rate risk exposure resulted in wholesale failures of banks and companies.

It would be inappropriate to attribute this debacle to credit risk and ignore its marketswide root, namely exchange rate risk exposure. Credit risk is firm specific, but market risk impacts equally on all companies that have foreign currency loans on their books. The omission of market risk from the loan book not only seriously underestimates the total risk that banks bear but also has implications for the valuation of their loan portfolios. While the Bank for International Settlements (1996) mentions the risk of so-called "structural" (i.e., nondealing) foreign exchange positions, it fails to provide an adequate risk-measurement and -management framework.

We propose to integrate market risk and its measurement and management into banks' loan portfolios. The novel features of our approach are as follows. First, we investigate market risk in the commercial loan portfolios of banks that arises as a result of economywide events such as an exchange rate collapse or the cyclical ups and downs in economic activity. Second, we apply the value-at-risk framework to assets that are not traded in the market. This entails, on the one hand, estimating the present value of loans and, on the other hand, expanding the time dimension of the holding period from about ten days in the case of the trading book to several years for a portfolio of loans. We commence with an overview of the risk-measurement and -management structure that is now in place.

TRADITIONAL RISK-MANAGEMENT APPROACHES

In the past, banks and their respective national supervisors employed a variety of risk-management techniques. For example, U.S. banks and regulators focused on the CAMEL features of banks.[2] A well-managed bank carries an adequate amount of capital, holds quality assets (few loan write-downs and highly rated securities), is run by capable managers, generates healthy earnings streams, and maintains sufficient liquid reserves.

In addition, banks use credit scoring methods, where loan customers are rated on the basis of a number of criteria to manage default risk. Credit scoring is an indispensable control tool of the credit officer to screen loan customers. Information regarding their employment status and history, whether they own a house or rent, have other assets, are burdened by debt, and even their family situation provide valuable clues which enable the bank to grade customers into good and poor credit risks.

Some banks also practice match funding in order to control interest rate risk exposure. Here the bank carefully matches the terms (interest rate and maturity) of each loan exactly to its funding source. While this effectively eliminates the problem, it also reduces potential profits from changes in market rates of interest. Moreover, it has the serious disadvantage in practice of being very cumbersome to implement, especially for a large bank with many loans. However, these traditional hedging approaches do not lend themselves to application across national boundaries for banking regulation on a global basis. In addition, they fail to address the issue of market or position risk which arises out of the trading book of banks. Needless to say, these traditional risk-management approaches ignore the market risk of commercial loans.

THE NEW RISK ENVIRONMENT

The increasing integration of national economies and in particular the process of globalizations of financial markets requires a concerted effort by supervisors to introduce uniform prudential norms. The Bank for International Settlements in Basle, which is owned by the major central banks, was charged with this task.

Credit Risk

The BIS started from the premise that credit risk, of all the various banking risks, poses the greatest threat to the viability of financial institutions. Credit risk arises mainly from defaulting consumer and commercial loans in banks' banking books. Concern for the banks' vulnerability to credit risk resulted in the 1988 Capital Adequacy Requirement Accord (see Figure 13.1). Banks now hold at least 8 percent of their risk-adjusted asset is the form of tier 1 and tier 2 capital.

Figure 13.1
Major Banking Risks

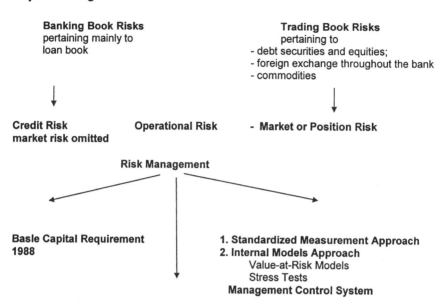

Banking Book Risks
pertaining mainly to
loan book

Trading Book Risks
pertaining to
- debt securities and equities;
- foreign exchange throughout the bank
- commodities

Credit Risk   **Operational Risk**   **- Market or Position Risk**
market risk omitted

Risk Management

Basle Capital Requirement   **1. Standardized Measurement Approach**
1988   **2. Internal Models Approach**
                                                Value-at-Risk Models
                                                Stress Tests
                                            Management Control System

Operational Risk

The complexity of derivatives and the enormous unhedged positions they allow banks to take through leveraged deals opens the door for rogue traders to engage in unauthorized or illegal trading. Resulting losses may not become apparent for some time, accumulate, and eventually wipe out the bank's capital (e.g., Barings Bank). Furthermore, even small errors with derivatives and computer systems failure may translate into large losses. Banks have to address these operational risks through the implementation of management control systems.

The BIS developed risk-measurement and -management proposals regarding the three main types of risks: credit risk, operations risk, and market risk. For the purpose of this chapter, we focus only on market risk.

MARKET RISK ANALYSIS

In recent years, banks have increasingly added the trading of securities and derivatives to their traditional banking activities, which include the taking of deposits, other borrowing activities, the granting of loans, and investing in debt securities and to a lesser extent also in equities. For this reason, banks now distinguish between their banking book and their trading book (see Figure 13.1). These two activities of banks are each associated with its own distinctly different kind of risk. Banks and supervisors soon realized that the trading book had the potential of posing an even greater threat to banks' viability than credit risk in the banking book. First, increased volatility of interest and exchange rates and of other asset prices caused earnings and assets/liabilities of banks to fluctuate appreciably. Second, banks increasingly moved away from their traditional core business of taking deposits and the granting of loans to the generation of fee income through trading of securities and derivatives and other off-balance-sheet activities. These transactions on the trading book of banks contain positions of securities and derivatives which are only held for a very short period, say a couple of days on average. Credit risk therefore does not play a role, but market risk caused by fluctuating rates and prices can affect the value of the trading book appreciably on a daily basis. For this reason, banks and supervisors now attempt to measure and manage market or position risk.

Market or position risk is defined as the risk that the value of on- or off-balance-sheet positions will decline as a result of unexpected changes of market prices before the positions can be liquidated, hedged, or offset with other positions. It is generally assumed that banks are able to offload or cover positions within ten business days. Market risk stems from unexpected broad changes in market interest rates, currency rates, and prices of stocks and commodities. Market risk arises out of the bank's trading book. The BIS defines the trading book as the bank's proprietary positions in financial instruments (including derivatives products and off-balance-sheet instruments) which are intentionally held for short-term resale and/or which are taken on by the institution with the intention of benefiting in the short term from actual and/or expected differences between their buying and selling prices, or from other price or interest rate variations, and positions from market making or positions taken in order to hedge other elements of the trading book. The trading book comprises all on- and off-balance-sheet debt securities and equities. Banks are required to value these securities and assets daily on a mark-to-market basis; that is, at the price they are worth in the market. For the purpose of capital charges to cover market risk, banks have to include in their trading book all of their foreign exchange and commodities positions.

Market risk is also called position risk, as it arises when banks take positions in securities, foreign currencies, or derivatives whose market prices may change unfavorably. For example, the global rise in interest rates during 1994 caused bond prices to fall. Banks with large bond holdings suffered substantial capital losses and their earnings were significantly curtailed. Likewise, the U.S. stock market crash of October 1987 shaved off a large slice of banks' portfolio values and caused the asset side of balance sheets of banks to shrink. As their liabilities remained the same, the threat of insolvency emerged.

During 1994, the BIS started to release discussion papers dealing with the measurement and disclosure of market risks of financial institutions. Subsequently, in January 1996, the BIS issued an "Amendment to the Capital Accord to Incorporate Market Risk." In this paper, the BIS lays down the rules for banks' capital charges in respect of their market risks in addition to their credit risks. The BIS requires banks for risk-measurement and -management purposes to slot all of their on- and off-balance-sheet instruments into banking book or trading book activities. The former predominantly contains credit risk and the latter market risk. They each require their own risk-measurement and capital charges.

MARKET RISK IN THE BANKING BOOK

Market risk not only afflicts the trading book; it can also arise from the banking book. The Basle approach recognizes position risk in the banking book that is due to interest or currency rate changes and price variations of shares or commodities. For example, whenever an unwanted interest rate gap or foreign currency, equity, or commodity risk exposure arises on the assets or liabilities sides of the banking book, the treasury division (trading book) provides hedging instruments which exactly offset these risks. The banking arm purchases, for example, the derivative from the trading arm, and it is accounted for on an accruals basis, at historic cost in the banking book and at market cost in the trading book.

This has the advantage of transparency, as it quarantines market risk from credit risk and enables the bank's total interest rate and currency exposures to be measured and managed in a single specialist center. Seen in this context, the interest rate risk, as the cause of traditional banking collapses, now becomes simply a part of the general market risk management of the trading arm. Ultimately, all the interest rate and currency risks of banking will therefore come under the umbrella of standardized value-at-risk management.

This market risk-management approach turns a blind eye to the possible presence of market risk in the commercial loan portfolio of the banking book. That is, the Basle approach fails to deal with a significant measure of market risk that remains in the loan book. Commercial loans are included in the balance sheets of banks at their book values or their credit-risk adjusted fair values. The Basle classification of risks in banking completely ignores market risk in the loan book that is caused by business cycles or cycle-related events. Focusing on banks' hedging of interest rate and currency risks on their books creates a false sense of security. Obviously, when a sharp rise in interest rates and a currency collapse leads to economywide failures of companies, even the most elaborate hedging structures cannot protect the values of the loan portfolios.

Market Risk and Loan Values

Market risk is associated with changes in the values of financial instruments that are due to fluctuations in prices affecting the whole market. Changes in investor sentiment regarding the growth prospects of a region, the earnings outlook, deflation, or the stance of monetary policies can depress or lift markets. Sometimes the source of a market disturbance may originate from a single adverse event, such as the downfall of a government, the reassessment of an emerging market, or the outbreak of international conflict. Conversely, positive news may provide an uplifting momentum for the whole market. Market risk is well understood with respect to the foreign exchange, bond, and share markets. We usually do not associate market risk with the loan portfolio of banks, even though their values appear to fluctuate appreciably and systematically over the business cycle.

Financial Cycles and Loan Valuations

Business cycles have a profound impact on the loan-granting behavior of banks and on the quality, and thus the value, of their loan portfolio. The relevant literature appears to be slow in accepting this feature. A first step in the right direction was taken by Chirinko and Guill (1991), who relate the credit risk of a loan portfolio to relevant macroeconomic variables. Randall (1993) examines the implications of financial cycles for credit quality of banks and other financial institutions in examining the causes of failed insured U.S. banks since the early 1970s. Problem loans resulting from commercial real estate lending caused the majority of bank failures. Loans to less-developed countries and financing for leveraged buyouts also damaged the banking industry. In fact, Randall's assiduously collected evidence attributes three-quarters of the bank failures (as measured by assets) during this period to cycle-related causes. Very few banks actually failed because of mismanagement.[3]

Australian banks' commercial lending behavior during the second half of the 1980s and the beginning of the 1990s clearly reflected a similar boom–bust mentality, prompting the governor of the Reserve Bank of

Australia to make the following comment: "During this period [in the late 1980s], banks were falling over themselves as they chased prospective customers. Throughout the second half of the 1980s, business credit was easily the fasted growing component of total credit, expanding by close to 25 per cent per annum. We all know now how unsound the fruit of much of that borrowing frenzy was" (Fraser 1994, 17).

Banks are inclined to assess loan applications more sympathetically when economic conditions improve. They may get carried away by waves of optimism and embark on a lending spree. Marking these loans on the basis of book values implies a concomitant expansion of the balance sheet. Assume, for example, a company launches an investment project during an economic boom period and obtains finance through a share float and from banks. Due to sanguine earnings expectations of $10 million and a low discount rate of 5 percent, formed on the basis of a bright, riskless economic outlook, the investment project, an inner-city shopping complex, is valued at $200 million. If bank finance is obtained for half of the value of the project, loan write-downs are inevitable when during the next recession earnings are pared to $2 million and the discount rate rises to 10 percent. The market value of the investment shrinks to $20 million. As a consequence, the bank would experience loan losses when the cash flow is inadequate to service the loan. While this example is hypothetical in nature, it presumably typifies the borrowing behavior of entrepreneurs and the lending conduct of many banks during the second half of the 1980s.

Even a bank's existing loan book does not remain unaffected, even though loan values have an upper ceiling. No matter how buoyant the economy and rising values of customers' share capital, the value of the loan cannot, in general, be written up above its contractual amount. However, this does not rule out the possibility of the bank's assets rising in line with the fortune of its loan customer. First, for equity participation loans, where the loan-granting bank acquires a share in the venture, the value of the equity in the company that has been financed rises in line with the latter's fortune. Second, the value of collateral which banks commonly require appreciates commensurately with rising asset prices. While the impact of rising collateral prices on the bank's net worth is extremely complex, as a rough approximation it is probably fair to say that the bank's assets rise. Frequently, customers top up loans in line with the increase in the collateral. Third, with rising asset prices, projects of customers that previously would not have received finance due to lack of insufficient collateral now become viable. A clear manifestation of the presence of market risk in the loan portfolio of banks are the forced sales of collateral assets backing risky loans in weak markets. The collapse of the asset price bubble of the late 1980s is a pertinent example.

WHY MARKET RISK IS IGNORED IN THE LOAN BOOK

Surprisingly, in the literature the impact of market risk on loan values appears to have been overlooked, even though the consequences may be quite severe for financial institutions and borrowers. We are not aware of any attempt to compute values of loans that take into account market risk, perhaps by adjusting expected cash flows for the possibility of an asset price collapse. As the BIS failed to develop a procedure equivalent to that embodied in the value-at-risk approach to effectively deal with market risk, the danger of mispricing of loan portfolios exists.

Several reasons may be given for this omission. First, the loan value changes associated with business cycles are a comparatively rare occurrence. While some banks may revalue their loans periodically, the assessment methods are not made public and they may vary from bank to bank. Therefore, the possibility for future loan evaluations on the basis of expected values and standard deviations of loan values derived from past business-cycle experience is not immediately obvious. We will address this issue later.

Second, the variabilities of market prices, yields, or interest and currency rates are commonly taken as a given constant and not subject to analysis in relationship to the loan book. The capital asset pricing theory serves as a pertinent example for this approach, where the volatility of the market portfolio serves as the benchmark for the rest of the market. Applied to the problem at hand, this means that banks regard the sequence of bulging loan books during boom periods and the subsequent write-downs when the economy skids into recession as outside their risk-management task.

Third, as the fortunes of companies wax and wane over the business cycle, default rates drop and rise in unison. Thus, default risk analysis would capture that part of market risk which is reflected in the cyclical movements of the economy.

Fourth, money and capital markets are frequently depressed by extreme pessimism or excessively buoyed by a sanguine economic outlook. To the extent that banks and firms become engrossed in these cycles of moods, they are, of course, unable to diagnose their own state of mind correctly.

TRADITIONAL ACCOUNTING STANDARDS FOR LOANS

For risk-management purposes, we require a valuation system that allows us to adjust the book values of loans to their correct discounted values. The main difficulty arises from the fact that loans commonly are not traded.

Of course, if values of assets and liabilities of a bank or a firm remained unchanged over time, historical cost accounting would effectively fulfill the main functions of an accounting system. That is, it
would provide us with a control-system routine, indicate how the resources of the bank are employed, and equip us with performance
measures.[4]

Due to a variety of factors, the values of loans are continually subject to valuation adjustments, making historical cost accounting a mis-
leading record-keeping system.[5] In particular, a range of risk factors
impinge on a bank's balance sheet items. Foremost among these are
default risk, interest rate risk, foreign currency risk, and market risk.
While the implications of the first three risk factors for some balance
sheet entries are subject to prescribed risk-management systems under the general supervision of the BIS, the importance of market risk
for banks' assets and liabilities appears to have been overlooked.

Changes in market risk cause loan values on the balance sheets of
financial institutions to fluctuate. For this reason, some kind of economic value accounting is required. The most prominent among these is
the market value accounting (mark-to-market) principle. Market value
has been defined as "the amount obtainable from the sale, or payable on
the acquisition, of a financial instrument in an active market" (International Accounting Standards Committee 1994). Market value accounting is most readily accepted for securities that banks hold and for which
the market establishes benchmark prices on a daily basis.

However, marking to market is not possible in cases where the market fails to establish a benchmark price or where trading occurs only
intermittently. Under these circumstances, banks have to estimate fair
values of the financial instruments. The International Standards Committee defines the fair value as the amount at which the asset could be
exchanged, or a liability settled, between knowledgeable, willing parties in an arm's length transaction. This valuation principle is particularly appropriate for loan portfolios of banks, and in the following
section we investigate how fair values of commercial loans may be
determined and whether it takes account of market risk.

Fair Values of Loan Portfolios

An important determinant of the fair value of a commercial loan is
default risk. Deterioration in the creditworthiness of a loan customer's
situation reduces the probability that interest payments are made in
full and on time and casts doubt on the eventual repayment of the
loan. As a consequence, the expected future cash flow falls. Given the
discount rate, the present value of the loan falls. How much the loan
has to be marked down to its fair value is difficult to say because com-

mercial bank loans are in general not traded in the market. Several techniques exist for the derivation of the fair value of loans. We may factor the deteriorating creditworthiness of a loan customer into the contractual cash flow associated with the loan or adjust the discount rate. We commence with a discussion of the latter method.

Risk-Adjusted Discount Rate

The present values of contractual loan payments (PV) are obtained from

$$PV = \frac{\sum_t CP_t}{(1 + r)^t} \tag{1}$$

where CP measures the dollar amount of the contractual payments at time (t) and the discount rate (r) equals the internal rate of return on a financial instrument which comparable default risk features require (Berger, Kuester King, and O'Brien 1991). While this approach has simplicity on it side, it faces the practical problem of selecting the appropriate discount rate from the range of market securities with similar credit quality, prepayment risk, and rate flexibility. Several methods have been applied to obtain an appropriate discount rate.

First, for credit-rated customers the bank management could conceivably obtain reliable market data from the rise in interest rates on securities that is commonly associated with the downgrading of firms. This avenue for obtaining market-based information about the default premium suggests itself for banks' bond holdings of private-sector issuers (Altman 1993, 15). However, the rating outcomes can conceivably also be applied to loans of rated firms. Financial securities with maturities comparable to those of loans of downgraded firms provide in-principle reference risk premia.

As the contractual cash flow of such securities is now discounted by a higher interest rate, we obtain the present value of expected cash flows. The variable CP becomes the contracted (or promised) cash flow. It remains unchanged after the loss in creditworthiness; the greater risk is entirely captured in upward adjustments of r. Uncritical application of the rating data to the loan portfolio would, however, be misplaced. Research by Randall (1989) casts doubt on the ability of rating agencies to identify banks with a buildup of problem loans.

Second, for unrated companies or where the rating information is of limited value, the following methods predominate. First, Berger, Kuester King, and O'Brien (1991) discount the contracted payments by a risk-adjusted internal rate of return on a financial instrument with similar default probabilities. The resulting present value of a loan provides an implicit measure of its market value. The problem with this approach consists in finding an interest rate on a compatible security. Mengle (1990) suggests matrix pricing to overcome this problem. A risk-determined yield spread (spread over prime or LIBOR [London Interbank Offer Rate]) is regressed on specific features of the loan customer such as firm size, risk, industry, loan type, and so on that explain the risk features of the loan.

Third, estimates of company-specific betas could be translated into risk premia in a variety of ways. For example, a firm's risk premium is set in relationship to the industry's average. In this case, the industry's excess return over the risk-free rate is multiplied by the company's beta, resulting in the appropriate company-specific risk premium.

Risk-Adjusted Cash Flows

An alternative approach attempts to assess the probabilistic value of the contractual cash flows. However, we lack a generally accepted method of evaluating the various factors that conceivably contribute to a deterioration of the creditworthiness of firms. Nevertheless, Australian banks appear to assess the full collectability of the cash flow emanating from loans on a periodic basis, for example, in their half-yearly reports to the Stock Exchange. To the extent that the recoverable amounts of problem loans are captured, a version of fair value accounting is already in place. The whole adjustment procedure, however, appears to be afflicted by a large dose of subjectivity. According to Berger, Kuester King, and O'Brien (1991), it thus lacks accuracy and comparability across financial institutions. Moreover, the projected cash flows depend on the cycle environment in which they are made. During an expansionary phase they are presumably too generous, and they tend to be downward biased when the business outlook is bleak.

Periodic Sales of a Small Proportion of Loans

Benston (1989) suggested that banks may overcome the problem posed by missing market values by engaging, from time to time, in loan sales. While sales of securitized mortgages are by now commonplace in U.S. capital markets, the secondary market for commercial loans remains largely undeveloped. However, a market is developing for Small Business Administration (SBA) guaranteed loans. A number of inherent weaknesses account for this situation.

First, individual loans are difficult to standardize; they differ with respect to riskiness, collateral, maturity, and other characteristics. Second, sales of loans encounter the well-known "lemons problem" (Beaver, Datar, and Wolfson 1992). Potential buyers, suspecting that the selling bank is in possession of private information of a negative nature, depress loan prices. Third, bankers, on the other hand, knowing that their operations are partly indemnified against losses through deposit insurance, by de facto government guarantees (in the cases of large banks) or lender-of-last-resort facilities available from the central bank, may dispose of the high-quality loans in their portfolios. In this way, the bank management fully utilizes the value of the deposit insurance. In the case of continuing successful operation, the bank reduces the cost of funds, while in the event of failure, a large part of the bankruptcy costs are borne by a third party. Therefore, the opportunities of obtaining market-value data that are relevant to loan portfolios are severely restricted.

ACCOUNTING FOR MARKET RISK
IN COMMERCIAL LOANS

The foregoing valuation approach is only relevant for expected loan losses at a point in time; it does not tell us anything about the uncertainty of loan losses. In terms of equation (1), for example, the uncertainty could be measured by specifying a probability distribution for the discount rate or the present value. Thus, the assessment of banks' loan portfolios on the basis of their fair values essentially ignores market risk. This is mainly due to two features of commercial loans. First, firms with an established banking relationship normally obtain finance on a medium- to long-term basis. The maturity of their loans may range over an indeterminate period, as happens when a revolving credit facility is granted to a fixed term of several years or longer. The longer-term nature of loans requires a risk-assessment horizon of matching length.

Second, banks appear to base their assessment of the riskiness of commercial loans on the business conditions they currently experience. This state-dependent nature of risk measurement entails the danger of extrapolating the buoyant (depressed) profit outlook during a boom (recession) into the future, when the business cycle may have run its course and firms face drastically altered business conditions.

Let us assume a firm has obtained a five-year variable-rate loan or a one-year loan that can be expected to be rolled over four times during an expansionary phase of the economy. On the strength of buoyant profit outlook the loan is classified as low risk. After two years, interest rates are raised by the central bank in order to combat the buildup of inflationary pressure, with the result being an ensuing downturn in the economy. The higher borrowing costs and the subsequent slide into recession cause profits of companies to evaporate; many suffer losses, asset prices become depressed, and loan defaults mount. Banks and other financial institutions are forced to write down bad loans, restructure loan agreements, and foreclose. For the same loan, two completely different risk ratings will be made; one during the period of business buoyancy, the other when tight monetary policy raises borrowing costs and pushes the economy into recession.

Business cycles are a fact of life. Since World War II, Australia, for example, has experienced ten business cycles (Pagan 1996), each lasting on average about two years from peak to trough and three years from trough to peak. Prudent banking behavior would suggest that the economic conditions prevailing during the cyclical ups and downs have to be factored into the market-risk rating of commercial loans. Banks are then able to measure market risk of commercial loans just as they do for the value-at-risk calculations of their trading book. It is worth mentioning that the market risk of loans is distinctly different from their credit risk. Conceptually, they may be separated, assuming away business cycles and measuring the probability of loan defaults. The difference between the overall chance of loan write-downs and cycle-free loan defaults then provides a measure of the market risk of loans.

VALUE-AT-RISK OF COMMERCIAL LOANS

In 1997, J. P. Morgan announced CreditMetrics, a statistical model used to assess credit portfolio risk, including bonds, loans, letters of credit, commitments, derivatives, and receivables. CreditMetrics is a value-at-risk approach to credit-risk management. That is, it incorporates the volatility of value due to changes in obligor's credit quality, defaults, upgrades, and downgrades to estimate the probability of decline in portfolio value, or losses, in a given period of time. The probability of losses usually ranges from 1 to 5 percent, and the time horizon may be any length, but it is usually short term. Since the introduction of CreditMetrics, other firms have developed competing models with different features.[6]

Despite the existence of such models, we examine the value at risk of the commercial loan portfolio from a more abstract point of view. From the bank's point of view, the difference between the expected rate of return from loans (r^e) and the cost of funding the loans (r^c) provides a measure of comfort or discomfort regarding the prospect of timely interest payments and principal repayments. A wide return-minus-funding-cost margin or net rate of return ($r^n = r^e - r^c$) signals a generous cushion, and a thin one suggests possible loan write-downs in the future.

The expected rate of return on a loan is defined as the product of the loan rate (r^l) and 1 minus the probability (p) of the loan defaulting (i.e., $r^e = r^l[1 - p]$). While the risk-adjusted loan rates are available, the probabilities of loan default have to be estimated by banks from firm-specific information, such as the internal rate of return of investment projects for which bank finance has been granted and the behavior over time of the cost of funds. A bank would have to collect expected rates of return for its loan portfolio over a longer-term time horizon for types of loans as well as data for the behavior of the cost of its funds.

For instance, a bank would obtain monthly or quarterly data on expected rates of return on loans for, say, the last twenty years for the various branches of the retail sector, the computer industry, the manufacturing sector, and those other parts of the economy to which it lends. A breakdown into expected returns on short-term and long-term loans would yield additional information. In order to measure the probability of default, the bank draws up risk profiles of the loan customers in the various activities for the purpose of determining the appropriate risk premium on loans. Likewise, data for the cost of loan funds on a monthly or quarterly basis, covering the same time period, have to be collected.

We now translate the information into a value-at-risk gauge and apply the BIS (1996) model to commercial loans.[7] Assume a bank has loans to the retail sector on its books with an average holding period of one year. The following steps are involved (see J. P. Morgan/Reuters 1996):

1. The fair value of the loans has been determined, say as $L_0 = \$100$ million.
2. On the basis of twenty years' quarterly data for r^e and r^c, the bank computes a mean net rate of return of $\bar{r}^n = 1.45$ percent, measured on a quarterly basis. As it expects this rate of return to prevail over the next four quarters, the future value of the loan portfolio for the first quarter is $L_1 = L_0(1 + \bar{r}^n)$ or $I_1 = \$100$ million $(1.0145) = \$101.45$ million.
3. Next, the bank uses measured monthly or quarterly standard deviation of returns, $\sigma = 0.82$ percent, to forecast the quarterly rate of return $\hat{r}^n$ in such a way that there is a 5-percent chance of the actual return being less than $\hat{r}^n$. Assuming that the return of the loan portfolio is distributed unconditionally normal, we obtain $\hat{r}^n = 1.65\sigma + \bar{r}^n$ or $\hat{r}^n = 1.65 \times 0.82\% + 1.45\% = 0.02803$. The worst-case loan value becomes $\hat{L}_1 = L_0[1 - (1.65 + \bar{r}^n)]$ or $\hat{L}_1 = \$100$ million $(1 - 0.02803) = \$97.197$ million. As is well recognized in the literature, the application of the mean-variance analysis to the loan portfolios of financial institutions is not without problems, as loan returns are not symmetrically distributed. However, for relatively short return measurement periods (monthly or quarterly), a normal return distribution serves as a first approximation.[8]
4. The value-at-risk may now be computed as $VAR = L_0 - \hat{L}_1 = \$2.803$ million.

Figure 13.2 contains a distribution curve depicting the return on commercial loans. The mean of the distribution ($\bar{r}^n$) measures the long-term average of the margin. It amounts to 1.45 percent or $1.45 million in money terms. It has, of course, to be positive; otherwise, a bank would suffer losses.

Figure 13.2
Distribution of Quarterly Loan Returns

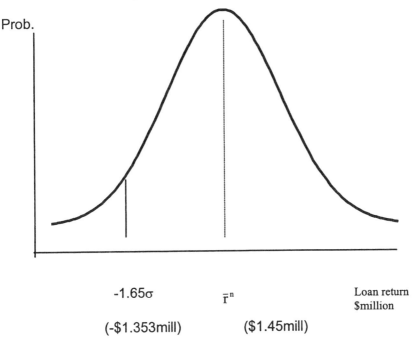

Prob.

-1.65σ $\bar{r}^n$ Loan return
                                                         $million

(-$1.353mill)   ($1.45mill)

The VAR of the loan portfolio equals that amount by which the worst possible outcome—a loss of $2.803 million—exceeds the expected outcome of $1.45 million. Using the normal distribution curve, the bank selects a one-tailed confidence interval of 95 percent, which corresponds to 1.65σ. The bank can now be 95-percent certain that its loss on the loan portfolio will not exceed the 1.65σ limit, which corresponds in Figure 13.2 to the horizontal distance between the mean return, $\bar{r}^n$, and 1.65σ.

For a one-year holding period, this amount has to be scaled up by the square root of four; that is, multiplied by two. Note we are computing σ and not variance. The resulting sum of $5.606 million, known as the value-at-risk, indicates the maximal loss over some time interval (one year) for a given level of probability (confidence interval of 95%).

At the same time, with a 95-percent confidence interval, the bank expects that there is a 1 in 20 (5%) chance that the actual loss over any given day will be greater than that corresponding to a negative rate of return of –1.353 percent on the loan portfolio.

The higher (lower) the confidence interval, the lower (higher) the probability that quarterly losses will not surpass the value-at-risk figure. However, the higher the confidence interval, the higher is the VAR. This becomes immediately apparent from Figure 13.2. The 95-percent confidence interval corresponds to the –1.65σ range, which implies a rate of return of –1.353 percent. A 99-percent interval, which is recommended by the Basle Supervisory Committee for trading book positions, would be further to the left and thus imply a higher expected loss on the loan portfolio, causing a greater potential loss for the institution, though the loss is expected fewer times than with a lower confidence interval.

The limitations of this approach have to be understood. The VAR focuses solely on the probability of losses larger than a specified amount, which in our case amounts to $2.803 million per quarter. It completely passes over the vital point of the extent of the expected losses when the confidence interval is breached. In our example, we computed the loss for exactly the 1.65σ cutoff point. In reality, however, losses during a quarter may occur at two, three, or even higher standard deviations.

CONCLUSION

The Basle proposal restricts the measurement and management of market risk to the trading books of banks. It fails to realize that market-risk factors also affect the commercial loan portfolio of the banking book. Our approach to developing a VAR framework for part of the banking book captures the cyclical and monetary policy determinants of market risk in banks' commercial loan portfolios. Quarterly data of expected rates of return on loans for a long historical time period reflect the ups and downs of the economy. Likewise, the statistical data regarding the cost of funds contain information about the sequence of tight and easy monetary policy stances. Both variables together provide a gauge for the expected losses from loans. The VAR measure can be used for the computation of required capital in addition (or in lieu) of the tier 1 capital requirement.

NOTES

1. Our analysis applies equally to nonbank financial institutions' loan books.

2. As of January 1997, the Federal Reserve and other federal regulators added a sixth component, the sensitivity to market risk (S), to the CAMEL rating, which is now referred to as CAMELS instead of CAMEL. S indicates whether a bank is able to identify, measure, monitor, and control market risk.

3. Park (1994) provides three reasons for the increased riskiness of U.S. banks in the 1980s: first, increased incentives for risk taking by bank shareholders; second, desperate attempts by managers to increase profits by assuming additional risks; and third, unexpected economic shocks. However, his analysis is confined to the last decade which would be too short for a cyclical analysis.

4. The introduction of historical cost accounting in 1938 in the United States carried with it the hope that this "accounting standard would encourage banks to focus on the long-run 'intrinsic' values and to eschew the pursuit of speculative market gains." Since all too frequently the opposite happened in subsequent decades, we are now on the verge of adopting marking to market. Embracing it uncritically could turn out to be even more disastrous than the past accounting regime.

5. In addition, it induced gains trading among banks. When market interest rates fell, for example, fixed coupon bonds would be sold for a capital gain while the capital losses associated with interest rate rises would be hidden behind their historical cost. This behavior increased the likelihood of bank failures and bail-outs by the taxpayer.

6. Information about CreditMetrics is available on the Internet at http://www.jpmorgan.com/RiskManagement/CreditMetrics. Also see Simons (1996).

7. The BIS's internal models approach requires that banks compute the value-at-risk for their trading book on a daily basis, assuming a ten-day holding period. The holding period is deemed to allow banks to hedge any open positions that are affected by worsening market conditions or trade out of difficulties. We apply the VAR framework to the commercial loan portfolio of the banking book. However, since the holding period for loans is on average measured in quarters (four) rather than days, we have to make the appropriate adjustments to VAR of a loan portfolio.

8. Gollinger and Morgan (1993) and Altman and Saunders (1997), for example, apply the mean-variance framework to financial institutions' loan portfolios.

REFERENCES

Altman, E. I. 1993. "Mark-to-Market and Present Value Disclosure: An Opportunity or a Costly Annoyance?" *Financial Analysts Journal* (March–April): 14–16.

Altman, E. I., and A. Saunders. 1997. "Credit Risk Measurement Over the Last 20 Years." *Journal of Banking and Finance* (December): 1721–42.

Bank for International Settlements. 1994. "Public Disclosure of Market and Credit Risks by Financial Institutions." Discussion paper prepared by the Working Group of the Group of Ten countries, Basle, September.

Bank for International Settlements. 1996. "Amendment to the Capital Accord to Incorporate Market Risk." Basle Committee of Banking Supervision, January.

Beaver, W. H., S. Datar, and M. A. Wolfson. 1992. "The Role of Market Value Accounting in the Regulation of Insured Depository Institutions." In *The Reform of Federal Deposit Insurance: Disciplining the Government and Protecting Taxpayers*, edited by J. R. Barth and R. D. Brumbaugh. New York: HarperCollins.

Benston, G. J. 1989. "Market-Value Accounting: Benefits, Costs and Incentives." *Proceedings of a Conference on Bank Structure and Competition*. Chicago: Federal Reserve Bank of Chicago.

Berger, A. N., K. Kuester King, and J. M. O'Brien. 1991. "The Limitations of Market Value Accounting and a More Reliable Alternative." *Journal of Banking and Finance* 15: 753–83.

Chirinko, R. S., and E. D. Guill. 1991. "A Framework for Assessing Credit Risk in Depository Institutions: Towards Regulatory Reform." *Journal of Banking and Finance* (September): 785–804.

Fraser, B. 1994. "Foreign Banks in Australia." *Bulletin* (Reserve Bank of Australia), September, 16–22.

Gollinger, T. L., and J. B. Morgan. 1993. "Calculation of an Efficient Frontier for a Commercial Loan Portfolio." *Journal of Portfolio Management* (Winter): 39–46.

International Accounting Standards Committee. 1994. *Financial Instruments* (Exposure Draft E48). London: International Accounting Standards Committee.

Jorion, P. 1997. *Value-at-Risk: The New Benchmark for Controlling Market Risk.* Chicago: Irwin.

J. P. Morgan/Reuters. 1996. *RiskMetrics—Technical Document.* 4th ed. New York: J. P. Morgan/Reuters.

Mengle, D. 1990. "Market Value Accounting and the Bank Balance Sheet." *Contemporary Policy Issues* (April): 82–94.

Pagan, A. 1996. "The Rise and Fall and Rise . . . of the Business Cycle." Discussion Paper, Centre for Economic Policy Research, Canberra.

Park, S. 1994. "Explanation for the Increased Riskiness of Banks in the 1980s." *Review* (Federal Reserve Bank of St. Louis), July–August, pp. 3–23.

Randall, R. E. 1989. "Can the Market Evaluate Asset Quality Exposure in Banks?" *New England Economic Review* (Federal Reserve Bank of Boston), July–August, pp. 3–24.

Randall, R. E. 1993. "Safeguarding the Banking System from Financial Cycles." Conference series no. 37, Federal Reserve Bank of Boston, pp. 17–64.

Simons, K. 1996. "Value at Risk: New Approaches to Risk Management." *New England Economic Review* (Federal Reserve Bank of Boston), September–October, pp. 3–13.

14

Problem Bank Resolution: Evaluating the Options

Anthony M. Santomero and Paul Hoffman

The banking systems in too many countries are insolvent. Whether one looks at Japan, Malaysia, Thailand, Korea, China, or Russia, the same situation is uncovered. Bank balance sheets have weakened, and there are real questions about the solvency of the entire system. At first, regulators and policymakers do not want to look, hoping that time will redress the ills and raise the value of troubled assets. However, in most cases, they come to recognize the obvious—some sooner than others. When this time comes, regulators look first for causes then for scapegoats, but eventually they look for answers. They slowly recognize the need to resolve their financial structure problems. At this point they are frequently offered expert advice, but rarely offered a survey of the full range of alternatives. They are often offered vague references to past experience, but they are rarely offered a full review of the recent relevant experience. This is the goal of this chapter.

Here, we look at the various options available to deal with problem institutions and evaluate their usefulness. Beyond enumeration and a theoretical description, we present a realistic analysis of the set of options that are available and have been available to bank regulators. Then we examine how they have been employed in three cases from different parts of the world. The result of the effort is not a simple prescription, however. We will show that there are a series of remedies for problem institutions, each with something to recommend it and problems associated with its use. In the end, the regulator has to weigh many factors before choosing an optimal path in his own environment. He must select from the choices available given the circumstances at hand. Yet knowing what can and has been done, plus what the likelihood of success depends upon, ought to aid us all in understanding both the past and the future paths of bank resolution.

The Role of Institutions in the Financial Sector

The discussion of bank crises and options for resolution can not begin without a recognition of the perceived importance of the banking sector to policymakers and economists alike. One worries about bank problems because banks are viewed by both of these groups as warranting special attention.

The current view of the role of these intermediaries is that they serve two primary functions that are essential for the smooth operation of an aggregate economy. First and foremost, they are generators or creators of assets. These assets are obtained from either the government, to finance deficits, or from the private sector. In the latter case, they are expected to screen the set of borrowing opportunities presented to them, using an expertise and specific capital that is unique to this sector (Diamond 1984; Bhattacharya and Thakor 1993). Projects found worthy are financed and monitored until repayment. This second phase of the lending function, ongoing servicing and monitoring, is critical for a number of reasons. First, once the loan is made, it is frequently illiquid and difficult to value without substantial effort (Gorton and Pennacchi 1990). Second, such oversight by firms who are responsible for financing the investment project often leads to higher returns from the endeavor, as investors respond to ongoing monitoring by increasing effort and closer adherence to the proposed purpose of the loan (Allen and Gale 1988). In both cases, the existence of a monitoring institution improves the performance of the project returns accruing to the stakeholders of the intermediary itself.

The second function of the intermediary sector is the channeling of savings resources to a higher purpose. This is achieved in two distinct ways. For transaction balances, the financial sector has developed the capacity to use idle balances, even while the payment system functions efficiently. From the perspective of the institution, it provides depository services in order to finance the lending activity outlined. Yet the fact that financial institutions are central to the clearing process suggests a need for regulatory concern and oversight (viz., the integrity of the payment system) (Goodfriend 1989). For standard savings balances, return must warrant risk and delayed consumption. The institution offers standard financial assets to the public which must be priced to permit a positive return for deferred consumption.

As an intermediary, the financial institution provides both of these functions simultaneously (i.e., it makes loans and assumes liabilities).

In fact, it often does so with assets that have maturity lengths that differ substantially from the average maturity of its liabilities. In so doing, the standard asset-transformation function includes maturity transformation as well as resource mobilization. While these can be viewed as mostly complimentary services, at times the use of relatively liquid liabilities to finance illiquid and longer-term risk assets generates an inherent instability in the system (Diamond and Dybvig 1983; Gorton 1988), yet it is central to providing the economy its value-added activity of mobilizing savings assets into productive real investment.

The Instability of the Sector

Given this description of functions performed by the sector, it should be transparent that some regulatory oversight of this sector is appropriate. Financial institutions are structurally vulnerable because they finance the holdings of direct claims that can be valued only imperfectly with short-term liabilities that are viewed as redeemable at par. In addition, they provide the valuable service of maturity transformation, which is mutually beneficial to borrowers and savers, but which may, nonetheless, place the financial institution itself in jeopardy (see Kareken and Wallace 1978; Jacklin 1987; Santomero 1992). In addition, marketability and valuation are likely to be fundamental characteristics of most of the direct claims held by these institutions. Therefore, holders of their claims (liability holders) cannot readily evaluate the solvency of the institutions by affirming that the market value of its assets exceeds the promised value of its aggregate liabilities.

Nonetheless, depositors and many other liability holders place funds in these institutions fully expecting to be able to withdraw them whenever they choose. In most circumstances, their withdrawals are purely random and statistically predictable. However, if liability holders become concerned about the solvency of the institution, withdrawals may become systematic and jeopardize the liquidity and solvency of the entire industry (Gorton 1988; Jacklin and Bhattacharya 1988).

Runs, once begun, tend to be self-reinforcing. News that the depository institution is selling direct claims at distressed prices or is borrowing at very high rates will further undermine the confidence of current and potential depositors. Even those who believe that with sufficient time the financial institution would be able to redeem all of its liabilities have a motive to join the run. They have reason to fear that the costs from the hurried liquidation of direct claims in response to the run by other creditors might render such an institution insolvent. This is the story that Diamond and Dybvig (1983) relate so forcefully.

This vulnerability to runs is more than the strictly private concern of an individual depository institution and its customers. It becomes a public policy concern when a loss of confidence in the solvency of the sector or many of its members leads to a contagious loss of confidence in other institutions. This will destroy not only the specific capital of the institution under pressure but also diminish the capacity of the financial sector to economically fund viable projects and monitor them to a satisfactory conclusion (Bernanke and Gertler 1989, 1990; Gertler 1988). This is a particularly serious problem when there are a few large institutions with national or international franchises. The larger the institutions, the greater the likelihood that the failure of any one will attract public attention and undermine confidence in the financial system in general and in other similar large financial institutions in particular.

The Financial Safety Net

It is for this reason that regulators everywhere have chosen to establish a mechanism to address the problem of weakness in the financial-institution sector. The financial safety net, an elaborate set of institutional mechanisms for protecting the financial system, has been constructed, and has largely succeeded in preventing contagious runs in the financial sector. Through this mechanism, most countries have developed a regulatory structure that prevents the amplification of shocks through the financial system. This safety net can be viewed as a set of preventive measures that can and should be triggered at various stages in the evolution of a financial crisis.

However, the safety net has worked only moderately well over the past half century. The chartering and prudential functions, so key to the integrity of the financial sector, have been responsible for maintaining a reasonably good reputation for the sector as a whole, worldwide. While crises of confidence occasionally arise, they are the noted exception, not the rule. Likewise, since the 1930s remedies aimed at the last stages of contagion control, the lender-of-last-resort function, and the monetary neutralization of a crisis have been largely successful.

Regulators and policymakers have had less success in dealing with a situation when a large institution or the industry as a whole is faced with a solvency crisis. Some regulators have been successful in navigating through these waters, closing troubled institutions early and containing a solvency crisis to a subset of the industry. All too often, however, when problems are the result of anything more than idiosyncratic behavior on the part of one entity, the record has been decidedly mixed. Sectors have fallen victim to contagion, governments have been left with large bills, and the institutional structure has been badly damaged.

This is in part due to the political nature of the process, but it is also due to lack of clear understanding of the options available. All too frequently, policy is made on limited information and great pressure by special interests—hardly a recipe for optimal policy choice. It is for this reason that a review of the options available for problem bank resolution may prove helpful.

OPTIONS AVAILABLE FOR THE RESOLUTION
OF PROBLEM INSTITUTIONS

We will consider the case where a regulator finds a single institution in trouble, as well as when the entire structure of financial institutions is weakened. These situations nearly always are the result of a sudden decline in the value of capital associated with a precipitous decline in asset value. In such cases, the regulatory authority has to resolve a situation of a troubled institution or institutions with little or no capital. What are the choices facing the regulator in this situation? How do the circumstances surrounding the crisis effect the outcome?

Understanding the Conditions Associated
with Resolution Options

To answer these questions, this section begins by evaluating the generic answers, and goes on to a finer, more detailed list. At the outset, however, two points warrant mention. First, it is not at all clear that the selection of the appropriate resolution option is related to the cause of the crisis. Second, the choice selected probably does depend on the breadth and depth of the problem. While more will be said about this, these two points warrant early attention.

We take as given that the choice of the resolution mechanism should be made based upon the minimization of the social cost of the financial-sector problem at hand. As such, the regulator must recognize that the solution sought is aimed not at the cause of the bank solvency itself, but on its effect on the financial structure. To a large measure, the cause of the crisis is irrelevant; it is a matter for historians, lawyers, and politicians, not economists. The latter ought to look for the optimal regulatory response to a hampered institutional structure. Their interest should rest on how to assure a return to status quo ante (i.e., an environment in which needed investment capital flows to the highest bidder in a relatively efficient manner, and savers regain their confidence in the system). Their role should not be one which attempts to impose penalties on the institutions or the managers involved. Nor should it necessarily be to renovate the workings of the system. This can be left to a later time.

Nevertheless, it should be recognized that any specific action which is taken will have repercussions. As the regulator addresses the current problem situation, he is sending clear signals to the market. In short, he is informing market participants as to the likely resolution option which will be used the next time a crisis arises and building expectations into the system. In this regard, therefore, actions taken today will affect the workings of the system tomorrow, by affecting expectations and defining the expected cost of failure for the next cycle.

The second point mentioned relates to the scale of the problem to be addressed. Often economists are quick to argue that failure should have a rapid and brutal response. Failed private institutions should pay the private penalty for default. However, while this result may be viable in theory, it is never employed in practice. In reality, the options open to the regulator will depend not only on the state of the institutions involved, but also on the state of the industry and the broader financial market itself.

Resolution options open to an isolated failure of a single institution are different than those available to the regulator when facing system-wide failure or the collapse of a whole market. This is true for at least two reasons. First, if the institution is part of a collapsing financial system, the reasons for establishing a safety net in the first place become critical. The regulator has no interest in closing the entire banking system because of a financial collapse or a sectoral decline which renders capital ratios negligible or indeed negative. The resultant cost of such a move, in terms of investment disruption and consumer confidence, is in all likelihood far larger than the regulatory process would tolerate, to say nothing of the political costs attendant to such a crisis. Likewise, given the systemic nature of a problem which could wipe out an entire sector, it is not at all clear that the immediate liquidation of financial assets to satisfy creditors is an appropriate strategy. Firesale prices, large bid–ask spreads, and the virtual lack of bids are common elements of a mass liquidation. The regulator accomplishes little by adding to the frenzy.

This having been noted, systemic problems must be addressed. No central bank has the capacity, nor should it have the authority, to sustain a bankrupt structure indefinitely. The issues that arise must be addressed and a resolution achieved. We are all too familiar with banking systems that remain bankrupt for long periods of time. The inevitable result is neither efficient funding of capital projects central to growth nor a stable depository structure in which depositors have confidence. The result is inefficiency, distrust, and subsequent collapse.

Enumeration of Options

With this as a starting point, let us look at the generic options available for problem resolution. At their core, there are only three: (1) permitting continued operation under some restrictions, (2) forcing a merger with another institution, oi (3) closure of some form. Let us examine each in turn.

The Continued Operations Options

The obvious first option is to allow the institutions to operate in spite of its hampered financial condition. The determination of whether a bank will be permitted to continue as a distinct institution, however, is dependent upon a number of factors, including the health of its balance sheet, public attitudes toward continued operation, and regulators' view of the likelihood of acceptable long-run performance. The ideal resolution for a problem situation is the return to strong financial performance and solvency. Regulators may use the tools of forbearance and even provide a capital infusion toward this end. However, the goal must be in sight; that is to say, this option may not be efficacious if the initial condition of the institution or institutions involved is severely troubled or the conditions result from a severely weakened asset base.

A somewhat more harsh remedy may take the form of continued operation with some form of regulatory control and management. This action is taken when it is thought that current management cannot orchestrate a turnaround. Regulatory control is generally viewed as a temporary measure along the way to either liquidation or merger. Regulators are usually considered to be caretakers, as they do not generally have the skill or staffing to maintain management control indefinitely.

Extreme financial stress may prompt the government to provide a rescue with a substantial capital infusion. At the limit, such an action is tantamount to de facto if not de jure nationalization. This is undertaken when the institution is considered to be of such critical importance to the financial system that its continued functioning is a matter of national urgency. Even if this is the case, nationalization is only undertaken when other avenues are closed and national sentiment does not preclude this option.

The Merger Options

A next-best solution from the standpoint of long-term corporate viability which also retains some of the bank's franchise value is a merger with another, hopefully healthier institution. However, merger of this form frequently requires enhancement of the balance sheet in order to entice prospective partners. This may range from partitioning of assets so that only some are transferred to the acquiring entity, all the way to the partitioning of the entire bank in the form of a good-bank, bad-bank split. Both measures are essentially forms of purchase and assumption. The real distinction is in how much of the old entity can be transferred to the new organization.

Payout Options

Regulators may ultimately conclude that liquidation is the most efficient, indeed the only, solution. However, this choice is usually made only after the going-concern value of the entity is considered and weighed against the taxpayer cost of maintaining the surviving firm. In the event this decision is taken, there is still the issue of which class of liability holders share in the associated loss. The tallying of total cost must incorporate a decision as to which depositors should be and will be reimbursed. If the country possesses explicit deposit insurance, only a decision concerning uninsured depositors is needed. In other jurisdictions, de facto implicit insurance leaves the issue of coverage and co-insurance to the regulator, in conjunction with the political process. Last, a plan for the disposal of assets must be determined.

Complete List of Options Available

The choices are, however, a bit richer than this enumeration would suggest. There are several ways to continue operations, to force a merger, or to liquidate. We will consider seven options that have been employed around the world. The commentary illustrates that many also have suboptions.

Forbearance

An institution which is experiencing financial distress may be able to resolve its problems if given time. The granting of time for a management turnaround, the orderly disposal of problem assets, and/or the generation of positive profits against which to charge off losses is defined as forbearance.

As this suggests, forbearance can occur for two separate reasons. Either the firm is thought to be bankrupt but the timing of the liquidation is deferred for market reasons, or the firm is perceived as salvageable if given enough time to recover from an unexpected and large loss. In the first case, it is sometimes alleged that immediate liquidation of assets is not possible in the real world. It is argued that pressure to liquidate assets can lead to returns which do not reflect fair market value. Therefore, to achieve maximum return an institution is given leeway to liquidate its assets as favorable bids are received.

However, the institution is viewed as managing to liquidation, rather than solvency.

The success or failure of forbearance to achieve true financial recovery can often hinge upon the diligence and/or flexibility of regulatory monitoring. Monitoring can be passive or active. In the passive mode, bank management is allowed the freedom to pursue its own means and strategy of turnaround, as long as risk exposure is considered reasonable by regulators. Active monitoring entails management submitting a strict plan for recovery and being closely watched for adherence. Some circumstances warrant substantial oversight, while others deserve a greater degree of flexibility.

Various mechanisms can be used in support of forbearance. Small cash-flow problems can be ameliorated by allowing access to central bank funding, using either direct borrowing lines or refinancing vehicles. Lines of credit drawn on the central bank or arranged by it through private-sector institutions are another approach that has been employed. Such arrangements usually come with implicit government guarantees along with promises of further capital infusion or deposit backing if financial conditions deteriorate. Kryzanowski and Roberts (1993) attribute this method to allowing many insolvent Canadian banks time to regain their health in the period from 1922 to 1940. The same could be said for First Pennsylvania in the United States or Nordbanken in Sweden, over different periods of time.

A strong argument against forbearance is based upon the management-moral-hazard argument, a line of reasoning that raises relevant concerns both for the assisted institution and for the signal such actions send to other solvent institutions. If a troubled insolvent bank is aware that a further government bailout is an option, management may feel it has nothing to lose by further increasing risk in the hope of achieving solvency. It may then invest in high-risk strategies at the expense of its government guarantor. This attitude has often resulted in subsequent higher closure costs and has frequently been associated with the thrift crisis in the United States. For this reason, regulators are wary of forbearance and usually implement it only in combination with strict monitoring.

Capital Infusion with Existing Management

Many of the arguments put forth for forbearance also extend to favoring direct capital infusion to hampered institutions. According to proponents of this approach, it is frequently the case that a bank's insolvency is not the fault of current management, or may be easily correctable by an accounting recognition of the problem. Current management may be able to regain solvency with forbearance and a sufficient capital infusion provided by government authorities. In this way, it is allowed to put its problems behind it and have its coffers replenished.

Infusion may take many forms, including increased access to the discount window, loan guarantees, and direct loans. However, the real need is to raise capital. Toward this end, the bank may attempt to raise capital through equity or debt offerings with government guarantees lowering the required interest rate. Alternatively, the government may directly provide the institution with the needed capital, as has been done in both the United States and Western Europe. However, prudent use of capital infusions is advisable because competitors may rightly view it as a subsidy, and subsequent privatization and/or liquidation may prove difficult.

Regulatory Control

Problems may be so severe that regulators do not think current management is capable of turning things around. This may be attributed to the severity of condition, a lack of faith in management competence, or concerns as to possible malfeasance as a cause of the problem being addressed. Once regulatory control is decided upon, authorities must decide whether to personally manage or delegate responsibility. In the first case, government employees take on the role of management, while in the second, outside experts are hired to provide these services. The latter, while preferable, is fairly expensive and, again, leads to problematic incentive issues. New management derived from the banking industry is the preferred method, as it is commonly thought that bureaucrats should not be in the business of day-to-day bank operations, following the usual comparative-advantage arguments. In any case, it should be clear that regulatory control is not a permanent solution. The goal is to return the bank to health or enough so to attract a merger candidate.

De Facto Nationalization of the Institution

Balance-sheet problems may be so severe that none of the previous solutions are capable of leading to a satisfactory outcome. A major capital infusion may be required, or buyers are in short supply. In such a situation, an offering may still proceed, with the government guaranteeing purchase of unsold shares. However, in this case, despite its intent, the government may well end up with a controlling interest. In such a case, the bank is in fact and in law an extension of the state. It is a nationalized institution. Minority interest is of little consequence.

Use of this method of financial rescue of a troubled bank is often country dependent. Countries such as the United States find this solution philosophically unpalatable, although they have come close on several occasions. Others, most notably in Western and Southern Europe, have been traditionally more comfortable with nationalization.

Opponents argue that a nationalized bank may evolve into an arm of government economic policy. With this comes incentive problems. As a major shareholder, the government may not be able to require that the bank be efficient and profitable. Bank workers may essentially become bureaucrats and the institution unable to compete without continued government indulgences. Indulgences then may lead to the expectation that the bank carry out political objectives. France using Crédit Lyonnais to bolster national employment is a case in point.

Once nationalized, an institution can be difficult to privatize. A bank that has been protected from the market grows inefficient and may be unable to survive without government help. Prospective equity owners will find valuation difficult and should be wary that their investment may be wiped out by future renationalization or restrictions on new management's ability to rationalize the firm's operations.

Good-Bank, Bad-Bank Split Model

In the 1980s, another method of problem resolution emerged, known as a good-bank, bad-bank split model. This method has been employed several times since and is often viewed as a mechanism to be used in preparation for future merger. Essentially, the bank is divided into two parts. The good bank retains performing assets, while nonperforming assets are transferred to a bad-bank shell. The rationale is that the good bank can now operate more efficiently and raise capital with greater ease and at lower rates. The bad bank can then direct all of its efforts at loan recovery and self-liquidation. Funds recovered from problem loans are channeled into dividends and/or interest payments to shareholders of the residual-asset bad-bank entity. This focusing of bank personnel improves overall efficiency.

The bank must decide on the exact form of the bad-bank structure. Choice may be dependent upon securities laws, but possibilities include a subsidiary of the bank, a separate bank complete with separate charter, or a trust-company form. In any case, the bad bank purchases nonperforming assets from the parent bank. The key issue, however, is funding the entity, as such debt can be difficult to place. Some funds are derived from reserves formerly allocated to the assets, but equity or debt sales are the primary source of bad-bank funds.

The first use of this method was in the mid-1980s, when high-yield debt capital was relatively easy to come by. The subsequent collapse of the junk bond market has raised costs and reduced the attractiveness of this alternative.

The winding down of the Thrift Crisis has lessened the necessity of problem-bank resolution in the United States. Accordingly, this approach has not been used recently in the banking sector of the United States. The good-bank, bad-bank approach has more recently been used internationally, as other regions have experienced similar banking difficulties.

Purchases and Assumption

This is basically a form of acquisition. An acquirer may either purchase the entire bank balance sheet or just the retail deposit base and a subset of the assets. If the whole bank is purchased, the acquirer may receive a government payment covering the difference between the market value of assets and liabilities. If only some deposits are purchased, the acquirer may be given the option of purchasing any of the others and get their pick of bank assets. What is purchased is decided upon through either negotiation or prior partitioning by regulators.

The purchase and assumption agreement (P&A) is often enhanced by government guarantees. These often take the form of putbacks, whereby the government promises to buy back the assets at a stated percentage of value within a specified time frame. The percentage is a declining function of time; therefore, there is an incentive for the acquirer to quickly identify problem assets. This guarantee is essentially a put option issued by the banking authorities.

The offering of a put can distort incentives, resulting in some loans being liquidated when they in fact have a greater value if worked out (James 1991). Rosengren and Simons (1994) therefore advocate that loans should be transferable. With the guarantees intact, the borrower can search for a bank that is willing to assume the loan. If successful, the government is likely to save money. If it is not, the loan would be returned to the liquidation pool.

Liquidation with and without Government Assistance

Regulators have often shown great reluctance to liquidate banks. Perhaps this is because in many countries liquidation must proceed through the court system. However, it may also be because banks are seen as unique in their importance to a country's financial base. A loss of confidence in banking could result in a severe economic contraction, as has been noted. However, as we also point out, this aversion to liquidation can lead to perverse incentives. If aid is offered, it is essentially rewarding an inefficient bank. It is for this reason that many economists and politicians have concluded that if a bank is poorly run, it should be allowed to fail. It is felt that resolution decisions should be based solely upon a least-cost basis, taking into account franchise value but nothing more.

While many would argue that this perspective ignores the cost of bank failure to the economy as a whole, there are clearly cases where closure is a preferred solution. In such cases, if a bank chooses an unaided liquidation, regulators must ensure that bank management and shareholders do not profit from the liquidation. Their primary loyalty is supposed by charter to be to depositors. A shortfall in assets may lead to some insured and all uninsured depositors not being compensated. The government will then be left to step in to pay off the insured depositors where direct explicit insurance exists, and decide whether the uninsured depositors should be compensated at all or in part. However, in most cases liquidation occurs with some government resources. Government assistance in the liquidation is usually provided in order to give the bank time to efficiently dispose of assets and clearly satisfy its liability holders of various types. Help may come in the form of an advance or a permanent cash infusion. The latter is done reluctantly and only when it is deemed to lower eventual payouts.

A more extensive and expensive liquidation procedure results when regulators eject bank management and oversee the liquidation themselves. Insured deposits are paid off or transferred to another institution. A decision is then made as to what if anything uninsured depositors should receive. Assets are sold individually or sorted into pools in order to make valuation and disposal easier. Bids are then accepted for the disposal contract. A proviso is usually made in such cases that liquidation should not unduly affect local markets.

A BRIEF REVIEW OF WORLDWIDE EXPERIENCE AND AN EVALUATION OF RESULTS

With the options reviewed in some detail, it may be useful to summarize the actual experiences prior to the current crisis. Therefore, three different regions where we have seen use of the resolution options enumerated will be reviewed, and the results evaluated. The United States has had the most experience because of the sheer size of its banking sector, so this will be reviewed first. Scandinavia has recently gone through a financial crisis which is reviewed next. Finally, we touch on activity in France for a somewhat different experience.

U.S. Experience

Perhaps the best place to begin in the United States is to review the decline in the U.S. thrift industry. Forbearance was initially the primary tool used in an attempt to resolve the Thrift Crisis of the 1980s. This was by directive of the Federal Home Loan Bank Board (FHLB) and drew justification from earlier banking acts, such as the Garn–St. Germain Depository Institutions Act of 1982.

Nakamura (1990) points out that forbearance was supported by those who felt the state of the economy required caution, considering the deep recession of the early 1980s. Dissolving or merging insolvent thrifts would have been difficult in this environment, it was argued at the time. Regulatory authorities firmly believed in an imminent economic recovery and the lowering of interest rates. In addition, a practical consideration was the possibility that the FSLIC's (Federal Savings and Loan Insurance Corp.) insurance fund was insufficient to undertake widescale closure. Replenishment would likely be politically unpopular. Unfortunately, the dissipation of the recession in 1982 made these constraints of less importance, but the policy of forbearance was continued.

The effectiveness of forbearance was hindered by two key problems that were part of the thrift crisis. Capital requirements were not risk based, and there was inadequate FHLB staffing for oversight. On top of this, along with forbearance came new accounting practices. Thrifts were given the option of using less stringent regulatory accounting practices (RAP), rather than generally accepted accounting practices. This created the illusion of healthier balance sheets than was, in fact, the case. The results were disastrous.

Dellas, Diba, and Garber (1996) find that the average time from insolvency to closure was thirty-eight months. The Congressional Budget Office (CBO) estimated that over $60 billion of additional costs can be attributed to the delay in closure. However, the CBO reported that, by 1991, 345 thrifts had recovered, resulting in a savings of $1.5 billion over closure. But, of the 345, a disturbing 70 percent were still considered to be under financial stress. The dour good news was counterbalanced by the concurrent loss of 1,600 thrifts which were unable to regain their health.

In 1986, the FDIC unveiled the Capital Forbearance Program. Brinkman, Horvitz, and Huang (1996) examine the performance of the 325 banks which were accepted into the program from 1986 to 1989. It is found that there was no substantial improvement of the capital ratios of the chosen institutions. A further examination was done to see whether there were ex-ante identifiable characteristics that could be attributed to the expectation that these institutions could return to solvency. The finding is that there were not. Thrift improvement was linked to the general improvement in local economic conditions, lower credit risk arising from improved economic conditions, private-sector capital infusion, extraordinary income items, and greater franchise value. Determining ex-ante which thrifts would benefit from forbearance was therefore futile, except in the cases where there was a strong likelihood of improvement of local economic conditions.

Access to the Federal Reserve's discount window did not seem to mitigate the crisis or its cost either. As is well known, such borrowing is allowed only in order to meet short-term liquidity problems. Nonetheless, many thrifts availed themselves of this option during the Thrift Crisis. Critics have voiced the view that the Fed was too lenient in allowing troubled thrifts to habitually use this source of cash during this period. It became, in a sense, a form of forbearance.

In 1991, the House Banking Committee found that 90 percent of institutions receiving credit at the discount window from January 1985 to May 1991 subsequently failed (see Dellas, Diba, and Garber 1996). It was stated that troubled institutions which were assigned CAMEL-5 status stayed open an average of ten to twelve months. The implication was that without this source of liquidity, thrifts would have failed earlier, thereby saving taxpayer money.

Gilbert (1994) dissents from the view that Federal Reserve lending increased the FDIC's losses. After being rated CAMEL 5, both borrowers and nonborrowers lasted a median of 20.5 months before failure. He does point out, however, that banks which borrowed in their last thirteen weeks tended to have been rated CAMEL 5 for a period of 9.5 months, as opposed to 7 months for nonborrowers. Borrowers were also statistically more likely to exhibit worse loss ratios. Nonetheless, Gilbert argues that these facts do not prove a direct link to increased FDIC losses.

Regulators have also had the option of direct cash infusion as a tool toward regaining a thrift's financial health. Open thrift assistance (OTA) was used sparingly by the FDIC because it was felt that aid of this sort would take away management and shareholder's incentive to regain solvency. The FDIC's rule was that neither group should be allowed to profit from OTA. Nonetheless, it was widely viewed as a form of subsidy that allowed unhealthy institutions to take market share away from healthy thrifts, hardly a desirable side effect of the resolution option.

A more prevalent method of raising capital has been through the issuance of private subordinated debt. Issuance of subordinated debt provides a capital infusion which may return an institution to solvency or, secondarily, attract merger interest. However, such issues have been floated without guarantees of any kind. Troubled banks that issue this debt have had to do so at market rates which incorporate the perceived risk of the bank. This is rightly viewed as a form of risk-based capital. However, Osterberg and Thomson (1992) correctly argue that the effectiveness of market pricing of risk is mitigated by deposit insurance and implicit government guarantees. Therefore, FDIC forbearance and insurance increases the value of subordinated debt and alters required rates of return. Subordinated debt will not reflect risk unless insurance premiums also do so. It is, however, a start and a move in the right direction.

Overall, James (1991) has shown that the cost of bank failure has been quite high in the United States, on the order of 10 percent of direct costs. This figure is much higher than that found in nonfinancial firms. James adds that returns on nonperforming assets are maximized when loans are transferred to purchasers. This and other studies lend credence to the FSLIC's priority of returning a thrift to health or its next best alternative of merger with a stronger institution. Toward this end, initial merger attempts involved noncompetitive bidding. In retrospect, this has been considered unfair, but it can likely be attributed to a lack of bidders. Bidder scarcity eventually led the FSLIC to open bidding to nonthrifts to increase investor interest.

In addition to the complaints concerning noncompetitive bidding, FSLIC incentives, such as future payments for capital losses, yield maintenance guarantees, and tax benefits, were all criticized for creating moral hazard and adverse selection problems. However, Gosnell, Hudgins, and MacDonald (1993) investigated whether there were in fact abnormal wealth increases experienced by acquiring institutions. It is found that under the FSLIC a few small institutions did experience wealth effects that are attributed to implicit guarantees for continued operation (the Resolution Trust Corporation [RTC] discontinued these guarantees). However, in general, from 1984 to 1991 there are no wealth effects found.

With the establishment of the Resolution Trust Corporation in 1989 came a much more formal and efficient process, including detailed directives and guidelines, better evaluation techniques, competitive bidding, increased auction participation, and limited time limits on asset putbacks. Prices for problem institutions improved, and the cost of insolvency resolution declined.

Throughout the period, mergers in both the thrift and the banking industries continued, both assisted and unassisted. Assisted mergers were termed P&As. In a P&A, the buyer assumes either all or only insured deposit liabilities and purchases a portion of the assets. Assets that are not purchased are further marketed and, if unsold, placed in an agency pool earmarked for liquidation. Details of P&A agreements over the period were quite flexible, with the unique method now known as a good-bank, bad-bank structure first used in the 1984 bailout of Continental Illinois. For this transaction, a subsidiary was created which became the repository of the institution's bad loans. The subsidiaries' sole purpose was the liquidation of these loans. This is one of the techniques open for such transactions, as we have noted. A good overview of the generalized process can be found in Herlihy and Wasserman (1992).

However, an interesting variation of the good-bank, bad-bank method was used in 1988 by Mellon Bank. Mellon created a new institution, Grant Street National Bank (GSNB) which was the repository of problem loans carrying a written-down book value of $1 billion, further written down to $640 million at the time of sale. GSNB purchased the loans with $123 million of cash which was paid in by Mellon and the issuance $513 million in Drexel Burnham Lambert junk bonds. What makes the Mellon case unusual is that Mellon was not insolvent. It independently decided (with regulatory approval) that it would be more efficient with restructuring (Santomero 1989). Two years after incorporation, GSNB Chairman William B. Eagleson (1990) reported that Mellon's and GSNB's experience had been positive. He does, however, point out possible areas of difficulties for banks attempting to emulate their example, including high cost, difficult fundraising, insufficient staffing of the bad bank, and determination of the most efficient corporate form.

With the collapse of the junk bond market, raising capital for the creation of bad banks has become more difficult. This and the winding down of the Thrift Crisis has resulted in a decline in the use of this method for problem-loan resolution in the United States. But it has spread to other areas, such as insurance liability structures.

In retrospect, it is generally agreed that liquidation of failed banks has been expensive in the United States. Indeed, it has been much more costly than bankruptcies in other industries, as James (1991) pointed out. This is why the regulatory authorities seemingly put a premium on rehabilitating troubled banks. Ultimately, however, decisions must be based on cost/benefit analysis. If it is less expensive to close a bank, it must be closed. In such cases, liquidation entailed the payoff of insured, and many uninsured, depositors in the early days of the Thrift Crisis. This caused a tremendous drain on the insurance funds and ultimately led to the inadequacy of the FSLIC fund. FDIC disposal of assets was then contracted out under a Standard Asset Management and Disposition Agreement (SAMDA). This followed the sorting and grouping of assets into homogeneous pools. Contractors then submitted proposals and bids for management and disposal. Costs fell and the efficiency gains reduced the expenses of the troubled-bank resolution.

Ultimately, approximately 40 percent of savings and loans were liquidated. Closure was initially slow under the FSLIC, but accelerated under the RTC. At the end of 1995, when the RTC itself was closed, over 1,600 thrifts had been liquidated. The total cost of the Thrift Crisis has been estimated in the neighborhood of $150 billion. Regulatory authorities were clearly unprepared for the magnitude of the Thrift Crisis. Costs were multiplied by initial inaction and bureaucratic inefficiency. There was a steep learning curve, which by the 1989 creation of the RTC began to level off. Unlike countries that subsequently experienced similar problems, the United States was fortunate that the thrift problem was small in relation to the total size of the financial system.

Scandinavian Experience

The Scandinavian experience is really the story of three bank crises, one each for Norway, Sweden, and Finland. We will consider each in turn.

Prior to 1984, Norway had experienced low unemployment and low real interest rates. Credit expansion was rapid in this environment, at 40 percent in 1985 and 1986. Expansion was aided by the liberalization of Norway's financial markets, which began in 1984. The collapse of oil prices in 1986 began the disruption of Norway's banking system. Inflation rose as savings declined. Credit losses mounted in 1987 as property values declined precipitously. Heiskanen (1993) points out that new accounting standards magnified the appearance of a weakening balance sheet. The position of savings banks, which prior to 1988 had no capital requirements and were typically undercapitalized in comparison to Norway's neighbors (6% of tier 1 capital [Bennett 1993]), grew precarious.

By 1991, the banking crisis had become systemic. Shareholder equity and the insurance funds were exhausted. The government then took its first vigorous steps by nationalizing the banking system. The Government Bank Insurance Fund and Government Bank Investment Fund infused the industry with NKr 28 billion. The government did not interfere in day-to-day operations, but did prompt changes in senior management, workforce reductions, and cost reduction. Individual banks, such as Christiania (CBK), were forced to institute strict loan screening, loan portfolio monitoring, and a reduced international presence.

Despite these actions, 1991 legislation was surprisingly vague. The Kredittilsynet (Banking Inspection Board) was overhauled and the Banking, Insurance and Securities Commission was strengthened, but no long-term banking or crisis-management policy was elucidated. Guidelines were issued which indicated that resolution should be at the lowest possible cost, capital adequacy ratios must be restored, and the regulatory authorities would determine the level of claim coverage. However, the political process did little to lay down an explicit timetable to achieve those goals, leaving this to the Banking Inspection Board for implementation.

Rising oil prices and emergence from recession improved the prospects of Norway and its banks. By 1992, household savings was at 6 percent, a sizable improvement from the −13 percent experienced in 1987. The September 1995 equity sale of Focus Bank was very successful. Bolstered by this success, the government reduced its stake in the two largest banks, Den Norske Bank and Christiania, to 50 percent in 1997.

Looking across to Norway's problems, Sweden thought that it was protected by its diversified economy. Unlike Norway and Finland, there were no external shocks to the economy. However, high inflation, rapid credit expansion (primarily in the real estate sector), and a recession in exports all contributed to Sweden's distress. Heiskanen (1993) pinpoints the primary problem as nonperforming loans in the property sector. This then led to increased bankruptcies, falling collateral value, and, finally, new, tougher accounting standards.

The evolution of the crisis was fairly clear-cut. From 1989 to 1993, metropolitan property values declined 70 percent, causing finance companies to be the first to experience distress (Bartal 1994). Swedish banks, some having as much as 75 percent of their loan portfolios in property, were also strongly affected. Banks lost an estimated SKr 100 billion from 1990 to 1992 (Lexner 1993).

The floating of the krona on November 19, 1992, then led to a 25-percent depreciation which catalyzed large bank losses in the foreign exchange market and foreign-denominated currency loans. Many banks were already in precarious positions, with capital-adequacy ratios at dangerous levels. Gota and Förningsbanken's capital adequacy ratios were 3.4 percent and 6.9 percent, respectively, in 1993. The government took interim action by infusing Nordbanken with SKr 25 billion of capital and Sparbanken Första with SKr 10 billion in loans and guarantees. This effectively nationalized both institutions.

An extensive rescue of the banking industry (and some affiliated institutions) was passed in the legislature on December 18, 1992. Sederowsky (1994) summarizes the essence of this bill as targeting protection of the payment system and safeguarding the supply of credit. The Bank Support Authority (BSA) was to receive advice from a string of outside consultants. Guarantees were provided on all retail deposits, senior and subordinated debt, problem assets, loans, and new equity issues. Banks were to bear the full costs of any government intervention, and cash infusion was achieved via loans at commercial rates. If a bank accepted an aid package it had to fully open its books and submit to government-directed restructuring and cost cutting. These features led the two largest private banks to strive to avoid requesting aid and all of the disclosure that it would involve.

The good-bank, bad-bank method of problem-loan resolution was extensively used in the Swedish bailout. Nordbanken channeled SKr 67 billion of its nonperforming loans into a bad bank, Securum. This split was augmented by a SKr 10-billion capital infusion by the government into Nordbanken and SKr 40 billion into Securum. Gota created bad-bank Retriva and transferred SKr 38 billion in bad loans to it. Gota was subsequently sold to Nordbanken for SKr 3.1 billion, thus creating Sweden's largest bank.

Svenska Handelsbanken (SHB) and Skandinaviska Enskilda Banken (SEB) were, prior to the Nordbanken–Gota merger, the two largest Swedish banks. Both were able to survive without government aid, despite dark days. Their strength was attributed to conservative policy, which was evidenced by their strong capital-adequacy ratios throughout this period. SHB had a very strict loan policy and avoided entanglement with finance companies. SEB sought relief by capital infusion through equity sales, the selling of loans to a bad-bank subsidiary (Diligentia), and an 8-percent staff reduction.

The health of Swedish banks improved with falling interest rates. Fee income has increased and nonperforming loans are generating lower costs. Unaided banks such as SHB and SEB have seen vast improvements in their stock prices (700% by SEB in 1993 alone). SHB has subsequently purchased two Norwegian banks. The cost to the Swedish government has been estimated at well over SKr 60 billion and the bailout has not been praised by all. Good banks, such as SEB and SHB, feel that the government went too far. It is felt that troubled banks such as Nordbanken received an unfair competitive advantage by essentially having their balance sheets wiped clean with government help. The merger of Nordbanken and Gota, and its resultant expansion, is seen as an unjustified reward for poor performance.

In Finland, the 1980s saw steady economic expansion. Unemployment was a steady 5 to 6 percent, and GDP growth was at 3 percent. During this time, banking embarked upon massive expansion in the credit market and major investment in corporate equity (export companies especially). For the most part, growth was financed by debt.

Akin to Norway's oil crisis, Finland's recession was spurred by the exogenous effect. In their case, it was the Soviet Union's collapse. Trade with the Soviets declined 65 percent in 1991. This reinforced declining domestic demand, which resulted in a drop of 7 percent in GDP. Property values, which had increased 68 percent from 1987 to 1989, declined precipitously. By year end, listed companies showed a negative Fm 10 billion in aggregate profits. After a loss of Fm 475 million in the first eight months of 1991, Skopbank became the first bank taken over by the central bank. The number of savings banks declined from 275 to 86. The remaining banks were consolidated into the Saastopankki Suomi (Savings Bank of Finland). Kansallis-Osake-Pankki (KOP) experienced losses of Fm 250 million in currency-market speculation and another Fm 270 million in dealings with a single Finnish investor, Pentti Kouri.

The government was slow to react to these signals. Legislative action in April 1992 infused the Government Guarantee Fund (GGF) with Fm 28 billion in order to back the three existing deposit guarantee funds. The newly created Savings Bank of Finland revealed that it was in deep trouble in the summer of 1992, which then resulted in the GGF taking over its operation. By the end of 1992, all insurance funds were exhausted.

Banks wrote off Fm 21 billion in nonperforming loans in 1992, leaving an additional Fm 55 billion on their books. The *eduskunta* (parliament) authorized an additional Fm 20 billion for insurance funds, but required it to be held by the Ministry of Finance as opposed to the GGF. In addition, it pledged to back the banking system under all circumstances, underscoring this statement with guarantees of up to a ceiling of Fm 35 billion.

The GGF was successful in selling the Savings Bank of Finland to competitors in October 1993. However, many banks did accept capital from the GGF over the entire crisis period. This capital infusion occurred using a total of Fm 8 billion of fifty-year floating rate certificates. These instruments were unusual, in that interest payment was at year end, and only one payment is required in the first three years. After three years of nonpayment, the government retained the option of conversion to equity, and after ten years the interest rates would be ratcheted upward.

Faced with this government alternative, some banks chose to raise capital on their own. In 1993, KOP, for example, experienced increased income and a steadying of their nonperforming assets. They decided not to ask for government help, instead raising Fm 2.85 billion in debt and equity issues, which raised their capital adequacy ratio to 10 percent. Concurrently, KOP reduced staff by 8 percent, cut costs by Fm 500 million, and reduced its international presence.

French Experience: Crédit Lyonnais

Crédit Lyonnais's expansion beginning in the 1980s was massive in scope. From 1988 to 1993, the value of its industrial holdings increased nearly 500 percent, to FFr 49 billion. Lending doubled in the five years ending in 1992. CL lent extensively to high-profile individuals who eventually defaulted: Bernard Tapie (FFr 1 billion owed), Robert Maxwell (FFr 1 billion owed), Florio Fiorini (his company, SASEA, went bankrupt owing $3.8 billion), and Giancarlo Parretti (whose takeover of MGM eventually cost Crédit Lyonnais $2 billion). The Crédit Lyonnais empire began to unravel in 1993, when Parisian commercial property values declined significantly. Heavy lending to property developers and others led to a FFr 6.9 billion year-end loss. The government came to CL's aid in the form of a FFr 23 billion bailout in 1994 and an additional FFr 45 billion in 1995. Estimates of the eventual cost to the government have run as high as FFr 135 billion.

Many of Crédit Lyonnais's competitors have voiced their displeasure at the seemingly unending bailout. However, it has always been difficult to disentangle Crédit Lyonnais and the government's dealings. According to former CL President Haberer, the industrial expansion was with the blessing, if not prodding, of the Socialist government. President Chirac has in the past scolded CL for not lending more to business to protect jobs. Many have questioned the lack of government supervision. The government has justified its bailout by pointing to CL's asset size, which totals one-quarter of France's GDP. The reasoning is that CL's failure would destabilize France and extend to the world banking system. The French government has promised the taxpayers that they will not have to pay for the bailout; costs will come out of CL's future profits.

To facilitate the rescue, the government has allowed FFr 135 billion in assets to be transferred to a CL subsidiary, Consortium de Realisation (CDR), which will act as its bad bank. The transfer was financed by a loan from a state-owned entity which in turn will be reimbursed by a twenty-year FFr 145 billion loan from CL. Other measures include trimming its workforce of 38 thousand by 10 percent and the replacement of top management. In addition, the European Competition Commission has mandated that CL sell 35 percent of its nondomestic assets (worth an estimated FFr 330 billion) by the end of 1998. The outcome, however, is still in doubt.

THE IMPLICATIONS OF INTERNATIONAL EXPERIENCE

As is apparent, there are any number of ways in which the regulatory authority can intervene in the financial sector. In the three regions examined, we have seen the full array of the seven models discussed. In each and every case, regulatory intervention is described as essential, and the circumstances unique. In each case, regulators attempt to limit the impact of the crisis by some form of forbearance. Capital inflow usually follows, and merger talks are not far behind. Often, merger is tantamount to liquidation, as a forced P&A has the effect of liquidation with government assistance. In the end, costs are higher than expected, and the industry structure changes more than anticipated. If there are lessons from the experience, several come to the surface:

1. Costs of intervention are generally larger than anticipated.
2. Interventions aimed at preserving the current institutional structure generally do not achieve the expected outcome.
3. The only sure resolution appears to come from confronting the insolvency directly and addressing its financial implications, no matter how large.

Regulators, however, often delay action in the hope of a turnaround. If the regulator is lucky, a change in the aggregate economy will remedy the financial imbalance. However, regulators are rarely lucky, at least in recent history. Resolution options available to regulators only permit them to delay the effects of a massive asset-valuation change on bank structure in the hope of a return to financial viability. If they do not set off a series of counterproductive incentive effects, they may offer both the regulator and the bank manager time to shore up balance sheets and improve profitability. But they offer only a little time and often require considerable luck. If the banking system cannot correct its problems in short order, as was the case in the U.S. Thrift Crisis, or if the economy continues to deteriorate, as in the Scandinavian case, or if the losses are too large, as in France, the policy will not achieve its end. On the edges, these policy options may offer some hope to sustain the institutions' lending capacity and consumer confidence for a short period of time. However, in the end, all of these options are no replacement for sound bank management and a sound balance sheet.

REFERENCES

Allen, Franklin, and Douglas Gale. 1988. "Optimal Security Design." *Review of Economic Studies* 50: 639–46.

Allen, Franklin, and A. M. Santomero. 1997. "The Theory of Financial Intermediation." *Journal of Banking and Finance* 21: 1461–85.

Bartal, David. 1994. "Sweden: Strong Recovery for Swedish Banks." *Institutional Investor*, June.

Beim, David O. 1992. "Why Are Banks Dying?" *The Columbia Journal of Business*, Spring.

Bennett, Rosemary. 1993. "Good Bank, Bad Bank." *Euromoney*, October.

Benston, George J., and George G. Kaufman. 1988. *Risk and Solvency Regulation of Depository Institutions: Past Policies and Current Options.* Salomon Center Monograph Series in Finance and Economics, Monograph 1988-1. New York: New York University Graduate School of Business Administration.

Bernanke, Ben, and Mark Gertler. 1989. "Agency Costs, Net Worth, and Business Fluctuations." *American Economic Review* 79 (1): 14–31.

Bernanke, Ben, and Mark Gertler. 1990. "Financial Fragility and Economic Performance." *The Quarterly Journal of Economics* 105 (1): 87–114.

Bhattacharya, S., and A. V. Thakor. 1993. "Contemporary Banking Theory." *Journal of Financial Intermediation* 3: 2–50.

Brinkman, Emile J., Paul M. Horvitz, Ying-Lin Huang. 1996. "Forbearance: An Empirical Analysis." *Journal of Financial Services Research* 10: 27–41.

Butkiewicz, James L., and Kenneth A. Lewis. 1991. "Bank Bailouts and the Conduct of Monetary Policy." *Southern Economic Journal*, October.

Calomiris, C., and C. Kahn. 1991. "The Role of Demandable Debt in Structuring Optimal Banking Arrangements." *American Economic Review* 81: 497–513.

Chisholm, Derek. 1985. "Bailing Out Insolvent Banks." *Canadian Business Review*, Winter.

Crockett, John H. 1988. "The Good Bank/Bad Bank Restructuring of Financial Institutions." *The Bankers Magazine*, November–December.

Davies, Sally M., and Douglas A. McManus. 1991. "The Effects of Closure Policies on Bank Risk-Taking." *Journal of Banking and Finance* 15.

Dellas, Harris, Behzad Diba, and Peter Garber. 1996. "Resolving Failed Banks: The U.S. S&L Experience." Discussion Paper 96-E-22, Institute for Monetary and Economic Studies, Bank of Japan.

Diamond, Douglas W. 1984. "Financial Intermediation and Delegated Monitoring." *Review of Economic Studies* 51: 393–414.

Diamond, Douglas W., and Philip Dybvig. 1983. "Bank Runs, Deposit Insurance and Liquidity." *Journal of Political Economy* 91: 4001–19.

Dreyfus, Jean-Francois, Anthony Saunders, and Linda Allen. 1994. "Deposit Insurance and Regulatory Forbearance: Are Caps on Insured Deposits Optimal?" Part 1. *Journal of Money, Credit, and Banking* 26.

Eagleson, William B. 1990. "How Good Is a Bad Bank?" *The Real Estate Finance Journal*, Summer.

Gertler, Mark. 1988. "Financial Structure and Aggregate Economic Activity: An Overview." *Journal of Money, Credit & Banking* 20 (3): 559–88.

Gilbert, R. Alton. 1994. "Federal Reserve Lending to Banks That Failed: Implications for the Bank Insurance Fund." *Federal Reserve Bank of St. Louis Review*, January–February.

Goodfriend, Marvin S. 1989. "Money, Credit, Banking and Payment System Policy." In *The U.S. Payments System: Efficiency Risk and the Role of the Federal Reserve*, edited by D. Humphrey. Boston: Kluwer Academic Press.

Gorton, Gary. 1988. "Banking Panics and Business Cycles." *Oxford Economic Papers* 40: 751–81.

Gorton, Gary, and G. Pennacchi. 1990. "Financial Intermediaries and Liquidity Creation." *Journal of Finance* 45: 49–71.

Gosnell, Thomas F., Sylvia C. Hudgins, and John A. MacDonald. 1993. "The Acquisition of Failing Thrifts: Returns to Acquirers." *Financial Management*, Winter.

Gup, Benton E. 1998. *Bank Failures in the Major Trading Countries*. Westport, Conn.: Quorum Books.

Heiskanen, Reijo. 1993. "The Banking Crisis in the Nordic Countries." *Kansallis Economic Review* 2.

Herlihy, Edward D., and Craig M. Wasserman. 1992. "Making the Good Bank/Bad Bank Structure Work." *International Financial Law Review*, April.

Herring, Richard J., and Prashant VanKudre. 1987. "Growth Opportunities and Risk Taking by Financial Intermediaries." *Journal of Finance* 42: 583–99.

Herring, Richard J., and Anthony M. Santomero. 1991. *The Role of Financial Structure in Economic Performance* (in Swedish). Stockholm: SNS Forlag.

Jacklin, C. 1987. "Demand Deposits, Trading Restrictions, and Risk Sharing." In *Contractual Arrangements for Intertemporal Trade*, edited by E. C. Prescott and N. Wallace. Minneapolis: University of Minnesota Press.

Jacklin, C., and S. Bhattacharya. 1988. "Distinguishing Panics and Information Based Bank Runs: Welfare and Policy Implications." *Journal of Political Economies* 96: 568–92.

James, Christopher. 1991. "The Losses Realized in Bank Failures." *The Journal of Finance* 46.

Kane, Edward J. 1985. *The Gathering Crisis in Federal Deposit Insurance*. Boston: MIT Press.

Kareken, J., and N. Wallace. 1978. "Deposit Insurance and Bank Regulation: A Partial Equilibrium Exposition." *Journal of Business* 51: 413–38.

Kaufman, George G. 1988. "Bank Runs: Causes, Benefits, and Costs." *Cato Journal* 7: 559–87.

Kryzanowski, Lawrence, and Gordon S. Roberts. 1993. "Canadian Banking Solvency, 1922–1940." *Journal of Money, Credit, and Banking* 25.

Lexner, Sven. 1993. "Emergency Ward for Swedish Banks." *International Financial Law Review*, February.

Moland, Torstein. 1994. "Economic Policy and Financial Distress." *Norges Bank Economic Bulletin*, March.

Nakamura, Leonard I. 1990. "Closing Troubled Financial Institutions: What Are the Issues?" *Business Review* (Federal Reserve Bank of Philadelphia), May–June.

Osterberg, William P., and J. Thomson. 1992. "Forbearance, Subordinated Debt, and the Cost of Capital for Insured Depository Institutions." *Economic Review* (Federal Reserve Bank of Cleveland), p. 3Q.

Puglisi, Kenneth F. 1988. "Assessing Mellon's 'Bad Bank' Strategy." *Bank Administration*, October.

Rose, Peter S. 1989. "The Good Word on 'Bad' Banks." *Canadian Banker* 96.

Rosengren, Eric S., and Katerina Simons. 1994. "Failed Bank Resolution and the Collateral Crunch: The Advantages of Adopting Transferable Puts." *Journal of the American Real Estate and Urban Economics Association* 22.

Santomero, Anthony M. 1989. "Techniques of Problem-Loan Management Theory and Experience." *Bank of Israel Banking Review* 2.

Santomero, Anthony M. 1992. "The Banking Firm." In *The New Palgrave Dictionary of Money and Finance*, edited by P. Newman, M. Milgate, and J. Eatwell. New York: Macmillan.

Santomero, Anthony M. 1996. "Effective Financial Intermediation." In *Proceedings of the Conference on Policy-Based Finance and Alternatives for Financial Market Development: Application to Latin America of the East Asia Experience*. Washington, D.C.: Inter-American Development Bank.

Sederowsky, Peter. 1994. "Sweden-Legal Report." *International Financial Law Review, Special Supplement*, July.

Selgin, George. 1993. "In Defense of Bank Suspension." *Journal of Financial Services Research* 7 (December).

15

Resolving, Recapitalizing, and Restructuring Insolvent Banks and Banking Systems

George G. Kaufman

Many of the macroeconomic problems experienced by countries throughout the world have been ignited or, more frequently, intensified by problems in financial institutions and markets, either in their own country or in other countries. Moreover, sustained recoveries in macroeconomic activity appear to require correction of financial-sector problems. That is, historical evidence clearly suggests that breakdowns in the financial sector are costly to an economy, in terms of lost output from unemployed labor and capital resources, misallocation of real resources, likely devaluation of domestic currency and resulting increased inflationary pressures, and increased uncertainty, as well as in terms of transfer costs to resolve the insolvencies. Resolution requires the use of government (taxpayer) funds to finance the negative net worths of banks and other financial institutions, whose assets fall short of the par value of their deposits and other liabilities that are explicitly or implicitly insured or guaranteed by the government. This chapter briefly reviews the causes of financial breakdowns and the implications for macroeconomic activity, discusses ways to resolve bank insolvencies and recapitalize banks, and suggests a structure for reducing the probability of future financial crises.

FINANCIAL PROBLEMS AND MACROECONOMIC STABILITY

In market-oriented economies, financial institutions and markets mobilize savings and channel them to the most potentially productive uses. The more efficient this transfer, the more efficiently are real resources allocated and the greater is the aggregate welfare of the economy. Financial institutions also assist in monitoring the performance of borrowers for ultimate lenders and in policing corporate governance. Recent empirical evidence supports earlier arguments that banking matters; namely, the more developed the financial sector is in a country, the faster real per capita macroeconomic growth is (Goldsmith 1969; Gurley and Shaw 1955; McKinnon 1973; Levine 1997a). Moreover, countries that have both developed banking markets and liquid (stock) capital markets appear to grow faster on average than countries that have only one developed market, which in turn grow faster than countries in which neither banks nor capital markets are well developed (Levine 1997b).

Although the evidence suggests that the behavior of banks importantly affects the macroeconomy for both good and ill, the predominant focus to date has been on the bad—breakdowns in banking spreading to breakdowns in the macroeconomy. A large number of studies report that the frequency of bank failures in industrial countries is inversely correlated with the stage of the business cycle—rising during recessions and falling during expansions—although the relationship appears stronger in the United States (for a review of the literature, see Benston and Kaufman 1995; Bordo 1986; Kaufman 1994; Mishkin 1997). For example, the correlation between annual changes in the number of bank failures and industrial production between 1875 and 1919 in the United States was –0.42, and in only two periods of sharp increases in bank failures did industrial production fail to decline (Benston et al. 1986). The studies differ on how banking crises begin—whether bank problems exogenously ignite the macroeconomic problems or are ignited by the macroeconomic or other exogenous forces and, in turn, feedback and intensify the magnitude and duration of the macroeconomic problems.

Among more contemporary economists, Minsky (1977) and Kindleberger (1985, 1996) are the major proponents of banks exogenously igniting problems that spread first throughout and then beyond the banking and financial sectors. Like most economic agents, banks get caught up in the euphoria of budding economic expansions and expand credit rapidly to finance increases in economic activity, particularly in areas subject to the greatest increase in demand and consequently also in prices (e.g., stock market and real estate). Moreover, the credit is often collateralized by the assets purchased. The credit expansion fuels and accelerates the economic expansion, accelerates asset price increases, and encourages additional speculation. Both lenders and borrowers fall victim of "irrational exuberance." Through time, borrowers become more highly leveraged and turn increasingly to shorter-term debt. Their margin of safety in covering their debt service payments from operating revenues or continued increases in asset price declines and approaches zero. Increasingly, debt servicing is financed out of new debt (in Minsky's terms, "Ponzi finance"). Given the high leverage, any slight decline or even slowdown in expected revenues, no less the bursting of asset price bubbles, and even moderate increases in interest rates can cause defaults. The financial system crashes due to its own weight. This leads to a self-feeding sequence of distress selling, fire-sale losses, further defaults, business failures, bank runs, and bank failures, and the expansion turns into a macroeconomic downturn. Bank problems precede macroeconomic problems.

Most contemporary analysts, however, view the bank problems during macroeconomic downturns as caused primarily by the accompanying increase in business failures and rising unemployment, which in turn are often caused by some exogenous shock, including government policies that reduce aggregate bank reserves and therefore the money supply, and the bursting of asset price bubbles (Bordo, Mizrach, and Schwartz 1998; Hubbard 1991). Increased business failures and unemployment and sharply lower asset prices increase defaults on bank loans and also the perceived risk of performing bank loans. Banking problems make it increasingly difficult for depositors to evaluate the financial health of their banks and to differentiate financially healthy from sick institutions (Mishkin et al. 1995). As a result, in the absence of deposit insurance, they are encouraged to run from deposits at their banks into currency outside the banking system, rather than to other "safe" banks. Unless the accompanying loss in aggregate bank reserves is offset by a central bank lender of last resort, a multiple contraction in money and credit is ignited (Kaufman 1988). This, in turn, feeds back onto the macroeconomy, transmitting and magnifying the initial downturn. Kaminsky and Reinhart (1996) have recently examined twenty-five banking crises worldwide between 1970 and the early 1990s and developed a series of stylized facts. These are shown in Figure 15.1. It can be seen that, on average, the banking crises are dated a number of months after declines in output and the stock market and increases in real domestic credit and bank deposits.

Asset price bubbles have contributed importantly to banking problems in many countries; for example, bubbles in real estate and energy in the United States in the mid-1980s, bubbles in real estate and stock prices in Japan in the early 1990s, and bubbles in real estate and stock prices in Korea and Southeast Asia in the mid-1990s. Financial institutions are particularly sensitive to abrupt asset price declines, because many of them engage in asset-based lending in which the in-

Figure 15.1
Empirical Regularities during Banking Crises

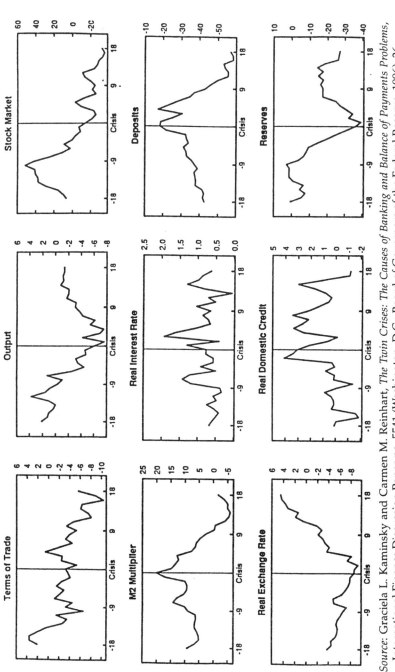

Source: Graciela L. Kaminsky and Carmen M. Reinhart, *The Twin Crises: The Causes of Banking and Balance of Payments Problems*, International Finance Discussion Paper no. 5541 (Washington, D.C.: Board of Governors of the Federal Reserve, 1996), 26.

Note: The real exchange rate and the real interest rate are reported in levels while all other variables are reported in twelve-month changes. All of them are relative to "tranquil" times. Vertical axes are percentages, and horizontal axes are the number of months.

stitutions finance the acquisition of assets, which are pledged as collateral. If asset prices decline abruptly, the institutions must either require additional collateral or sell the assets to repay the loans. If the asset sales are not quick enough, the banks may generate insufficient funds to retire the outstanding amount of the loans. The banks will suffer losses and, if these losses are large enough, may be driven into insolvency.

Because banks tend to be more highly leveraged than firms in other industries, smaller losses may drive them into insolvency than are necessary elsewhere. Explicit or implicit government-provided insurance and guarantees of bank deposits and other liabilities have effectively encouraged banks to substitute public for private capital, and have permitted them to operate at even lower private-capital levels than otherwise. The lower private-capital ratios for banks before the introduction of government safety nets were permitted by private market forces. This suggests that banks were generally perceived to be less risky than other firms. Empirical evidence, at least for the United States, indicates that, before the establishment of the Federal Reserve in 1914, fewer banks failed annually on average than nonbanks, and losses to their depositor-creditors averaged less than those for creditors at failed nonbank firms. However, in light of the large number of bank failures recently, the still lower capital ratios after the safety nets appear too low to permit banks to absorb shocks that they previously might have absorbed. This has been particularly true in many Asian countries, where banks were generally more highly leveraged than in Western countries. Moreover, other industries in many of these countries also tended to be relatively more highly leveraged. Adverse shocks in the macroeconomy thus drove them into insolvency more quickly, forcing them to default on their bank loans and igniting banking problems.

Capital-impaired banks are likely to cut back on their new lending until their capital is replenished. Moreover, abrupt price declines increase general uncertainty. In such an environment, even solvent banks encounter difficulties in evaluating the value of risky assets and ventures and are likely, in the absence of deposit insurance and other government guarantees, to reshuffle their loan portfolios toward safer projects; the more so, the closer the bank is to insolvency. Combined with the cutbacks in total bank lending, this behavior creates a "credit crunch" that makes it more difficulty to ignite and/or sustain recoveries in macroeconomic activity. This pattern is currently being observed in most Asian countries that are experiencing macroeconomic and financial problems. In some of these countries, government guarantees have, at times, mitigated the reluctance of banks to lend, but frequently only at the cost of directing credit to the very borrowers with whom they have close ownership, political, or other ties and who had defaulted earlier and had been a major cause of the banks' ongoing problems. Such a solution to a credit crunch is not conducive to sustained economic recovery. Rather, banks need to be recapitalized on a freestanding basis, so that they are politically independent, able to freely allocate credit in response to market forces, and able to withstand losses from historically normal macroeconomic shocks without becoming insolvent. How this may be done is described in the next section.

RESOLVING AND RECAPITALIZING INSOLVENT BANKS

Banks become economically insolvent when the market value of their assets declines below the market value of their deposits. At this point, the market value of their private capital is negative and, unless conditions change for the better, they are unable to repay their deposits in full and on time. In the absence of government-provided guarantees, knowledgeable depositors would have run on their banks in an attempt to withdraw their funds at par value. Unless the insolvent bank is recapitalized, sold to a solvent institution, or legally declared insolvent and resolved through receivership, satisfying depositor claims in full on a first-come, first-served basis is unfair, as it shifts the losses totally to the later claimants. In the process, the bank must sell off (is stripped of its remaining best assets, on which it experiences the smallest fire-sale losses). At some point, the bank will begin to experience sufficiently large losses on its asset sales to prevent it from satisfying further depositor claims in full, and will suspend operations. At this point, the solvency problem has resulted in a liquidity problem that forced an end to the unstructured liquidation and introduced a more formal structured resolution that treats the remaining claimants more fairly.

Because it negates the rationale for runs, government-provided guarantees effectively shift the timing of the resolution of insolvencies from the private market to the bank regulators. The guarantees relieve the liquidity problem, but not the solvency problem. The guaranteed deposits at economically insolvent banks are effectively implicit off-budget liabilities of the government that should more appropriately be recorded as explicit on-budget government debt obligations.[1] To the extent insolvent banks are permitted by the regulators to continue to operate, they are likely to continue to generate losses, both by continuing to lend to the same insolvent borrowers and by increasing their risk exposure further by "gambling for resurrection." If they win, they may be able to regain solvency and reclaim private ownership. If they lose, the losses are borne by the deposit insurance agency and/or the government. Continuing losses from ongoing operations is particularly likely for state-owned banks (SOBs) and state-controlled banks (SCBs), where much credit is directed at favored sectors or borrowers at times, regardless of ability to repay. These institutions often are effectively arms of government policy rather than traditional banks, whose major concern and bottom line is maximizing shareholder wealth.

Resolving insolvent banks requires official recognition of their negative net worth and allocating the loss among involved parties—the deposit insurance agency or government standing in the shoes of the insured deposits, uninsured depositors and other creditors, and shareholders of privately owned banks. Governments generally find neither of these two actions politically easy or painless. Official recognition implies both a public admission of a government failure to perform adequately and an admitted increase in its deficit and debt. Allocating losses will likely be resisted by the potentially harmed nongovernment parties, even if these parties were not explicitly insured ex ante. Moreover, governments at times may not wish to impose losses on some or all of these parties for fear that the losses might be disruptive to the payments system or because these parties may be politically powerful or political allies. The latter reason often appears to extend even to private shareholders, who should rightfully be wiped out in insolvencies.

Because deposits are a major part of most countries' money supplies, imposing loss-sharing on uninsured depositors, even if politically feasible, must be undertaken carefully so as not to disturb the payments system. If resolution of insolvent banks occurs through the normal bankruptcy process, uninsured depositors in most countries would receive the recovery value (par value less the prorata share of any loss) of their claim only after a considerable period of time, not infrequently stretching over a number of years. This procedure is so economically and politically disruptive that few governments are willing to chance it, even when the uninsured depositors had been explicitly notified ahead of time that they would not be protected.

Such loss-sharing arrangements are, however, feasible if the private uninsured claimants receive their payments immediately and the losses are not usually large. This is the procedure used in the United States. Insolvent banks are not resolved through the usual bankruptcy process to which other corporations are subject to. Rather, because they have a special charter of incorporation, they are resolved by their primary regulatory agency. The FDIC is appointed as receiver. Particularly since the enactment of the FDIC Improvement Act in 1991, which requires prompt corrective action (PCA) for troubled banks and least cost resolution (LCR) of insolvencies, bank examiners are familiar with a troubled bank's balance sheet before its ultimate insolvency. As a result, they have the opportunity to value the assets and liabilities. Indeed, in some instances, the regulators require this knowledge to search out potential buyers for the bank and prepare them for the bidding. Thus, the examiners can make an approximate determination of the recovery value of a troubled bank's assets and liabilities shortly before its resolution.

Resolutions are typically initiated at the close of the bank's business day. In all resolutions, insured depositors receive full access to the par value of their funds the next business day, either at the bank that has assumed the deposits or at the insolvent bank in receivership. In resolutions in which the lowest cost to the FDIC involves sharing any loss with uninsured claimants, the FDIC will generally advance each depositor the next business day an amount equal to a conservative estimate of the expected recovery value available at the bank in receivership.[2] If, in retrospect, this amount is less than the actual amount recovered, the depositors are paid the difference. If the FDIC overestimated the actual recovery value, it is not reimbursed. If the regulators are efficient in carrying out the provisions of FDICIA and resolve the institutions as soon or shortly after its equity capital/asset ratio declines to the minimum 2 percent required in the law, except in cases of major fraud, losses to creditors should be small, particularly relative to the losses these same investors would suffer in insolvencies of nonbank firms (Kaufman 1994). In addition, because the uninsured depositors effectively receive their funds immediately, the economic and political disruptions of imposing loss-sharing on large depositors are minimized. That is, removing banks from the normal bankruptcy process and following a procedure similar to that described is effectively a necessary prerequisite for imposing losses on uninsured bank depositors in the real world, regardless of any provisions in the statutes against protecting uninsured claimants.

Unless there is only weak demand for banking services, insolvent banks need not be liquidated. They can be sold or otherwise recapitalized, either as a complete entity or as one or more smaller entities. However, potential buyers will bid for these institutions only if their estimated present value net worths are at least positive. Thus, in order to receive bids, the negative net worths of the institutions cannot exceed their estimated franchise values. If they do, the government must inject public funds or reduce uninsured depositor and other stakeholder claims to the point that this condition is satisfied.[3] As noted earlier, this is not always easy. In particular, public support must be obtained for the use of taxpayer funds. Because many bank insolvencies are associated by the public with fraudulent, unethical, or self-serving behavior by either or both bank management and bank regulators, the public is reluctant to provide support until it is convinced that the funds will not be used to perpetuate such behavior or reward the alleged perpetrators. Moreover, if the funds are used incorrectly once, the government loses considerable credibility and the public becomes even more reluctant to support additional commitments.

The recent experiences of the United States and Japan are informative. The U.S. Thrift Crisis began in the late 1970s, primarily as an interest rate risk problem. To a considerable extent encouraged, if not forced, by government policy to extend long-term fixed-rate residential mortgage loans financed by short-term deposits, the savings and loan associations were exposed to large interest rate risk. Such exposure would probably not have occurred in the absence of government-provided deposit insurance, as the depositors would have fled to safer, less-exposed institutions. When interest rates jumped abruptly in response to a sharp acceleration in the rate of inflation, many thrifts were driven into economic insolvency. By 1982, some 90 percent of all savings and loans were unprofitable, and two-thirds were market-value insolvent (Kaufman 1995). The regulators were unprepared for this crisis and rather than resolve the insolvencies, provided forbearance in the hope that interest rates would decline. They won their bet and rates did decline.

But many insolvent or undercapitalized institutions either unintentionally, because of economic recessions in their market areas, or intentionally, by "gambling for resurrection," replaced their interest rate risk with credit risk. The resulting losses were accompanied by widespread media publicity about fraudulent and self-serving behavior. Although an increasing number of insolvent institutions were resolved, in many cases the regulators again postponed taking stronger actions and the number and size of insolvencies increased. Afraid to give official recognition to the large and smoldering problem, the government denied its size and promised that only industry-provided funds were necessary to resolve the insolvencies. Only after these proved insufficient and the debacle expanded to the point that it could no longer be contained without the use of large amounts of public funds did the government give official recognition to the problem and persuade the public that withholding such funds would only increase the need for more funds later and that the funds would be used only to make good the government guarantee on deposits. None would be used to support shareholders or management at insolvent institutions and that vigorous actions would be undertaken to recover misused funds from culprits.

Indeed, the legislation enacted to appropriate some $150 billion of taxpayer funds was entitled the Financial Institutions Reform, Recovery and *Enforcement* Act (FIRREA) (emphasis added). A new government agency, the Resolution Trust Corporation, was authorized to replace management at insolvent institutions and to resolve the institutions by selling the assets on a timely basis. In all, it took some four years from the time that it became evident to independent observers that public funds would be necessary to resolve the S&L insolvencies in the mid-1980s to the authorization for such funds in FIRREA in early 1989. Because the government appeared to have kept to most of its promises thereafter, the public did not object when, two years later, the government requested additional funds (which turned out not to be needed) for troubled commercial banks. In retrospect, the RTC resolved the thrift insolvencies reasonably efficiently and quickly and, combined with fundamental deposit insurance reform enacted in FDICIA and the sustained noninflationary economic expansion, both the commercial banks and remaining thrifts recovered quickly and played an important role in financing the macro expansion.

In contrast, Japan has been unable to resolve its banking insolvencies and the resulting credit crunch has hampered its ability to recover from its prolonged macroeconomic recession. From the beginning, the Japanese government has been unwilling or politically unable to either use or promise to use taxpayer funds only to support depositor claims on insolvent institutions. It has used and effectively promises to continue to use such funds to maintain both management and the existing shareholder interests. As a result, banks receiving such aid are effectively SOBs or likely to behave at least like SCBs. At the same time, reports of mismanagement, fraud, influence peddling, and self-serving scandals involving the Ministry of Finance and Bank of Japan have increased in frequency and seriousness. Not unexpectedly, the Japanese public has become increasingly reluctant to support the use of its funds for resolving bank insolvencies. As a result, the Japanese banking system remains largely insolvent, continues to be progressively downgraded by the rating agencies, and is a drag on the macro-economy, therby hampering recovery.[4]

Thus, countries have an option. They can follow the U.S. model to recovery or the Japanese model to stagnation. Unfortunately, some recent reports suggest that Korea may be deciding to follow the U.S. model more than the Japanese (Schuman 1998). It would be wise for Korea to reconsider this strategy.

MAINTAINING BANK SOLVENCY AND EFFICIENCY

After the banking system is recapitalized, it is important to impose a prudential regulatory structure that will both maintain solvency and encourage efficiency. One such structure is the scheme of structured early intervention and resolution (SEIR) that I described in earlier research and was enacted in modified form in the United States in the PCA and LCR provisions of FDICIA. The details of SEIR have been discussed elsewhere and will not be discussed here (Kaufman 1997a). Its major provisions are shown in Table 15.1. Basically, the scheme keeps the best of government-provided deposit insurance—ensuring small depositors of the safety of their funds and discouraging runs by them

Table 15.1

Summary of Prompt Corrective Action Provisions of the Federal Deposit Insurance Corporation Improvement Act of 1991

Zone	Mandatory Provisions	Discretionary Provisions	Capital Ratios (percent) Risk Based Total	Tier 1	Leverage Tier 1
1. Well Capitalized			>10	>6	>5
2. Adequately Capitalized			> 8	>4	>4
3. Undercapitalized	1. No brokered deposits except with FDIC approval	1. Order recapitalization	< 8	<4	<4
	2. Suspend dividends and management fees	2. Restrict interaffiliate transactions			
	3. Require capital restoration plan	3. Restrict deposit interest rates			
	4. Restrict asset growth	4. Restrict Certain other activities			
	5. Approval required for acquisitions, branching, and new activities	5. Any other action that would better carry out prompt corrective action			
	6. No brokered deposits				
4. Significantly Undercapitalized	1. Same as for Zone 3	1. Any Zone 3 discretionary actions	< 6	<3	<3
	2. Order recapitalization*	2. Conservatorship or receivership if fails to submit or implement plan or recapitalize pursuant to order			
	3. Restrict inter-affiliate transactions*	3. Any other Zone 5 provision, if such action is necessary to carry out prompt corrective action			
	4. Restrict deposit interest rates				
	5. Restrict pay of officers				
5. Critically Undercapitalized	1. Same as for Zone 4				<2
	2. Appoint receiver/conservator within 90 days				
	3. Appoint receiver if still in Zone 5 four quarters after becoming critically undercapitalized				
	4. Suspend payments on subordinated debt				
	5. Restrict certain other activities				

Source: Board of Governors of the Federal Reserve System.

*Not required if primary supervisor determines action would not serve purpose of prompt corrective action or if certain other conditions are met.

into currency—and corrects the worst—excessive moral hazard risk-taking behavior by insured banks and poor agency behavior by bank regulators who are motivated to delay imposing sanctions on financially troubled institutions. The scheme requires regulatory sanctions and behavior that mimics market sanctions and behavior, invokes mandatory regulatory sanctions when discretionary sanctions are ineffective in preventing a bank from deteriorating through the capital-asset zones, encourages market discipline by large depositors to supplement regulatory discipline, focuses on sufficient economic capital, and imposes a resolution or "closure" rule at a low but positive capital ratio.[5] Inefficient or unlucky banks will still fail, although probably in smaller numbers, but the costs of failure will be greatly reduced or, at least in theory, almost eliminated.

By effectively forcing bank regulators to accept loss minimization as their primary goal, as private insurance firms do, the regulators and private market are goal compatible and SEIR is incentive compatible, so that all involved parties are rowing in the same direction. By minimizing, if not eliminating, negative net worths, SEIR also reduces the likelihood of systemic risk, which is ignited by losses from negative net worths cascading down the chain of interconnected banks. SEIR represents fundamental and effective deposit insurance reform.

The early evidence suggests that SEIR has worked well in the United States, even in a modified and weakened form, in strengthening the banking system and permitting it to finance macroeconomic recovery and prolonged expansion (Benston and Kaufman 1997). SEIR has a large number of advantages over other prudential regulatory structures that also make it desirable for countries other than the United States (Kaufman 1997b). These include the following:

- Maintains existing banking structure
- Maintains insurance for small depositors only
- Reduces the number of failures
- Reduces losses from failures (makes deposit insurance effectively redundant)
- Reduces bank insurance premiums and incorporates risk-based premiums
- Reduces probability of systemic (contagion) risk
- Reduces too-big-to-fail (protection of uninsured depositors)
- Encourages market discipline from large depositors to supplement regulatory discipline
- Reduces moral hazard behavior by banks
- Reduces agency problem for regulators
- Provides for carrots as well as sticks to improve bank performance
- Permits wide range of product powers for well-capitalized banks
- Reduces regulatory micromanagement of banks

But, because countries differ in significant ways, it is important to tailor the structure to the particular economic, social, political, legal, and cultural characteristics of the country (see Working Party on Financial Stability in Emerging Market Economies 1997).

To be effective, SEIR depends on the abilities of both the regulators and the marketplace to impose sufficient discipline to curtail bank risk-taking and losses, of bankers to manage their operations in a way to maximize value to both shareholders and the economy, and of governments to accept loss minimization in insolvencies as the primary goal of bank regulation. If these parties can agree to these preconditions, SEIR may be modified to be effective in the particular countries. The more important modifications required depend on the following factors:

- Macroeconomic instability
- Political instability
- Strength of private market and tradition of market discipline
- Structure of banking, including solvency and the importance of SOBs and SCBs
- Sophistication of bankers
- Sophistication of bank regulators, supervisors, and examiners
- Sophistication of market participants
- Credit culture
- Equity culture
- Bank control on nonbanks and nonbank control of banks
- Loan concentration in banks
- Quality of accounting information and disclosure
- Bankruptcy and repossession laws
- Bank reliance on foreign currency deposits

More specifically, the following features need to be tailored specifically to the country:

- Values of the tripwires for PCA and LCR
- Types of regulatory sanctions
- Division between regulatory rules and discretion
- Definition of "small" depositors
- Regulation of foreign currency exposure
- Bankruptcy (resolution) process for insured banks

In some countries, deposit insurance reform is being introduced at the same time as financial deregulation or liberalization and for the same reasons. The two reforms are not independent of each other. Because SEIR retains some government-provided deposit insurance, it retains the need for some government regulation, in particular for government supervision and examination to monitor banks on an adequate basis. Deregulation does not imply desupervision. Indeed, supervision may need to be intensified after liberalization, as many banks, after laboring for years under a repressed system, are often ill-prepared to suddenly operate in a market structure with penalties as well as rewards. In particular, they are likely to have weak if any credit cultures and engage in insufficient credit analysis and monitoring. Thus, bank risk exposures are likely to virtually explode following a sudden changeover from financial repression to financial liberalization, unless the liberalization is structured correctly (Working Party on Financial Stability in Emerging Market Economies 1997). Unfortunately, this was not recognized sufficiently in many countries, including the United States in the early 1980s and Japan in the late 1980s, and was an important cause of the banking debacles. Banking liberalization must be phased in or sequenced in such a way that at any one time regulatory discipline is not reduced by more than market discipline is reasonably able to replace: The weaker the sum of market and regulatory discipline or total discipline on banks, the higher the need for required private-capital ratios to achieve the same degree of stability.

The greater the macro and political instability in a country, the higher the numerical values of the tripwires for the PCA and LCR tranches need to be, particularly for resolution of potential insolvencies. If these zones are stated in terms of capital asset ratios, it is important to note that assets must include both on- as well as off-balance-sheet activities and that the Basle capital ratios are minimum requirements for large, international banks in industrial countries with relatively high macroeconomic and political stability. For most other banks and countries, the capital ratios for each zone need to be considerably higher. These values also need to be higher if the quality of accounting and reporting information is poorer. Although poor-quality accounting information may either overstate or understate true information, incentives are to overstate. Thus, banks almost universally underreserve for loan losses and find additional ways of at least temporarily hiding losses. Because the value of the final capital ratio tripwire for resolution determines the potential for losses to the insurance agency, assigning a value that is too low to prevent or minimize losses can defeat the objective of SEIR.

Resolving a bank before its capital becomes negative does not represent confiscation. Current shareholders are given first right to recapitalize the institution. It is only if they prefer not to do so, most likely because they believe that the bank's true capital position is even worse than the reported position, that resolution through sale, merger, or liquidation proceeds. Any proceeds remaining after resolution are returned to the old shareholders.

It also follows that the values of the tripwires for each capital zone need to be higher as the credit and equity cultures in a country become weaker; the bankers, regulators, and market participants become less sophisticated; the bank loan portfolios become more concentrated; the definition of "small" depositor becomes larger; and bank reliance on foreign currency deposits becomes greater. Likewise, these conditions suggest greater emphasis on regulatory rules than on regulatory discretion.

Foreign currency deposits are particularly important in smaller, open economies. Exchange rate (currency) problems and banking problems are often interrelated and easily confused. Banks that offer deposits denominated in foreign currencies assume exchange rate risk, unless offset by foreign-currency-denominated assets or hedged otherwise. The shorter term the deposits—the "hotter" the money—the greater the risk. Banks are particularly tempted to raise funds in foreign currencies when domestic interest rates greatly exceed those on foreign currencies. Economic theory, however, indicates that in equilibrium such rate differences should be matched by equal differences in the opposite direction between spot and forward exchange rates. This condition is referred to as interest rate parity.[6]

Any downward pressure on a country's exchange rate will impose losses on unhedged banks and, if large enough, may cause banking problems in previously strong banking systems or exacerbate problems in weak banking systems, such as in Korea and many other Asian countries in 1998. In addition, downward pressure on the exchange rate in a country with a financially strong banking system may encourage depositors in domestic currency to run into deposits in foreign currencies, possibly even at the same "safe" banks. This is a run on domestic currency, not on banks. The run exerts downward pressure on the country's exchange rate. If the country attempts to protect its exchange rate (maintain fixed exchange rates), it needs to sell foreign reserves. This reduces aggregate bank reserves. Unless this decrease is offset by infusions of reserves from other sources by the central bank, which would be difficult in these countries without intensifying the problem, it will ignite a multiple contraction in money and credit. This is likely to impair the financial solvency of the banks and may possibly ignite runs on banks.

Such a scenario is visible in the stylized facts on banking and balance of payments crises compiled by Kaminsky and Reinhart (1996). As shown in Figure 15.1, foreign reserves begin to decline before the banking crises. The banking impact, however, is offset temporarily by increases in the money (deposit) multiplier that permits both deposits and credit to continue to increase. At some point, the banking crisis occurs and sets in motion the series of adverse effects. In some countries, there is evidence that the rapid increases in deposits and credit before the banking crisis were fueled by increased bank reserves resulting from large capital inflows and government policies of maintaining fixed exchange rates, which required purchasing foreign currency.

Conversely, if a country with a strong foreign currency position but a financially weak banking system experiences depositor runs to domestic currency deposits at safe banks or into domestic currency, the banking problem will not spread to foreign currency (exchange rate) problems. But if the runs are from domestic currency deposits to foreign currency deposits at even the same safe banks, downward pressure will be exerted on the exchange rate and ignite an exchange rate problem. Thus, exchange rate problems can cause banking problems and banking problems can cause exchange rate problems, but because the causes differ, the solutions also differ.[7]

STRENGTHENING THE EQUITY CULTURE

One of the primary causes of the ongoing financial and macroeconomic crises in many Asian countries, including Korea, is the generally low private capital-to-asset or high leverage or bearing (asset-to-capital) ratio of bank and nonbank firms. For example, the book value asset-to-capital ratio for all nonbank corporations in the United States in the mid-1990s was between 200 and 250 percent. (As market values exceeded book values in the period, the market-value leverage ratios were lower.) In contrast, the asset-to-capital ratios in Korea averaged more than 400 percent, or nearly twice as high. Nor, as can be seen from Table 15.2, is the United States an outlier. The unweighted capital ratios of the fifteen OECD countries other than Korea averaged about 275 percent. Only Japan and Italy had leverage ratios as high as Korea. As capital is the first account to absorb losses, any losses in excess of this account must be charged against creditors and represents insolvency. Thus, an equally adverse stock is nearly twice as likely to drive an average Korean firm into insolvency as a U.S. firm.

Moreover, capital ratios are even lower in Korea for most large conglomerate firms or *chaebols*. Many had reported book value leverage ratios of more than 500 percent, and some that have experienced severe financial problems and sought bankruptcy protection had ratios of nearly 1,000 percent. Because the market value of capital was considerably lower than book values in recent years, the book value ratios understated their economic or actual condition. For many, the market value ratios were close to or less than zero, and explain their plight.

Table 15.2
Leverage Ratios for Nonfinancial Firms
in OECD Countries, 1993

Country	Percent[1]
Austria	241
Belgium	247
Canada	209
Denmark	219
Finland	276[2]
France	136[2]
Germany	158
Italy	436
Japan	488
Korea	413
Netherlands	227[2]
Norway	379[2]
Spain	264
Sweden	303[2]
United Kingdom	146
United States	212[3]
Average (excluding Korea)	272

Sources: Organization for Economic Cooperation and Development (OECD) *OECD Economies at a Glance* (Paris: OECD, 1996); Bank of
Korea, *Statistics of the Korean Economy: Business Management* (http://www.bok.or.kr/
kb/index-e.html, last visited June 1998).

[1](debt + equity)/equity.

[2]1992.

[3]From other sources, ranges up to 250 percent.

Capital represents the funds provided by shareholders. As owners, they
share in the profits of the firm. In order to increase the potential rate of
return, shareholders often lever their investment by offering other fund
providers a senior but fixed and ex ante smaller claim on the firm's revenues. The creditors agree to the lower expected return because the
shareholders will assume the first losses up to the value of their in-

vestments. If the firm's losses exceed the shareholders' investment, the shareholders lose their claim and ownership rights and the creditors become the shareholders. Thus, shareholders participate in both the upside and the downside of the firm's fortunes. Because losses have to be associated somewhere, the role of capital as the first absorber of losses is central to free enterprise and market economies. The fear of losses also restricts the incentive of shareholders to increase the firm's risk exposure from that if they only shared in the gains but not the losses.

If the government intervenes to protect shareholders from loss, the losses are shifted primarily to the government. But it receives none of the gains. The firm's gains are effectively privatized and its losses socialized. As their risk of loss is reduced, shareholders will respond by increasing the firm's risk-taking, in particular by reducing their capital contribution. This increases the risk of insolvency and losses to the government and other creditors.

The probability of future reoccurrences of the currently costly banking crises can be reduced by strengthening the equity culture in countries so that shareholders of both banks and nonbanks share in the downsides of their firms' fortunes as well as the upsides. This would require them to provide their firms with the amount of capital dictated by market forces in the absence of government guarantees to minimize the probability of insolvency from normal adverse shocks.

What is the appropriate capital ratios for banks in a particular country? Because deposit insurance insulates banks from full market discipline, the market solution in an insurance environment implicitly incorporates a provision for loss sharing and therefore understates the private-capital ratio that the market would require in the absence of the insurance. A proxy for this value may be obtained in each country by observing the ratio the market requires of nongovernment insured or guaranteed bank competitors (e.g., independent finance companies, insurance companies, etc.). In most countries, these ratios are significantly higher. Thus, increasing bank capital ratios to these levels does not increase their costs unfairly, but primarily removes a subsidy. Moreover, because from the point of view of the deposit insurance agency capital is effectively any claim that is subordinated to the insurance agency, it can consist of subordinate debt, which in some countries has tax advantages over equity. Because they do not participate in the upside earning potential of the bank beyond the coupon payment but may absorb much of the downside losses, subordinated debt holders are likely to monitor their banks very carefully. This reinforces the monitoring by regulators. For this reason, required use of subordinated debt has been recommended by a number of analysts and was recently adopted in Argentina.

It is particularly important to recapitalize and privatize SOBs and SCBs so that they become economically and politically independent.

As long as they remain in their present form, the public will reasonably perceive them as effectively government agencies, all of whose deposit liabilities are fully guaranteed. This provides unfair competition to private banks, whose deposits are insured only up to a maximum amount, unless the higher guarantee is extended to them. Moreover, because, as noted earlier, their bottom line may not necessarily be profitability, they can both undercut the loan rates charged by private banks and outbid these banks for deposits. Because of the ability to use SOBs and SCBs to carry out economic, political, and social policies, as well as bestowing political favors (often off-balance sheet and hidden), governments are reluctant to surrender this power and are generally willing to privatize almost any other industry before banking. Nevertheless, to reduce the probability of suffering another banking breakdown, it is necessary to do so. Use of government funding to resolve insolvencies—in Korea, basically, through the Bad Debt Resolution Fund—should be accompanied by full privatization as quickly as feasible and not involve increased government ownership. Foreign banks should not be precluded from bidding for these banks.

Permitting well-capitalized foreign banks to purchase SOBs in competitive bidding is desirable for at least four reasons. First, in some countries, the foreign banks will be relatively small units of much larger and well-capitalized organizations that may be perceived to be able to protect their small affiliates more securely than the domestic government can protect deposits at domestically owned banks through deposit insurance. Second, foreign banks are likely to bid a higher premium for insolvent or barely solvent institutions in order to get a toehold in the country, thereby reducing the need for any public funds to lower the negative net worth position of insolvent institutions to the level that domestic private parties are willing to absorb. Third, foreign banks are likely to enhance competition and encourage a more efficient domestic banking system, particularly in countries which are dominated by a few large domestically owned banks. Fourth, large international banks are likely to be better diversified than smaller domestic banks, particularly in smaller, less-diversified countries, and will reduce the vulnerability of the banking sector to adverse shocks.

CONCLUSION

Banking problems can cause and, more likely, magnify macroeconomic problems. In large measure, particularly in recent years, banking problems have been ignited by poor regulatory policies that direct bank credit without sufficient regard for profitability, and guarantee deposit liabilities, in some countries effectively even in foreign currencies. As a result, banks have operated with insufficient private capital to absorb losses from normal adverse shocks and many have been driven into insolvency. Capital-impaired banks are unable to extend the credit necessary to help the macroeconomy recover from its problems. Thus, recapitalizing banks and imposing a prudential regulatory structure that is directed at maintaining solvency and efficiency should be a high priority of national policy.

Recapitalization with public funds is politically difficult because it requires official recognition of the problem, which is an admission of government failure and increases the reported government debt. It also may involve imposing losses on private shareholders and depositors who are politically strong. The economic problems are considerably easier, and this chapter describes a process for recapitalizing banks efficiently.

This chapter also describes a regulatory scheme for structured early intervention and resolution that is designed to maintain the solvency of the banking industry while promoting efficiency. A modified form of SEIR was incorporated in the United States in 1991 in the deposit insurance reform provisions of FDICIA and appears to have contributed to the recovery of the U.S. banking system and permitted it to help finance the macroeconomic expansion. The scheme appears amenable to export to other countries. However, many of the features need to be modified to accommodate the economic, political, social, legal, and cultural characteristics of each country. It is also important in some countries, including Korea, to strengthen the domestic equity culture so that both bank and nonbank firms operate with sufficient private capital to absorb losses from normal adverse shocks and remain solvent. Governments must permit shareholders to share in their firms' losses as well as the gains. Banks should be required to maintain capital ratios comparable to those maintained by their noninsured competitors and should be resolved before their economic capital declines become zero. State-owned banks should be recapitalized and sold to private bidders so that they are independent both economically and politically and do not either provide unfair competition to private banks or direct credit on the basis of nonmarket incentives. Foreign banks should not be precluded from bidding on these banks.

NOTES

This chapter appeared in *Restructuring Korea's Financial Market*, Lee-Jay Cho and Yoon Hyung Kim, Editors, to be published by the KDI Press (Seoul, Korea) in 1999.

1. If these deposits had been recognized as official government debt, the debt ratio of a number of Asian countries now experiencing banking prob-

lems would have been substantially higher than the low and comfortable ratios reported earlier and possibly given earlier warning of the pending debacles.

2. In 1993, the United States adopted depositor-preference legislation that gives the FDIC, standing in the shoes of insured depositors, and uninsured depositors at domestic offices of insured banks equal priority in resolution to depositors at foreign branches of insured banks and nondeposit creditors, such as federal funds sellers. Thus, the newly subordinated claimants assume any losses before the FDIC and uninsured domestic depositors and effectively serve as capital for the latter. Both the static and dynamic implications of this provision are analyzed by Kaufman (1997c).

3. The appropriate use of taxpayer funds in restructuring and recapitalizing insolvent banks is often misunderstood. See, for example, Working Party on Financial Stability in Emerging Market Economies (1997, 41).

4. Recent articles have reported that the Japanese government was again considering letting banks fail and not protecting shareholders, but generally not until after the coming elections in July (Sapsford and Davis 1998; Strom 1998). But such statements have been reversed so often in the past that healthy skepticism is warranted. Moreover, reducing the number of banks per se, as is frequently advised in support of such a policy, is not an appropriate solution. What is necessary is to reduce the asset size of the industry, which is artificially maintained at above its equilibrium size by the underpriced government deposit guarantees. Reducing the number of banks without reducing the asset size of the industry only reduces competition and is the worst of all worlds.

5. It is important to note that closure of troubled banks does not necessarily imply physical liquidation, but generally resolution by recapitalization, sale, or merger so that banks or their successors effectively remain open for business. Physically closing a number of banks is likely to lead to public fears of further physical closings and the inability to convert deposits into currency. This would result in undesirable currency runs on the banking system, as occurred in the United States in the early 1930s in response to state-declared "bank holidays" and recently in Indonesia.

6. Before the recent crisis, banks in a number of Asian countries, including Korea, were borrowing heavily in short-term foreign currencies (primarily dollars) at low interest rates, and lending in domestic currency at much higher rates in amounts that may have suggested that they were operating under the illusion that their governments could and did repeal the law of interest rate parity. The BIS (1998) recently estimated that nearly 60 percent of the International Interbank borrowing by banks in Indonesia, Korea, Malaysia, the Philippines, and Thailand in 1995 and 1996 were in dollars and most of the rest in yen. Two-thirds had a maturity of less than one year. In Korea, deposits and borrowing in foreign currencies represented 13 percent of the total assets of domestic nationwide commercial banks at the end of 1996 and loans in foreign currencies made up 7 percent (Bank of Korea 1997). Foreign currency exposure probably increased in early 1997.

7. Kaminsky and Reinhart (1996) found that banking crises predict balance-of-payments (exchange rate) crises, but balance-of-payments crises do not predict banking crises.

REFERENCES

Bank for International Settlements (BIS). 1998. *68th Annual Report*. Basle, Switzerland: BIS.

Bank of Korea. 1997. *Financial System in Korea*. Seoul: Bank of Korea.

Benston, George J., Robert A. Eisenbeis, Paul M. Horvitz, Edward J. Kane, and George G. Kaufman. 1986. *Perspectives on Safe and Sound Banking*. Cambridge: MIT Press.

Benston, George J., and George G. Kaufman. 1995. "Is the Banking and Payments System Fragile?" *Journal of Financial Services Research* (December): 209–40.

Benston, George J., and George G. Kaufman. 1997. "FDICIA After Five Years." *Journal of Economic Perspectives* (Summer): 139–58.

Bordo, Michael. 1986. "Financial Crises, Banking Crises, Stock Market Crashes and the Money Supply: Some International Evidence, 1870–1933." In *Financial Crises and the World Banking System*, edited by Forrest Capie and Geoffrey E. Wood. New York: St. Martin's Press.

Bordo, Michael D., Bruce Mizrach, and Anna J. Schwartz. 1998. "Real vs. Pseudo International Systemic Risk: Some Lessons from History." *Review of Pacific Basin Financial Markets and Policies* (March): 31–58.

Goldsmith, Raymond W. 1969. *Financial Structure and Development*. New Haven, Conn.: Yale University Press.

Gurley, John G., and Edward S. Shaw. 1955. "Financial Aspects of Economic Development." *American Economic Review* (September): 515–38.

Hubbard, R. Glenn, ed. 1991. *Financial Markets and Financial Crises*. Chicago: University of Chicago Press.

Kaminsky, Graciela L., and Carmen M. Reinhart. 1996. *The Twin Crises: The Causes of Banking and Balance of Payments Problems*. International Finance Discussion Papers no. 5541. Washington, D.C.: Board of Governors of the Federal Reserve System.

Kaufman, George G. 1988. "Bank Runs: Causes, Benefits, and Costs." *Cato Journal* (Winter): 539–87.

Kaufman, George G. 1994. "Bank Contagion: A Review of the Theory and Evidence." *Journal of Financial Services Research* (April): 123–50.

Kaufman, George G. 1995. "The U.S. Banking Debacle of the 1980s: An Overview and Lessons." *The Financier* (May): 9–26.

Kaufman, George G. 1997a. "Banking Reform: The Why's and How To's." Paper presented at EWC/Korean Development Institute Conference, 7–8 August, Honolulu, Hawaii.

Kaufman, George G. 1997b. "Lessons for Transitional and Developing Economics from U.S. Deposit Insurance Reform." In *Regulation and Supervision of Financial Institutions in the NAFTA Countries and Beyond*, edited by George M. von Furstenberg. Boston: Kluwer Academic.

Kaufman, George G. 1997c. "The New Depositor Preference Act: Time Inconsistency in Action." *Managerial Finance* 23 (11): 56–63.

Kindleberger, Charles P. 1985. "Bank Failures: The 1930s and 1980s." In *The Search for Financial Stability: The Past Fifty Years*. San Francisco: Federal Reserve Bank of San Francisco.

Kindleberger, Charles P. 1996. *Manias, Panics, and Crashes: A History of Financial Crises*. 3d ed. New York: Wiley.

Levine, Ross 1997a. "Financial Development and Economic Growth: Views and Agenda." *Journal of Economic Literature* (June): 688–726.

Levine, Ross. 1997b. "Stock Markets, Economic Development, and Capital Control Liberalization." *Perspective* (Investment Company Institute), December, pp. 1–7.

McKinnon, Ronald I. 1973. *Money and Capital in Economic Development*. Washington, D.C.: Brookings Institution.

Minsky, Hyman P. 1977. "A Theory of Systematic Financial Fragility." In *Financial Crises: Institutions and Markers in a Fragile Environment*, edited by Edward Altman and Arnold Sametz. New York: Wiley.

Mishkin, Frederic S. 1997. "The Causes and Propagation of Financial Instability: Lessons for Policy Makers." In *Maintaining Financial Stability in a Global Economy*. Kansas City, Kan.: Federal Reserve Bank of Kansas City.

Mishkin, Frederic S., John B. Taylor, Ben S. Benanke, Mark Getler, Allan H. Meltzer, Maurice Obstfeld, and Kenneth Rogoff. 1995. "The Monetary Transmission Mechanism." *Journal of Economic Perspective* (Fall): 3–96.

Sapsford, Jathon, and Bob Davis. 1998. "Japan Vows Again to Repair Banking System." *Wall Street Journal*, 18 June, pp. A1–2.

Schuman, Michael. 1998. "South Korea Adds $35.5 Billion to Bank Bailout." *Wall Street Journal*, 21 May, p. A8.

Shaw, Edward S. 1973. *Financial Deepening in Economic Development*. New York: Oxford University Press.

Strom, Stephanie. 1998. "Japanese Seem Ready to Let Banks Fail." *New York Times*, 11 June, p. C4.

Working Party on Financial Stability in Emerging Market Economies. 1997. *Financial Stability in Emerging Market Economies*. Basle, Switzerland: BIS.

Index

About the Editor and Contributors

Kiyoshi Abe is a Professor of International Economics at Chiba University, Chiba City, Japan. After obtaining his Ph.D. from the State University of New York at Binghamton, he taught at the International Division of Sophia University, Tokyo, and was a researcher at Hitachi Ltd., and a research fellow at the Kiel Institute of World Economics in Germany. Dr. Abe has served on two government committees for the Economic Planning Agency and he chaired one for the Ministry of Posts of Telecommunication. He has published widely in economic journals and is the author of five books.

Philip F. Bartholomew is the senior international economic advisor at the Office of the Comptroller of the Currency, Washington, D.C. Prior to joining the OCC, Dr. Bartholomew was with the Congressional Budget Office, the Federal Home Loan Bank Board, and the Federal Housing Finance Board. Dr. Bartholomew taught at the University of Michigan, Dearborn. He has a distinguished list of publications in professional journals and books.

Marcelo Dabós is director of the Masters Program in Finance and professor at the Universidad de San Andres, Buenos Aires, Argentina. Dr. Dabós has his Ph.D. from the University of Chicago. He has been a visiting scholar at the International Monetary Fund; a researcher at the National Opinion Research Center, University of Chicago; a researcher at the Central Bank of the Argentine Republic; and an economist at Duff and Phelps Credit Rating Agency, Buenos Aires.

Benton E. Gup holds the Robert Hunt Cochrane—Alabama Bankers Association Chair of Banking at the University of Alabama. Dr. Gup has written eighteen books and more than ninety articles dealing with banking and financial topics. He serves as a consultant to government and industry. He was a visiting scholar at the Comptroller of the Currency in 1997. In addition, he teaches a course at the University of Melbourne, Australia, and is an internationally known lecturer.

Paul Hoffman is a senior fellow at the Wharton Financial Institutions Center, the Wharton School, University of Pennsylvania. His previous experience includes a position in the financial sector at Chase Manhattan Bank.

D. Johannes Jüttner holds the chair of the Bachelor of Applied Finance Program at Macquarie University, Sydney Australia. Dr. Jüttner is the author of twelve books and more than ninety articles dealing with economic and financial topics. He served as consultant to the OECD/Paris, the German Council of Economic Experts, and private-sector firms. As a visiting scholar, he also consulted with the Deutsche Bundesbank in Franfurt. He is the founder of Macquarie University's Center for Money, Banking, and Finance.

George G. Kaufman is the John J. Smith Jr. Professor of Finance and Economics at Loyola University in Chicago. Dr. Kaufman also directs the university's Center for Financial and Policy Studies. In addition, he is the co-chair of the Shadow Financial Regulatory Committee and is a consultant to the Federal Reserve Bank of Chicago. His extensive list of publications includes textbooks, monographs, and articles in leading journals dealing with financial economics, institutions, markets, and regulation. He has served as a consultant to numerous government agencies and private firms.

Laura Gómez Mera is a licenciate in economics at the Universidad de San Andrés, Victoria, Argentina. She was an exchange student at Babson and Harvard, and was a trainee at Chase Manhattan Bank, New York.

Doowoo Nam is a Ph.D. candidate in finance at the University of Alabama. His undergraduate degree is from Seoul National University, Korea. He has worked as a managerial and financial accountant for Yukong Limited (now SK Corporation), a major Korean oil company. He obtained his MBA from Syracuse University.

Anthony M. Santomero is the Richard K. Mellon Professor of Finance and Director of the Financial Institutions Center at the Wharton School of the University of Pennsylvania. Dr. Santomero has written more than 100 articles and monographs dealing with financial-sector regulation and performance. He has served as a consultant to leading financial institutions, including the Federal Reserve Board, the Ministry of Finance in Japan, the Swedish Central Bank, and others. He is currently serving on the board of trustees of the Blackrock Funds and two Zweig Funds.

Nancy A. Wentzler is the director of the Financial and Statistical Analysis Division at the Office of the Comptroller of the Currency, Washington, D.C. Dr. Wentzler was formerly Deputy Director of the Office of Thrift Supervision, and an economic advisor at the Commodity Futures Trading Commission and the Office of Management and Budget. She is an adjunct professor at Virginia Tech, Falls Church, Virginia.

ISBN 1-56720-283-7

9 781567 202830

90000>

HARDCOVER BAR CODE